PRAISE FOR
KEEPING AT IT

"Paul Volcker is the greatest man I have known. He is endowed to the highest degree with what the Romans called *virtus* (virtue): moral courage, integrity, sagacity, prudence, and devotion to the service of country. This book is more than an account of his life. It is his credo."　　　　　　　　　　　　—Martin Wolff, *Financial Times*

"If there were a Nobel Prize for government service, Paul Volcker's name would surely be on the short list....It paints an accurate personal portrait. The picture that emerges is of a man of granitic integrity, committed to what he perceives as wise policies—committed, that is, to what he calls The Verities: stable prices, sound finance, and good government....There are few people like Paul Volcker in the US government today, or in business, for that matter—respected and trusted by everyone."　　　　　　　—Charles R. Morris, *Atlantic*

"Any list of the ten most valuable US public servants over the past half-century would include Paul Volcker, who started in the administration of President John F. Kennedy and finished with President Barack Obama. With the economy in tatters in 1979, he took over as chairman of the Federal Reserve for eight years, restoring both national economic stability and the credibility of the central bank."　　　　　　　　　　—Al Hunt, Bloomberg Opinion

"Engaging....*Keeping At It* is part autobiography, part monetary history, part plea for the restoration of trust in American political institutions....Humility is one of the charms of both the man and his book."　　　　　　　　　　—James Grant, *Wall Street Journal*

"Delivers a powerful message."　　　　　　　　　—*Washington Post*

"Who is the most influential political figure alive? The Queen? Henry Kissinger? Donald Trump, Bill Gates, or the Google founder Larry Page? Wrong. It's Paul Volcker. Some of you may not have heard of this ninety-one-year-old American but it is hard to think of another."   —Ed Conway, *Times* (UK)

"[A] frugal and charming autobiography is filled with illuminating stories from Volcker's seven decades of public service."
                          —Richard N. Cooper, *Foreign Affairs*

"Never has a message like Paul Volcker's been more important. At a time of deep divisions in this country, his courageous fight for America's financial and economic stability—under six different US presidents—provides a model that should unite us all."
                          —President Jimmy Carter

"This book is a monument erected by a man who played a key role in the world financial affairs over more than fifty years. Paul Volcker was the only one to master inflation in the early 1980s. He devoted himself to public service with exceptional integrity and energy."
                          —Jacques de Larosiere, advisor to the chairman
                          of BNP Paribas SA, chairman of the strategic
                          committee of Agence France Tresor, and former
                          director of the International Monetary Fund

"Paul Volcker is an American hero who has seen more and done more to shape the world economy than anyone else over the last fifty years. His memoir, *Keeping At It*, is a must read."
                          —Ray Dalio, founder of Bridgewater As-
                          sociates and author of *Principles*

"*Keeping At It* is a delight to read. It is the story of the long and distinguished banking career of the remarkable Paul Volcker, who has dedicated his entire adult life to building a sound central banking system for the United States and beyond. When this pillar of wisdom and integrity tells us that effective governance in the US is broken, we must listen. And those of us who care about America's future must answer Paul's call to do whatever it takes to fix it."

—John C. Bogle, founder of
the Vanguard Group

"The arc of Volcker's career parallels sweeping economic changes in the US since World War II. As Federal Reserve chairman, Volcker broke the back of inflation in the 1970s, set the stage for a thirty-plus-year bull market in bonds, and gets way too little credit for the rampaging equities bull market of the 1980s and 1990s. He's arguably the greatest Fed chairman all time, and this book is at the top of my list."

—Barry Ritholtz, Bloomberg

"Thoughtful.... An orderly, winning book from the economist whose Volcker Rule limits risk-taking by banks."

—Kirkus Reviews

"This fine memoir, written with the assistance of financial journalist Christine Harper, reveals Volcker's personal traits. An amiable temperament. Great common sense. A clarity of thought and expression. An independence of mind without arrogance. Personal authority without self-importance. Rather, his natural disposition is one of wry self-deprecation. Volcker prizes loyalty and has striven to avoid conflicts of interest, so commonly abused nowadays on Wall Street and elsewhere. The possession of such personal integrity and old-fashioned civic virtues made Volcker an exemplary public servant. Now in his nineties, he is what the Japanese would call a 'living national treasure.'"

—Edward Chancellor, *Reuters Breakingviews*

"A memoir that is ultimately a cri de coeur from a patriotic American.... Refreshingly subversive and packed with the sort of perspective that only age can bring."

—John Cassidy, *New Yorker*

"A book that deserves to be read, if only because pure public servants like Paul Volcker have become all too rare, if not nonexistent, in today's America."
—Alan Murray, *Fortune*

"A book I strongly recommend and we can all hope to live up to some part of who he is."
—Jay Powell, chairman of the Federal Reserve

KEEPING
AT IT

KEEPING
AT IT

THE QUEST *for* SOUND MONEY *and* GOOD GOVERNMENT

PAUL A. VOLCKER

with CHRISTINE HARPER

PublicAffairs
New York

PublicAffairs
Hachette Book Group
1290 Avenue of the Americas, New York, NY 10104
www.publicaffairsbooks.com
@Public_Affairs

Printed in the United States of America

Originally published in hardcover and ebook by PublicAffairs in October 2018
First Trade Paperback Edition: March 2020

Published by PublicAffairs, an imprint of Perseus Books, LLC, a subsidiary of Hachette
Book Group, Inc. The PublicAffairs name and logo is a trademark of the Hachette Book
Group.

The Hachette Speakers Bureau provides a wide range of authors for speaking events.
To find out more, go to www.hachettespeakersbureau.com or call (866) 376-6591.

The publisher is not responsible for websites (or their content) that are not owned by the
publisher.

Editorial production by Christine Marra, Marrathon Production Services.
www.marrathoneditorial.org

Book design by Jane Raese
Set in 12-point Adobe Caslon

Library of Congress Control Number: 2018958758

ISBN 978-1-5417-8831-2 (Hardcover); ISBN 978-1-5417-8829-9 (Ebook);
978-1-5417-8830-5 (Trade Paperback)

LSC-C

Printing 3, 2022

To Anke,
who more than anyone deserves the credit for this wise
old parrot's ability to produce a memoir at age ninety.
Just one small reflection of a love story
too often left untold.

CONTENTS

Timeline   ix

introduction   The Wise Old Parrot   1

chapter 1   Growing Up   5

chapter 2   Getting an Education   15

chapter 3   Early Experience   30

chapter 4   Off to Washington   45

chapter 5   "The Best Job in the World"   59

chapter 6   Monetary Reform Frustrated   75

chapter 7   Back to the Beginning   93

chapter 8   Attacking Inflation   102

chapter 9   Financial Crises, Domestic and
              International   120

chapter 10 Unfinished Business:
              Repairing the Financial System   138

chapter 11 After the Fed   152

chapter 12   Mr. Chairman in Several Guises   166

chapter 13   The Search for Integrity   176

chapter 14   Setting Standards   193

chapter 15   The New Financial World:
               Breakdown and Reform   203

chapter 16   The Three Verities   220

epilogue   Credit Where Credit Is Due   241

               Afterword   247

               Acknowledgments   249

               Notes   251

               Index   276

Photo section appears after page 192

TIMELINE

September 5, 1927   Paul A. Volcker Jr. born in Cape May, New Jersey.

1930   Volcker family moves to Teaneck, New Jersey, where Paul Sr. becomes town manager for twenty years.

July 1944   International Monetary Fund (IMF) and World Bank are created.

1949   Volcker graduates from Princeton with highest honors for senior thesis on the Federal Reserve.

1951   Volcker leaves Harvard University's Graduate School of Public Administration after passing the general exam for his PhD.

March 3, 1951   Treasury-Fed Accord reestablishes the Federal Reserve's independence from the Treasury.

April 2, 1951   William McChesney Martin becomes Federal Reserve Board chairman.

1951–1952   Volcker is Rotary fellow at the London School of Economics.

1952   Volcker joins New York Fed as junior economist, moves to Brooklyn Heights, New York, close to the Brooklyn Dodgers.

September 11, 1954   Volcker marries Barbara Marie Bahnson in Jersey City, New Jersey.

August 20, 1955   Janice Louise Volcker born.

1957   Volcker moves to Plainfield, New Jersey, and joins Chase as a research economist.

May 10, 1958   James Paul Volcker born.

January 8, 1962	Volcker joins Treasury as director of the new Office of Financial Analysis under Robert Roosa and Secretary Douglas Dillon.
November 18, 1963	Volcker named to succeed J. Dewey Daane as Treasury's deputy under secretary of monetary affairs.
November 22, 1963	Kennedy assassinated, Lyndon Johnson becomes president.
December 31, 1964	Roosa leaves Treasury to join Brown Brothers.
April 1, 1965	Fowler succeeds Dillon as Treasury secretary.
October 6, 1965	Johnson clashes with Federal Reserve chairman Martin at White House, calls for delay in raising interest rates.
November 1965	Volcker joins Chase as director of forward planning and moves to Montclair, New Jersey.
January 20, 1969	President Richard Nixon inaugurated.
January 22, 1969	Volcker attends meeting with Nixon, David Kennedy, and Charls Walker in the Oval Office. Volcker officially nominated as Treasury under secretary for monetary affairs, "the best job in the world."
February 1, 1970	Arthur Burns replaces Martin as chairman.
February 11, 1971	John Connally sworn in as Treasury secretary.
May 28, 1971	Connally's international debut at banking conference in Munich, Germany.
August 15, 1971	Nixon closes gold window, ending official convertibility of the dollar into gold at $35 per ounce, as part of his "new economic policy."
September 15, 1971	Connally tells Group of Ten meeting in London that the United States wants a $13 billion swing in its balance of international payments.
November 30, 1971	Group of Ten meeting in Rome.
December 14, 1971	Nixon agrees with France's Georges Pompidou in the Azores to devalue dollar and revise exchange rates without restoring convertibility of the dollar into gold.

December 18, 1971   Group of Ten reaches multilateral Smithsonian Agreement on exchange rates; dollar devalued and official gold price rises to $38 an ounce.

May 16, 1972   Nixon names George Shultz to succeed Connally.

June 23, 1972   Committee of Twenty created to address international monetary reform.

February 12, 1973   Dollar depreciated by about 10 percent relative to other major currencies; official gold price changes to $42.22 an ounce.

March 9, 1973   Group of Ten meeting in Paris ends with acceptance of temporary float.

September 1973   Effort to negotiate new monetary system, led by Volcker, abandoned.

April 8, 1974   Volcker resigns and says he'll leave Treasury after Committee of Twenty meeting in June.

August 9, 1974   Nixon resigns, Gerald Ford becomes president.

September 11, 1974   Volcker named senior fellow of the Woodrow Wilson School.

August 1, 1975   Volcker becomes New York Federal Reserve Bank president.

December 27, 1977   President Carter nominates G. William Miller to replace Arthur Burns at Fed.

July 15, 1979   Carter's "malaise" speech.

July 19, 1979   Carter names Miller to replace Michael Blumenthal as Treasury secretary.

August 6, 1979   Volcker replaces Miller at Fed; Miller becomes Treasury secretary.

August 16, 1979   Board raises discount rate to 10.5 percent from 10 percent.

September 18, 1979   Board raises discount rate to 11 percent, but three of the seven members dissent: Charles Partee, Nancy Teeters, Emmett Rice. Gold and silver surge in wild speculative trading.

October 2, 1979	Volcker leaves IMF meeting early, flies back to DC.
October 6, 1979	Meeting of the Federal Open Market Committee (FOMC) to agree to new policy package, unveiled at 6 p.m. press conference. Plan includes increase in discount rate to 12 percent, new reserve requirements, and a new focus on controlling the money supply instead of short-term interest rates.
March 14, 1980	Carter unveils Anti-Inflation Program, including plans to submit a smaller 1981 budget (reduced by $13 billion) and to impose credit controls.
March 27, 1980	Silver price decline sets off margin calls against Hunt brothers' massive holdings, threatening Bache Group and other financial institutions.
April 28, 1980	First Pennsylvania Bank announces it has received a $1.5 billion rescue, sponsored by the Federal Deposit Insurance Corporation (FDIC) and Federal Reserve.
May 22, 1980	In midst of sudden recession, Fed rolls back most of the credit controls implemented in March.
October 2, 1980	Monetary policy tightening ahead of the election incites mild presidential criticism.
November 4, 1980	Ronald Reagan elected president.
January 20, 1981	Reagan takes office, nominates Donald Regan as Treasury secretary.
January 23, 1981	Volcker has lunch with Reagan at the Treasury Department along with Donald Regan, Council of Economic Advisors (CEA) chief Murray Weidenbaum and others.
June 30, 1982	Mexico is world's largest borrower, with $21.5 billion owed to US banks alone. Fed agrees to short-term swap line, conditional on the willingness of the new Mexican president to work with the IMF.
July 5, 1982	Penn Square Bank shut by banking regulators, exposing substantial credit losses on oil loans at major banks.

August 17, 1982   Salomon Brothers economist Henry Kaufman reverses prediction for higher rates, instead saying short-term and long-term rates will fall in response to Fed easing (following First Boston's Albert Wojnilower). Stocks rally, rates fall.

August 20, 1982   Mexican ministers meet with 115 creditors at the New York Fed, beginning the long process of dealing with the Latin American debt crisis with IMF support.

October 9, 1982   Volcker's remarks at Business Council in Hot Springs, Virginia, describe a change in monetary policy tactics, but not in the anti-inflation policy.

June 6, 1983   Volcker meets Reagan; tells him he would serve only a year or so of a second term if reappointed.

June 18, 1983   Reagan calls Volcker at 11 a.m. to ask him to serve a second term; announces it in his Saturday radio address.

May 17, 1984   Continental Illinois bank bailout, including $1.5 billion in new capital from FDIC.

July 23, 1984   Continental Illinois gets additional $4.5 billion rescue, including $3.5 billion loan from Fed to help FDIC buy Continental's problem loans.

July 24, 1984   Volcker meets with Reagan, James Baker in White House library.

February 4, 1985   James Baker replaces Donald Regan as Treasury secretary.

September 22, 1985   Plaza Accord agreed by group of five nations (United States, West Germany, Japan, Britain, France); first major effort since 1973 for international cooperation on exchange rates.

October 8, 1985   "Baker Plan" proposed in speech at IMF–World Bank meeting in Seoul, South Korea, modifying the established approach toward the Latin American debt crisis.

February 24, 1986	Federal Reserve Board revolt led by Preston Martin, calling for discount rate reduction.
March 7, 1986	Fed cuts discount rate half a point to 7 percent in coordinated move with West Germany and Japan.
March 21, 1986	Preston Martin resigns from Fed.
February 22, 1987	Louvre Accord between the United States, United Kingdom, France, Japan, West Germany, and Canada signals the end of the decline of the dollar over previous two years.
May 1987	Volcker tells Howard Baker and James Baker he doesn't want to be reappointed.
June 1, 1987	Volcker meets with Reagan and hands him a written resignation.
June 2, 1987	Reagan nominates Alan Greenspan as Fed chairman.
July 7, 1987	Volcker concludes his last FOMC meeting as chairman by saying, "I appreciate the cooperation of all, in these recent years in particular. This is a wild and woolly venture sometimes, with so many people. But it works and I trust it will continue with all your intelligent and forceful efforts. Thank you."
July 23, 1987	Volcker agrees to serve as chairman of the National Commission on the Public Service to study what he calls a "quiet crisis" in governmental administration.
March 2, 1988	Volcker announces he'll become a professor at the Woodrow Wilson School and chairman at James D. Wolfensohn Inc.
March 29, 1989	National Commission on the Public Service report presented to President George H. W. Bush.
September 23, 1990	Volcker delivers "The Triumph of Central Banking?" as Per Jacobsson Lecture at IMF–World Bank meeting in Washington.
June 1, 1995	James Wolfensohn becomes World Bank president; Volcker becomes CEO of James D. Wolfensohn Inc., which is renamed Wolfensohn & Company.

May 22, 1996   Bankers Trust New York Corp. agrees to acquire
                      Wolfensohn & Company.

May 1996   Independent Committee of Eminent Persons (the
                      "Volcker Commission") established to investigate
                      Swiss banks' holdings of assets belonging to victims
                      of the Holocaust.

June 14, 1998   Barbara Bahnson Volcker dies.

November 12, 1999   Financial Services Modernization Act of 1999
                      signed into law (Gramm-Leach-Bliley Act),
                      ending separation of commercial and investment
                      banking.

December 6, 1999   Volcker Commission releases report on Swiss banks'
                      Holocaust-era accounts.

May 2000   Volcker named chairman of nineteen-member
                      International Accounting Standards Committee
                      trustees, working to establish international
                      standards.

February–May 2002   Volcker chairs Independent Oversight Board for
                      Arthur Andersen (Andersen indictment unsealed
                      on March 14).

January 2003   Volcker's second National Commission on the
                      Public Service releases report.

April 16, 2004   Volcker named chairman of Independent Inquiry
                      Committee (the "Volcker Committee") to
                      investigate corruption in the United Nations' Oil-
                      for-Food program.

October 27, 2005   Volcker Committee releases 623-page report
                      detailing findings of corruption in the United
                      Nations' Oil-for-Food program.

February 2007   Volcker named by World Bank president Paul
                      Wolfowitz to chair Independent Review Panel
                      (the "Volcker Panel") to study the work of the
                      Department of Institutional Integrity and the
                      effectiveness of its anti-corruption efforts.

September 13, 2007   Volcker Panel submits report to new World Bank president Robert Zoellick calling for fundamental change in the anti-corruption effort.

January 31, 2008   Volcker endorses Barack Obama for president.

November 4, 2008   Barack Obama elected president.

January 15, 2009   Group of Thirty working group, chaired by Volcker, issues report proposing comprehensive financial reforms.

February 6, 2009   Obama names Volcker chairman of the President's Economic Recovery Advisory Board for a two-year term.

January 21, 2010   Obama announces he plans to support "Volcker Rule" in Dodd-Frank legislation.

February 11, 2010   Volcker marries Anke Dening.

July 21, 2010   Dodd-Frank bill signed into law.

May 26, 2013   Volcker Alliance launched to address the challenge of effective execution of public policies and to rebuild public trust in government.

December 8, 2019   Volcker dies at his home in Manhattan.

THE WISE OLD PARROT

Y*ears ago,* I was told a story that somehow seems relevant to this memoir. It's about a lonely old man. His wife had died, his children were gone, his business was closed. Yearning for company, he decided to buy a parrot. Off to the local pet store he went, pointed a finger at the first parrot he saw, and asked the price.

The proprietor said, "He's a fine parrot, and he costs $5,000."

"How is that one parrot worth $5,000?"

"Well, his native language is English, but he also speaks French, German, Italian, and Spanish—all of the important languages of the European Union."

"I'm old, I'm not working anymore, and I don't give a damn about the European Union. Give me that young one over there."

"Okay, but he's $10,000."

"How can he be $10,000? What's so special about him?"

"He's young but he's learning. He already knows Mandarin, Cantonese, Japanese, and he's working on Korean. He is just the right parrot for the twenty-first century."

"Look, I'm not going to live for long in the twenty-first century. How about that old one up in the corner with his feathers falling out and glassy eyes. He's for me. I'll take him."

"I understand, but he's $25,000."

"How can that grizzly old guy possibly be worth $25,000?"

"None of us can figure it out. All we know is the other parrots call him Mr. Chairman."

I've told that story maybe a hundred times. This will be the last. Even now I'm called Mr. Chairman fairly often and I actually still chair—these days mostly "honorably"—a few small organizations. One is the Volcker Alliance, which I created in 2013 as part of my effort to encourage training and education for public service. But when somebody stops me on the street or on the bus, which still happens every once in a while, they're usually thinking of when I was one particular chairman, of the Federal Reserve Board in Washington, some forty years ago. Inflation rising to record levels, 10 percent unemployment and interest rates topping 20 percent made a lasting impression.

We've seen plenty of financial crises since then, including the Great Recession that began in 2008. Sweeping reforms in financial regulation, including the so-called Volcker Rule, have followed.

Important as those events were in shaping my life, they aren't the reason I decided to write this memoir. I'm driven by a growing, and much broader, concern. We have for some time been experiencing a breakdown in the effective governance of the United States.

Polarization between (and even within) political parties, accompanied by the ever-growing influence of highly concentrated wealth, has paralyzed key elements of public policymaking: prudent budgeting able to finance programs ranging from our military services to old-age retirement; sensible strategies for international affairs, immigration policy, health care, and much more. Even needs as self-evident as rebuilding our infrastructure seem, for all the talk, beyond our capacity for action.

Less understood is the erosion in what Alexander Hamilton insisted at the very beginnings of the republic would be the true test of government: "its aptitude and tendency to produce a good administration." There has been a lack of attention for years to the need for effective governmental organizations staffed by talented, dedicated public servants. The result has been too many breakdowns, too little efficiency, and, most critically, too much distrust of government itself. Polls show fewer than 20 percent of Americans trust government to do what's right most of the time, down from about 75 percent sixty years ago.

In the early 1950s, when I first took a government job, it was a matter of personal pride, as it was for others. With strong leadership in both political parties, America supported Europe's economic recovery, helped restore democracies in the free world, and opened global trade and investment. The result seemed evident: unprecedented gains in the human condition, marked by growing populations over most of the world that were healthier and wealthier than ever before.

Looking back, I am forced to recognize that the United States, in leading the grand coalition of free and emerging states, could not entirely escape the mortal sin of hubris. We embarked on long, unnecessary, and ultimately unwinnable wars far from home. We failed to recognize the costs of open markets and rapid innovation to sizable fractions of our own citizenry. We came to think that inventive financial markets could discipline themselves. We underestimated how much the growing size, economic weight, and ambitions of other countries, most critically China, would come to upset the easy assumption of America's unique global reach.

The collapse of the Soviet Union and a more open, prosperous China at the end of the twentieth century made some believe we had come to the end of history—a victory of democratic values and perpetual growth around the world. Now, we find ourselves in a different mood. Our historic allies are perplexed and questioning our leadership. The vision of spreading democracy and the rule of law is in jeopardy.

Over the seventy years of my adult life I have had the good fortune of playing a small part in American governance, observing its great strengths—and some large blunders—firsthand. I hope this memoir provides lessons, particularly in matters of financial and monetary policy to which I have dedicated most of my life.

But I have come to understand something broader and more important: the need to restore trust in the full range of our governmental processes. My hope is that the Volcker Alliance can play a part. It will not be easy.

chapter 1

GROWING UP

*M*y *early life* was relatively comfortable given that I
grew up in the midst of the Great Depression and then
World War II. By good fortune, my hometown of Teaneck, New
Jersey, was growing rapidly. I was too young to serve in the war. But,
as I look back, there is no doubt that my father's prominent position
in local government had a huge impact on the way I view life and
the world.

A Model Town

"Government is a science and I am happy that the officials and the
people of this community agree that the man who is to manage it
should be thoroughly trained in the science of government."

That was my father, city manager of Teaneck, explaining in 1948
why he was hiring a successor, two full years before he planned to
retire.

My father cared deeply about making things work. The oldest
son of German immigrants, his childhood in Brooklyn, New York,
had included some gang battles (modest by recent standards) and
other mischief. But mostly he found comfort in the rigorous clas-
sical education he received at Boys High School and later as a civil

engineering student at Rensselaer Polytechnic Institute, where he stood high in his class both physically and academically.

A job helping to rebuild New York State's Erie Canal system took him to the small upstate town of Lyons. There he met my mother, a Vassar College graduate and the only child of one of the town's more prominent families. They married in 1915 and moved to Lebanon, Pennsylvania, when he was hired to be that town's engineer.

But he soon saw a greater opportunity. Government itself needed fixing too. That was certainly true in Cape May, New Jersey.

Once a favorite summer resort of wealthy Philadelphia families and even a president or two, its big old Victorian hotels had lost their luster. The city finances were extended to the point of bankruptcy. The local leaders decided radical change was needed. In 1925 they became the first in New Jersey to adopt a recently created system of city government: a nonpartisan part-time council and a professional city manager.

My father was drawn to city management, to the challenge of creating civic order out of disarray. So nobody was surprised when he joined a large number of applicants for the $4,500-a-year Cape May job. "As the first official in such a capacity, Mr. Volcker will, of course, have the eyes of the entire state upon him," the *Lebanon Daily News* reported on the day he was awarded the position. At age thirty-five he moved to Cape May with my mother and three sisters, two years before I was born.

It proved an excellent fit. He soon straightened out the city's finances and discovered a knack for publicizing "cool Cape May, twenty miles at sea," with "shaded streets and golden sands" that not so subtly contrasted with rival New Jersey resorts built on treeless barrier beaches with flimsy housing.

Atlantic City, forty miles north, was another story: much larger, with a nationally famous boardwalk and pier, majestic hotels, and big-time entertainment. In the twenties its promoters started a beauty pageant. Cape May usually sent a contestant.

Just weeks into his job, my straitlaced father made headlines by ending that practice. No young Cape May maiden should be encouraged to exhibit herself in a bathing suit before leering men in a city of questionable morals.

Meanwhile, a much larger municipality in northern New Jersey was falling into financial and governmental crisis. Voters decided to throw out the politicians and bring in the council-management form of government. Teaneck, a New Jersey township twenty minutes outside of New York City, hired my father in 1930, immediately saving money when he also agreed to be city engineer for no extra pay.

He turned Teaneck around too. In his two-decade tenure, which overlapped with the Depression and war, Teaneck's debt dropped to $1.8 million from $5 million and the population doubled. The town acquired ninety-five acres of parks. Taxes were cut.

Bespectacled, pipe-smoking, and six feet, four inches tall, my father cut an imposing and authoritative figure. On the wall behind his office desk he posted a framed quotation from George Washington to put favor seekers on notice: "Do not suffer your good nature, when application is made, to say 'yes' when you ought to say 'no.' Remember that it is a public not a private cause that is to be injured or benefited by your choice."

To the best of my knowledge, his local authority was seriously challenged only once. I was way too young at the time to understand the implications, but I did know it was highly unusual for him to come home early from a town council meeting, bringing along two or three of his close associates. Later I learned the full story.

Determined to professionalize the police and fire departments, my father told the council he would be hiring a new police chief from out of town. The contentious mayor fiercely objected, demanding that one of the local good old boys be promoted instead. My father refused, insisting that the law (which I believe he largely drafted) made the appointment his responsibility as city manager.

The council could fire him but knew it would lack public support. It equivocated by suspending his pay. The issue went to court, which promptly upheld my father. Teaneck got a professional police chief, the mayor lost his influence, and my father's salary was restored.

Behind his formality and reticence, my father concealed a dry wit and sophisticated political instincts. As I grew older he'd take me along sometimes as he consulted with the mayor, councilmen, or other influential citizens. He also made a point of visiting with the town's less influential workers. He was fanatic about disclosure. Every family would get a detailed annual report about the state of the town. He described the budget, spending and taxes, the number of police cars and fire engines, the condition of the town's facilities, and the salaries of employees, including his own.

By the standards of the day, the city manager was reasonably paid, starting out at about $8,000 a year. Only later did I discover that in the middle of the Depression my father volunteered to reduce that by $2,000, and it was a long time before it was restored.

The town's success, and the city-manager form of government, was publicized nationally and even internationally. In 1945 the Federal Bureau of Investigation's national statistics identified Teaneck as the lowest-crime town in the country. The *Saturday Evening Post* carried an article headlined "There's No Crime in Teaneck." While proud of the sizable juvenile recreation programs and professional police force that contributed to Teaneck's low crime rate, he made clear his discomfort about declaring such an absolute victory in a speech to the New York City Federation of Women's Clubs that he titled "There Is No Crime in Teaneck?"*

A little later the US Army selected Teaneck from ten thousand applicants as the model town to be featured in an exhibit used to educate occupied countries about democratic practices after the war. Through his dedicated, professional, and nonpolitical management, my father had created an example for his own parents' war-destroyed homeland—and for me.

While he often told me to pursue a career in business instead of government, I didn't know whether he really meant it. In any event, I didn't listen.

---

*Almost forty-five years later, I would unconsciously mimic this technique in my Per Jacobsson Lecture marking the end of the Great Inflation: "The Triumph of Central Banking?"

The Name Carrier

At about ten-thirty in the morning on Labor Day, 1927, in Cape May, New Jersey, Alma Volcker gave birth to a large baby boy. The congratulatory telegram soon arrived from Grandpa Volcker: *"Der Stammhalter ist da!"* ("The name carrier is here!")

Grandpa Adolf Volcker, himself one of ten children (nine boys and one girl) of the headmaster of a well-known *gymnasium* (high school) in a small German city, was the first to emigrate to the United States. He soon brought some brothers along. Two generations later I was the first and, for a long time, the only male descendent. I had three older sisters (another had died in infancy), so it had been a long wait. As I grew older, I came to consider it a bit of a hardship. It seemed that my sisters, and even my mother and father, bent over backward to ensure the lone male had no special sense of entitlement. My family called me "Buddy," which at least seemed better than "little Paul" or "Paul Junior."

I was pretty quiet as a child, hardly speaking for hours while playing with my pals. In my very first kindergarten report card, Miss Palmer (beautiful in my eyes) noted that "Paul does not take part in group discussion." How perceptive she was. That is a chronic difficulty to this day. While I have become quite at home in chairing a meeting, I tend to be uneasy in any group (from my sisters to presidential advisors) competing for attention.

My oldest sister, Ruth, flitted in and out of my life, appearing like a fairy godmother on special occasions. By the time I was in elementary school, she was away at Simmons College in Boston and then on to her lifetime professional career as a science librarian with Eastman Kodak and its affiliates. She left us all mystified when she spent a couple of years during World War II isolated in Oak Ridge, Tennessee. Unbeknownst to us, and maybe to her, the scientists she worked with were producing "Little Boy"—the Hiroshima atom bomb. She spent the rest of her life as an active supporter of the cultural institutions in Kingsport, Tennessee.

Louise, next in line, was emotional, artistic, athletic, ambitious, feminist by instinct. She annoyed her young brother no end by demanding so much parental attention. (Still I have no doubt that, for my emotionally repressed father, she was the favorite.) Later in life Louise, who became a social worker after obtaining degrees from Barnard College and the University of Chicago, introduced me to the worlds of art and Freudian psychology. She became my most enthusiastic supporter until she fell victim to cancer in 1966, at age forty-seven.

Virginia, with a calmer temperament and much closer to my age, was a natural childhood playmate, confidante, sometimes backseat combatant. She was the only one of my six-foot-tall sisters* to marry. She had five children and lived far away, but we became close when she and her family moved back east in later years. With her death in 2011, I became the de facto family patriarch.

Teaneck was as solidly middle class as you could get when I was growing up. There were no large estates or even visibly wealthy families. There was a very limited section of the town that could be characterized as poor, but in no way a slum. Most men commuted to New York City and mothers were home with children, who were in large supply. There was one black family. Teaneck voted solidly Republican, typically five or six to one.†

The country may have been in deep depression but to me it was hardly visible. The George Washington Bridge over the Hudson River had just been completed, driving a surge of residential development in Teaneck and adjacent towns. That magnificent monument to civil engineering, originally with six lanes of traffic and now with fourteen in a double-deck arrangement, has been absolutely essential to the economy of New York City and nearby New Jersey communities. Sadly, almost eighty years later, with our rail tunnels and subways at the breaking point, we're unable to conceive and finance the lesser pieces of infrastructure required for the twenty-first century.

---

*We lived on Longfellow Avenue, a source of much local amusement in Teaneck given our family's height.

†Teaneck today is proudly multicultural, featuring significant populations of Jewish, black, Latino, and Muslim residents. The residents vote Democrat five to one.

In many ways my horizons were limited by today's standards. There was virtually no air travel. Ocean liners took a week to cross the Atlantic. Long-distance telephone calls took time. Visiting grandparents in upstate New York was a day's journey.*

But there were compensations. At age twelve I could travel alone from Teaneck to Ebbets Field to see my beloved Brooklyn Dodgers—two bus rides and a subway transfer away. What mother would permit that trip today, even if the Dodgers were still in Brooklyn?

My mother ran the household. She was approachable, understanding, and a patient mediator of childhood squabbles. But she also laid down family law.

My father was more remote. Only fishing or a chance to explain some engineering principle created much rapport. He had a true passion for bass, freshwater or saltwater, acquired from his father. He once took me out of school, sending me back the next day with a note for the teacher explaining that he figured a day of fishing was worth at least a day of school.

Before World War II it was the family custom to rent a cottage for the month of July at a rural New Jersey lake, complete with a rowboat, canoe, and outdoor loo. Beaver Lake was filled with oversized sunfish and perch and an occasional largemouth bass. My father made a practice of coming up Wednesday nights and weekends and I was called upon to row him around the islands and coves as he cast, whether with a fly rod and "bass bugs" or with a casting rod and shiny "spoons." My first real angling achievement was one day, out alone, when I caught my first bass on a fly rod.

It was at Beaver Lake that I heard, on the radio, Lou Gehrig declare himself before sixty-two thousand fans at Yankee Stadium the "luckiest man on the face of the earth" in his farewell speech to his baseball career, cut short by what is now known as Lou Gehrig's disease. It still brings tears to my sentimental eyes. The "Iron Horse," even though a Yankee, was a true hero to this Brooklyn Dodgers fan.

---

*Later I realized that almost all of my parents' classmates at Rensselaer Polytechnic Institute and Vassar College, both top schools at the time, came from nearby communities easily reached by bus or train.

My view of Beaver Lake was colored by a few very-well-established houses, each with a sizable boathouse and a Chris-Craft that sped around the lake hauling water skiers. I longed to be part of the action and whined to my mother, "Why can't we have a Chris-Craft?"

"They have a mortgage," she responded. "We don't."

There in six words was the definitive expression of the Volcker family fiscal instincts. They have stayed with me all my life.

Being the son of the city manager, to me the town's most recognized and respected citizen, had its downside. It was unspoken but crystal clear that I should avoid anything that might reflect badly on my family. No mischievous street games like those my father played in Brooklyn a generation earlier. No joining the boys in shooting out streetlights. Taking a temporary city job shoveling snow or mowing the parks could look like nepotism. Most importantly, I was under strict orders not to hang out at the Teaneck Diner, known to cater to the "fast" crowd.

In fact, my teenage years were a social wasteland. I may have lived with older sisters but I was shy with girls. No dates or proms for me. Academics or athletics were not particularly challenging. I didn't aim to be number one in the big high school class—that would have marked me as a nerd. My objective was to appear laid back. One basketball season I took pride in not bringing home a single homework assignment. Nor, at a gangly six feet, seven inches, did I push myself hard enough to be a real basketball star.

And I took the easy way out when it came time to write the required senior research paper: I could do the research for my description of the council-manager plan for town government by interviewing my father at home. It still reads well today.

I recall a family council one evening at an earlier stage of my schooling. My parents asked if perhaps I'd be better off—more challenged, more disciplined, better educated—if I went off to a good private school? No deal. I was too comfortable at Teaneck High, and that's where I stayed.

There was never a question about going to college—that's what Volckers did, including all of my sisters. Our mother, we were occasionally reminded, had been valedictorian of her 1913 Vassar class, then the very cream of women's colleges. She was intensely loyal, then absolutely furious when Vassar considered joining with Yale and eventually went co-ed. She accepted Virginia's decision to go to Wellesley because, at least, it was still a women's college.

One family policy was never questioned. For sixteen consecutive years, tuition, room, and board at one of America's best educational institutions was a parental responsibility. Once in graduate school—also assumed—we were on our own financially.

My father expected me to follow in his footsteps at RPI, the Rensselaer Polytechnic Institute. (His Class of 1911 Rensselaer banner still hangs in my fishing room.) He believed that good engineering training, with its precision and implied responsibility, equipped you for any career.

But then, out of the blue, a family friend suggested I apply to Princeton, an Ivy League college well beyond my consideration. I wasn't from an exclusive "preppie" private school. A tall basketball center might be accepted from a public high school, but I wasn't that good. And my father didn't approve. He argued that I would be socially alone and struggle to compete academically with better-prepared students. Nonetheless, I decided to apply. To this day, I remember the application form's heavy parchment paper and images of neogothic campus buildings with their implications of wealth and exclusivity.

When I was accepted, there was another hurdle to be overcome. My mother said I would get an allowance of $25 a month, just as my sisters had.

"Don't you know that prices have doubled since the 1930s?" I complained. "I'll be with some rich kids and I'm a boy; we have more responsibilities."

Searching for help, I wrote to each of my sisters, who pledged support, and appealed to my father. But my mother was in charge and adamant. Twenty-five dollars was it.

She was a victim of what I later learned in economics is termed the "money illusion"—ignoring the impact of inflation on the value of nominal money. Or maybe she just thought it was good discipline.

I made up the financial shortfall in freshman year by manning the hotdog stand at football games.

My father took some solace in the fact that he was marginally acquainted with Harold Dodds, the then president of Princeton and professor of public administration. Dodds also had been chairman of the National Municipal League (now the National Civic League), which not only championed professional local government but played the leading role in establishing the council-manager model as an ideal.

Unknown to me, two other Teaneck graduates from an earlier class, both in military service, had also been admitted. About half of the Class of '49 came from public schools. Princeton even had a black student for the first time in memory thanks to the navy's integrated V-12 program. World War II made an impact on Princeton traditions.

My own military status had been in question. I reached draft age and was called for a May physical examination. Psychologically I was in a dilemma. I felt a responsibility to serve; after Pearl Harbor, it was an inherent part of American citizenship for young men. On the other hand, the war was obviously ending. The odds of engaging in lengthy training, much less actual combat, seemed low.

The dilemma was quickly resolved. The army was no longer in need of men taller than the six-foot-six-inch height limit. So, feeling slightly guilty, off I went to Princeton, to the fourth floor of North Dod Hall, along with my new classmate Don Maloney, also from Teaneck.

chapter 2

GETTING AN EDUCATION

P rinceton was underpopulated in early July 1945 when the freshly admitted Class of 1949 got started. Many of my future classmates were still in military service. Scattered veterans enrolled in earlier classes began reappearing. They seemed students apart: more mature, with hard-earned experience. New or old, we all celebrated Japan's surrender with a bonfire on Cannon Green.

I worked pretty hard in my freshman classes, afraid of failing to catch up with my presumably better-prepared prep school classmates. In the event I got top grades, including in the allegedly challenging math and science courses. And with my six-foot-seven-inch comparative advantage, I naturally played freshman basketball. Don Maloney was also able to keep up and became the class expert in Dixieland jazz. Disproving the qualms of my father, Teaneck High had prepared us well.

It wasn't long before I reverted to procrastinating. Studying waited until exam weekends. And without hard physical training to become a strong varsity basketball player, I spent two years basically sitting on the bench. Intramural softball and tennis, bridge and poker games in the dormitory, and pinball at the local eatery consumed my days.

Looking back, I realize the opportunities I squandered. Thankfully, I did take some courses that weren't required and that seemed a bit odd at the time. Modern art, which to this day permits me to distinguish a Manet from a Monet, a Velázquez from a Goya, a Picasso from a Braque. I retain at least a little knowledge of Sophocles, Aristophanes, Euripides, and Plato. My courses on constitutional law and world religions remain highly relevant today. (Incidentally, my youngest grandson, a recent Princeton grad, has already expressed a similar lament: too much lacrosse, too many mind-opening educational opportunities missed.)

I regret never establishing relationships with the professors whose lectures intrigued me. I saw them as distinguished scholars absorbed in their own research who would have little interest in a callow undergrad. My connection was limited to writing a final exam and almost always getting a good grade. I now wonder why the faculty didn't try to reach out to me. Nor did the basketball coach do much to instill me with discipline.

My indecision with respect to a future career was reflected in my choice of a college major. The relatively new program in the School of Public and International Affairs (SPIA) offered a limited number of students the ability to select advanced courses *à la carte* from across the economics, politics, and history departments. I didn't have to choose just one.

The trade-off was compulsory participation in the school's specialty: a conference in which a small group of students worked together in researching a public program, alternating each term between a domestic and international subject. Led by a few seniors, the conference participants presented a final report to the faculty advisor and other invitees. It was a challenge. We each had to research one aspect of the subject, then negotiate to get our viewpoints into the final conference report.

For me, and for many of my classmates, it was also the most memorable part of our Princeton education. I learned something of the political and bureaucratic challenges of one of the New Deal programs and then studied how the United States should approach China, torn apart at the time by civil war. In one way or another, SPIA (long since renamed the Woodrow Wilson School) has maintained a strong tradition that's viewed, I later learned from some of my own students, as the high point of their undergraduate careers.

In the 1960s a very generous gift allowed the creation of a graduate program for, in the words of the donors, "training and education of men and women for government service." Twice in my career I returned to teach at the Woodrow Wilson School, ultimately as a tenured professor after I left the Federal Reserve (itself created after Princeton president Woodrow Wilson became US president).

The Woodrow Wilson School's potential to be a leader in graduate education for public service has been a preoccupation of mine. Princeton's motto from the times of Woodrow Wilson was "In the Nation's Service." At the 250th anniversary it was changed by adding "and in the Service of All Nations," which I viewed as a bit of an overreach. Then, twenty years later, it changed again to "In the Nation's Service and the Service of Humanity," which strikes me as simple pomposity. That is a matter to which I will return.

Strange as it may seem from my later career perspective, I didn't major in economics. Nor did I take the proverbial Economics 101. The big introductory course with hundreds of students didn't strike me as challenging enough. Given my early academic success, I decided as a sophomore to jump directly into the most advanced economic theory course, limited to maybe a dozen or two older and better-qualified students.

That did require work. So did a course in traditional money and banking. Both were taught by distinguished refugee scholars of the classic Austrian liberal school of economics, Oskar Morgenstern and Friedrich Lutz. They emphasized the works of free-market advocates, including Ludwig von Mises and Friedrich Hayek from Eastern Europe. While it hardly seems possible, to the best of my memory John Maynard Keynes and his theories in the English tradition advocating active government policies to manage the economy received no attention.

I took a lot of the standard economics courses of the day—labor, public finance, accounting, and industrial organization among others. But it was only money and banking and monetary policy that really caught my attention. The seeming precision of balance sheets, with their carefully delineated assets, liabilities, and capital, appealed to my sense of order. The importance of the money supply and the "natural rate of interest" seemed clear enough.

Only later in life did the real world, with its amalgam of greed, risk taking, rational (or irrational) expectations, accounting irregularities, and regulatory lapses, impinge on the textbook world. The logic of orderly, competitive free markets plainly needed some qualification.

While I don't remember discussing economics with my mother in those days, I now realize that I should have. I recently found her 1911 economics textbook, *Outlines of Economics*, written by the Vassar College Professor Herbert Elmer Mills. I was struck by the clarity of the professor's description of economic theory at that time, two years before the Federal Reserve was created. Even more remarkable was the extent of my mother's scrawled notes in the margins—she was clearly an enthusiastic student. One handwritten sentence seemed particularly prescient in light of my later career: "Economic laws cannot be depended upon if we disregard psychology, etc."

By far the most significant challenge in my Princeton education was writing my senior thesis, a requirement for graduation. There was no falling back to family resources, no easy essay on the merits of the council-manager form of government.

Because of my early start in Princeton, my senior year began in February 1948. I spent the spring procrastinating, the summer in a clerical job in New York, and returned in September for my final four-month term without a required thesis subject, much less any research. Somehow I grasped at the idea of writing about the Federal Reserve, founded just thirty-five years earlier. Central bank policy had become a matter of growing public debate. I liked my money and banking course. There seemed to be a lot of potential material available. But I had not yet lifted a finger to start.

I remember my first visit to my designated faculty advisor, Professor Frank Graham. Unbeknownst to me, he happened to be one of the leading American scholars of international trade and was convinced that price stability was a key objective of public policy. When I told him about my idea and expressed concern that I might run out of time, he responded reassuringly: "Don't worry, May is a long time off."

"But I'm scheduled for a February graduation."

"Oh! We'd better get started!"

For once in my academic life I did. I holed up in a little carrel in the brand new Firestone Library and got to work. I studied the origin, the theory, and the practice of central banking, starting with Walter Bagehot, the mid-nineteenth-century British writer credited with defining the appropriate role of the long-established Bank of England as "lender of last resort." I ran through the theorists of the "real bills doctrine," Wicksell's "natural rate of interest," the practical interrelationships among the Federal Reserve's discount rate, open market operations, and reserve requirements. The role of "selective" credit controls, then enforced on consumer credit, and much else was on the table.

By mid-November, I was churning out a chapter a week, in bad handwriting on a yellow pad (just as I am writing today with even less legibility). On Thursday or Friday, I'd deliver a copy to Professor Graham. He faithfully returned it on Monday, with thoughtful and useful comments.

What student today would dare to present his senior professor with such incomplete and illegible materials? What professor would respond so promptly and constructively?

Professor Graham was implicitly providing a steady stream of encouragement about my work and what he saw as my potential as an economic scholar. In the end, he awarded my thesis a summa cum laude, highest honors. He went out of his way urging me to apply for a distinguished Marshall Fellowship or other graduate study opportunities.

Some of my thesis is a little embarrassing to reread, with difficult-to-follow detail about the twists and turns in postwar financial markets and policies. But the review of central banking theory and practice as it developed in the years after the Federal Reserve was established helped provide perspective. More notably, the concluding sections on the importance of price stability and the key role of monetary policy could have been written today.

Federal Reserve policy in those days was devoted to sustaining the pattern of low interest rates established in the late 1930s and maintained throughout World War II. The residue of Depression-era "easy money," with interest rates remarkably similar to those prevailing after the 2008 financial crisis, seemed important to the Treasury Department, and indeed to President Harry Truman. Borrowing costs were kept low and financial markets stable. President Truman remembered feeling cheated when the World War I Liberty bonds he purchased later declined in value. (Bond prices fall when interest rates rise and rise when rates fall.)

A combination of political pressure (including directly from the president) and the possibility of a slowing economy (even though it hadn't shown up in the statistical evidence) made the Fed reluctant to take even small steps that might reduce the availability of money. So much seems familiar: then, as now, central banks too often hesitated to deal with inflation pressures at early stages. As I write this, the Fed is presented with that recurrent question.

In my Princeton ivory tower I was unsympathetic to those concerns. The thesis ended with a strong plea to recognize price stability as the central bank's core objective and to make it independent of partisan politics. Subconsciously, my career path was set.

Harvard

My first priority after Princeton was to get a job. I had eight or nine months before graduate school, so some kind of internship seemed useful. Naïvely, I took a train down to Washington and spent a day or two knocking on the doors of federal agencies that might conceivably be interested in a brand new potential economist. Of course, I usually didn't get past the most junior personnel officer. The exception was the Federal Reserve Board.

I presume the fact that I wrote my senior thesis on the Fed was what caught attention. I had a long interview with two senior staff economists, both of whom I came to know well years later. The attention was gratifying, but the conclusion was preordained: The Federal Reserve Board didn't hire college graduates off the street. An internship would have to follow my graduate studies. (For a long time now, but not then, a PhD has been a requirement to get through the research department's doors.)

Back in New York I applied to a couple of the major banks' economic research departments. My big break came in an interview at the Federal Reserve Bank of New York,* arranged after a vice president of the bank who lived in Teaneck happened to chat with my father about my plans.

So there I landed, at a small desk next to the stenographic pool. One new colleague seated alongside regaled me with stories about his father-in-law, Professor Arthur Burns, the business cycle sage who had written a robust criticism of Keynesian economics. Little did I suspect how many times our paths would cross later on. My early Fed years also introduced me to Albert Wojnilower and Henry Kaufman, who became Wall Street economic gurus, later sometimes dubbed "Mr. Gloom" and "Dr. Doom" for their dire economic forecasts.

I had actual work to do, mostly involving long hours with the mechanical computing machines of the day. By the time I left for graduate school, I had become quite adept at calculating complicated seasonal adjustment patterns for factors affecting commercial bank reserves—"Federal Reserve float" and "currency in circulation." While it was routine data crunching, it was a necessary technical ingredient in determining how many government securities, if any, the New York Fed's trading desk should buy or sell each day to maintain the desired level of commercial bank reserves at the Fed. Without

---

*The Federal Reserve Bank of New York is one of twelve regional reserve banks that, along with the seven-member Federal Reserve Board of Governors in Washington, make up the Federal Reserve System.

going into details, the level of those reserves directly influences the growth of the nation's money supply (the quantity of money) and indirectly influences short-term interest rates (the price of money).* I labored for hours on what today takes a well-programmed computer just seconds.

Meanwhile, where to pursue graduate studies? I first visited Harvard's vaunted economics department. Its law school also seemed a reasonable option. Or Yale, where the law school was already building its strong public policy orientation? Given my Princeton record, any of the three were open to me. So, as usual, I procrastinated.

Finally, Harvard's law school and graduate school discovered that both had admitted me. I was pressed for a decision. Serendipity intervened: the relatively new Harvard Graduate School of Public Administration was offering a few administration fellowships to new college graduates. Each carried a stipend of, as I recall it, $1,200. That was almost enough to live on and far more than I could reasonably ask for elsewhere. Moreover, it was clear that, as with Princeton's SPIA, I would have wide latitude in course selection.

I could take all the economics courses I wanted and still get a slightly modified doctoral degree in political economy. The strong economics faculty had taken over the Littauer Center, as the new home for the School of Public Administration was known. The handful of Littauer students intermingled in graduate economics classes and the common library.

So that's where I went for the next two years. Perhaps subconsciously, procrastination had paid off once again.

In those days, Princeton economics and Harvard economics were in different intellectual worlds. The key Harvard professors were smitten by John Maynard Keynes and his general theory. The leading acolyte, Alvin Hansen, lectured and wrote with remarkable clarity. He illustrated with simple graphics and arithmetic how Keynesian "consumption functions" and "investment multipliers" could interact

---

*Over time, the emphasis the Fed placed on controlling interest rates and the money supply changed, as you'll see in later chapters.

with precision. One advanced student, Laurence Klein, managed to put it all in more formal mathematical form, building toward an early application of "econometrics."

As an empirical judgment, Hansen pronounced with confidence that the United States, after years of depression, was caught up in "secular stagnation." Only wartime spending and big federal budget deficits had rescued the nation from the Depression. Government deficit spending would need to be sustained.

Inflation, which had risen during World War II and again during the Korean War, didn't seem to be considered a serious threat. In fact, one of the less renowned professors, Arthur Smithies, lectured week after week about the importance of maintaining an inflationary bias in the economy—maybe only 2 or 3 percent a year, but inflation nonetheless.

They were dedicated teachers. But there was something in their analyses that put me off. Somehow, it seemed to me, the complexities of the economy couldn't be reduced so easily to so few variables. Surely, new private investment opportunities would reappear to stimulate the economy. That, after all, was the history of capitalism. And what was the economic purpose, and for that matter the morality, of the government inducing chronic inflation—intentionally debasing the nation's currency a little every year? My mother would see through that.

Harvard, and the then upstart Massachusetts Institute of Technology (MIT) economics faculty nearby, was successful in attracting a slew of young scholars—James Tobin, Jim Duesenberry, Bob Solow, and others. Paul Samuelson from MIT, already greatly respected, sometimes appeared. Later armed with Nobel Prizes, they came to question Hansen's simplistic certainty, but they played a major role in embedding Keynesian thinking in the political as well as the intellectual world.

At the same time, there were bridges to the older Austrian tradition. Gottfried Haberler and Willy Fellner taught international trade and finance and advanced economic theory. They could not be labeled inflationists. Thankfully, they spent their "retirement" years at Washington think tanks, where they would become a source of comfort and support to a new Fed chairman struggling to lead a war against inflation.

John Williams provided another counterpoint to Alvin Hansen. Together they ran the prestigious Fiscal Policy Seminar, where they debated the issues of the day with students and guests. Williams, who spent part of the week as an advisor to the New York Fed, was institutionally minded, instinctively suspicious of abstract theorizing.

At the time, his skepticism was directed particularly at the agreement to control foreign currency exchange rates reached by a summit of forty-four nations in Bretton Woods, New Hampshire. The delegates who had spent nearly two weeks at the Mount Washington hotel in July 1944—even as World War II raged in Europe and Asia—established a system of global economic cooperation they hoped would prevent another Great Depression and world war. As then–Treasury secretary Henry Morgenthau Jr. put it in his opening address:

All of us have seen the great economic tragedy of our time. We saw the worldwide depression of the 1930s. We saw currency disorders develop and spread from land to land, destroying the basis for international trade and international investment and even international faith. In their wake we saw unemployment and wretchedness—idle tools, wasted wealth. We saw their victims fall prey, in places, to demagogues and dictators. We saw bewilderment and bitterness become the breeders of fascism and, finally, of war.

So the stakes were very high. Postwar peace and prosperity seemed to depend on maintaining the agreements reached at the summit, the so-called Bretton Woods system. Gold, still seen at the time as the underpinning of all currency, was set at $35 an ounce. All other currencies' foreign exchange values were fixed against the dollar and the US Treasury promised to convert any nation's dollars to gold at the $35 price on demand.

Williams, however, doubted that the International Monetary Fund created in Bretton Woods could sustain and enforce the new exchange-rate system. In his view, more informal cooperation would be needed, beginning with an understanding between the United States and Britain because their two currencies were globally accepted, used around the world as so-called reserve currencies.

Later I spent years of my life trying to prove him wrong. I should have listened more carefully.

During my second year at Harvard, I lived in a new graduate dormitory with a pretty active intellectual and social life. It was easy to get to Boston's legendary Durgin-Park or to the Old Lobster House for an occasional good dinner for, as I recall, less than $10; or once in a great while to the infamous Old Howard burlesque house, long ago destroyed but then a hallowed Harvard tradition. And for me, still all too shy, a rare date with a Wellesley girl.

As I recall it, we students were almost unanimously critical of the unsophisticated Harry Truman from Kansas City, then known for its corrupt local politics. But most of us were eager for a career in government. I was, after all, enrolled in a school of public administration, taking a couple of required courses in government affairs. Even my friends majoring in pure economics had Washington in mind.

I deliberately missed one course that later came to dominate economics. My year was the last that didn't require economics PhD candidates to take econometrics: the new "more scientific" data-driven approach toward economic analysis. At the time, I thought that was a lucky break. I'd had some pretty advanced statistics courses and didn't see the need to refresh my mathematics.

As it happened, a team of econometricians drawn from various universities was being formed to help the US Treasury review how it estimated tax receipts. As a Harvard contribution, I was asked to collect raw data to feed the computers that were calculating the needed "regressions." Luckily, I was close enough to the leaders to get some feel for econometric thinking, approaches, and shortcomings. Only recently with the rise of the behavioral school of economics, with its emphasis on human psychology, has the primacy of the econometric approach been, in my judgment, sufficiently challenged.

At the end of the school year, I had passed the general examination for my political economy PhD. The idea was that I would go abroad, probably to England, to research and write a thesis about the contrasting approaches toward monetary policy and banking regulation in the United States and the United Kingdom.

The Treasury offered me a permanent position when and if I would return. As attractive as that appeared, I wasn't ready to make the commitment. We compromised. I was added to the Treasury rolls as an employee, but on leave for one year. That year turned out to be significant in one respect: forty years later, it counted toward my retirement benefits, adding a few pennies to my eventual government pension.

London

My plan to go abroad was made easier with a recently established Rotary Foundation fellowship for study outside the United States.

Applications had to be initiated by a local Rotary club. My father was an active member in Teaneck, where he had just retired after twenty years as township manager. A few of his friends suggested that I might be a suitable candidate.

The application required me to choose a university and present a reasonable study plan. England was the obvious choice, given my central banking interest and lack of fluency in another language. The Universities of Oxford and Cambridge were already hosting Rotary fellows, so I selected the London School of Economics (LSE) instead. Its faculty had a strong interest in finance. The promise of living in one of the world's greatest cities was an attraction in itself.

My crossing to Europe on the Holland-America Line's *Nieuw Amsterdam* cost $75 and took five days. First, I joined my two oldest sisters on a (greatly shortened) grand tour of Europe: Rome, Venice, Padua, Verona, Genoa, Lyon, Reims, Chartres, and Paris. Louise had already spent a year at Oxford on a Fulbright fellowship. She was ready to go home—to get warm, as she put it. For Ruth and me it was all new. Even so, we could be too sensible and frugal. Years later I regret overruling Louise's plan to splurge on a meal at Fernand Point's La Pyramide near Lyon, then and for a long time considered one of the top restaurants in all of France. The legendary chef Paul Bocuse spent part of his early career there. Ruth and I vetoed the visit as too expensive. (As it turned out, I found myself with extra money at the end of my year in Europe. I spent the remainder on a £40 Savile Row suit and a bespoke bathrobe from Harrods, which I still occasionally wear sixty-five years later for the sake of *auld lang syne.*)

Once in London, it didn't take long for me to get settled. The Rotary stipend, $2,000 or more as I remember it, could cover a lot in those days. A typical bed and breakfast in central London was £3 (about $8.50) a week. The rooms were tiny, the beds too short, and the electric heater required a shilling every couple of hours. The location was what counted.

Only six years after the war, London was far from rebuilt. I was well off relative to the English students, who found central London living costs too high. They lived on the city's outskirts and many had jobs. Brits made up only about half of the LSE's truly international graduate student body, including a fair share from the old empire.

The year was fascinating. I learned that class in England was still clearly defined by accent and occupation. (Foreign students generally got the benefit of the doubt as to whether they were gentlemen, who were addressed in the mail as "Mister.") Politics were exciting—I joined some new Labour Party friends in "knocking up" votes on the night Winston Churchill won back Parliament. Rotary clubs around England occasionally invited me to visit, often for a weekend, so I had ample opportunity to absorb upper-middle-class British life.

The academic side was a lesson in the persistence of bad habits. The leading scholar of British banking and financial markets was Professor Richard Sayers, the historian of the Bank of England who later chaired a prestigious official committee reporting on the appropriate (and, as he saw it, limited) role for monetary policy. Sayers, like Frank Graham at Princeton, was my advisor.

After a few weeks, I could no longer postpone meeting the professor, which was a more elevated title in an English university than
in the United States. When I explained the purpose of my visit, he
had, from years of experience, only one question: "Are you here to
work or to play?" I gulped. No doubt I exaggerated my sense of academic commitment.

I did regularly participate in Sayers's weekly seminars, to which
he would often invite leaders from "the City" (that is, banks and
other financial institutions). A point made forcibly by one such City
visitor has always stuck in my mind. He noted that international
banking and free currency markets had been effectively shut down
by the war, but they were on the way back. Speculation and excessive risk taking, à la the late 1920s, would reappear. He warned that
the inevitable crises would be easier to deal with if they were concentrated inside the regulated banking system rather than outside,
without official oversight.

I later recalled that warning while distinguishing between the
manageable Latin American banking crisis in the 1980s, in which
United States and foreign banks found themselves with huge portfolios of loans to countries in Latin America and other emerging
markets that couldn't repay them, and the subsequent highly damaging Asian monetary crisis little more than a decade later, complicated by contagious currency speculation and international capital
flows.

The temptation to travel through Europe with a friend or two
during the long intervals between academic sessions was impossible
to resist. The major German cities were still largely in ruins. Munich's center was so flattened that my hotel room was in a basement.
I had little success in meeting distant relatives and confirming my
role as the Volcker name carrier. Those continental trips reinforced
my sense of America's good fortune in escaping the ravages of war
as well as the importance of defending democratic values at a time
when some European countries were still tempted to turn eastward
to the Soviet Union for support.

As spring approached, I finally made some effort to begin serious research for my dissertation. Professor Sayers opened doors at

the top levels of Britain's commercial banks. To this day, I still have some five-by-seven-inch filing cards with notes on my conversations about the contrast between British and American central banking practices.

The Bank of England itself was, perhaps predictably, less accessible to an unknown American student. Time grew short. I had fallen head over heels in love with a warm and accomplished English grad student. Thoughts of completing my thesis drifted away.

Another question couldn't be deferred. Both the US Treasury and the Federal Reserve Bank of New York wanted to know: Was I ready to return?

I had become friendly with a young American, Sam Cross, who was serving as assistant Treasury attaché in the London embassy. It struck me as a comfortable and professionally interesting life for a neophyte, well paid by English standards and exposed to interesting policy questions. So, in the full flush of youth and confidence, I told the Treasury I would be glad to return if it would commit to appointing me as Sam's successor in London—or perhaps send me to Beirut, with its then entrancing and exotic reputation.

The reply was clear: Treasury, not some new recruit, would decide on the location of personnel. So my decision was made. I returned to the New York Fed with the rank of "Economist-C"—rather low on the totem pole but still near to policy questions that became a theme of my life.

chapter 3

EARLY EXPERIENCE

I returned to New York in 1952, too late to vote but still able to sense some of the enthusiasm Adlai Stevenson had generated among my peers during his campaign for president. With a quick wit and relevant experience away from Washington, Stevenson had provided a bracing contrast to the rather dour Dwight Eisenhower. It was enough to induce me to register as a Democrat, a designation that somehow stays with me on Wikipedia even though I abandoned any party affiliation decades ago.

Thanksgiving dinner at the Volcker home in Teaneck was always a large and boisterous family affair. That year my ex-roommate Don Maloney showed up as dinner was ending. He was accompanied by a recent Pembroke graduate named Barbara Bahnson, the sister of one of his University of Pennsylvania School of Medicine classmates. She would later say that she was impressed only by my traditional toast to the queen of England delivered just as she arrived. Barbara was pretty, shared an irreverent sense of humor, and my London girlfriend was far away. Within two years Barbara and I were married and she joined me in Brooklyn Heights, halfway between my job at the New York Fed and Ebbets Field. She soon came to share my passion for the Brooklyn Dodgers.

The New York Fed

For a young economist interested in finance, a chance to work at the Fed, particularly the New York Fed, was a favored career step. The bank also encouraged some short-term appointments, a year or so, for economists still early in their academic careers. There was a lot of informal debate and discussion around the lunch table. Alan Greenspan, starting his consulting career, joined us once in a while.

One tenet I don't remember ever being challenged within the bank's sturdy walls was that the Federal Reserve's overriding responsibility—the cornerstone of effective economic policy—was to maintain the stability of the currency. The Arthur Smithies–Alvin Hansen doctrine that a little inflation was a good thing had no constituency in the New York Fed.

Federal Reserve policy had been maintaining historically low interest rates (⅜ to ⅝ percent for three-month Treasury bills to 2½ percent for long-term bonds) from the Depression right through the World War II and early Korean War inflations. My senior thesis had excoriated that spineless approach of letting political pressure for low interest rates override the central bank's obligation to keep prices stable. If that was the way the Fed viewed its responsibilities, it might as well be part of the Treasury Department! Finally, only after an open clash with the Treasury and President Truman himself was the Fed's independence affirmed. It was in 1951, more than two years after my undergraduate thesis pleaded for that action.

The new chairman of the Federal Reserve Board, William McChesney Martin, had negotiated "the Accord" that freed the Fed from the Treasury's oversight while he was assistant Treasury secretary. He began to speak forcefully about the Federal Reserve's responsibility for maintaining price and financial stability. His statement that the role of the Fed is to take away the punch bowl "just when the party was really warming up" has become central banking lore.

Price stability was pretty much restored by 1952, followed by about fifteen years of economic growth and low unemployment. There were, to be sure, three short recessions, attributed in substantial part to recurrent and reversible periods of excessive home building and inventory buying. But overall, the US economy grew strongly and prices were stable. That helped put to rest some of my Harvard professors' fears that the country had entered a secular, or long-term, era of economic stagnation.

Not long after I arrived at the Fed, Milton Friedman came into prominence with his forceful exposition of the virtues of free markets and pure "monetarism." The monetarist policy advice—find the optimal rate of growth for the money supply and stick to it through thick and thin—seemed naïve at best and dangerously misleading. Applying such a hard and fast, almost mechanistic, rule to the conduct of economic policy essentially meant removing the Fed's human judgment. Unsurprisingly, the monetarist approach was distinctly out of fashion among my new Federal Reserve colleagues.

I had myself spent some time trying to make sense of the longer-term and cyclical relationships between the "money supply" and economic activity. Friedman declared that his analysis unambiguously indicated that over time the supply of money, a favored asset because it's liquid and widely accepted, would and should grow faster than the economy as measured by gross national product (GNP).* In the jargon of the time, money's "velocity" would slow. In fact, even then, and continuing for decades, the opposite trend prevailed.

More important in the short run, institutional changes made it difficult to precisely define what we meant by "money." Were savings accounts that paid interest the same as demand deposits? What about short-term "time deposits" (like certificates of deposit)? We ended up with two or three alternative measures of money—known as M1, M2, M3, etc.—as regulations changed and time passed.

---

* The market value of all goods and services produced by a country's residents in a year.

Friedman, fifteen years older than me and some sixteen inches shorter, surely ranks first among the most doctrinaire and persuasive economic gurus I have encountered. The simplicity of his advocacy of free markets and monetarism was almost impossible to challenge in debate if not in analysis. As a professor at the University of Chicago near Lake Michigan, Friedman came to command the "freshwater" movement in monetary analysis that contended with the "saltwater" economic theories out of America's East and West Coast universities. Among those in his camp was a young George Shultz, dean of the University of Chicago's business school and later a member of the Nixon and Reagan administrations. Friedman won the Nobel Prize in economics in 1976, although not specifically for monetary policy.

I came to appreciate Friedman's basic contention that the supply of money, even given its slippery and imprecise definition, has a fundamental significance for the inflation process. Much later I depended on the common sense of that relationship when, as chairman of the Federal Reserve, I tried to make clear the necessity for monetary restraint as the backbone for a forceful attack on inflation. But I also take some intellectual satisfaction from a report that, in his nineties, Friedman confessed that he had perhaps overemphasized the stability of the relationship between money, prices, and economic activity. A little late from my point of view.

Informality was not a characteristic of the New York Fed. Officers, from the president on down through the junior officers and managers, were a people apart—in fact, mostly a floor apart as well. Research memos went up and down through the ranks, rarely with brief notations from the president himself and seldom, if ever, a meeting.

I participated in one effort to break through the established ambiance. The governing body of the Federal Reserve's systemwide pension program included one elected representative from each of the twelve regional Reserve Banks. In New York, that position was typically filled by a vice president in uncontested balloting. So it was out of the ordinary when Madeline McWhinney, who had joined the bank in 1943 and was relatively senior in research, decided to compete for the position and asked me to be her campaign manager.

We had fun. I got together a makeshift four-man band to parade down each floor (except the hallowed executive floor), passing out "Win with McWhinney" campaign pins to every employee. We distributed our "platform." Statistician Vic Milkowitz, fluent in Polish, helped us address the large representation of Polish immigrants in the evening cleaning staff. McWhinney won in a landslide.* She joined me and Barbara to celebrate at our Brooklyn Heights apartment.

Later I was asked to chair the annual staff Christmas party at the old Astor hotel in Times Square, replete with a Guy Lombardo-style band. More than seventeen hundred people attended. Perhaps Chairman Martin's rule about the punch bowl was suspended for the party. In any event, management later decided that was one tradition the bank could do without.

One relatively young New York Fed officer stood out as the intellectual and policy leader. Robert Roosa, a bowtie-wearing economics PhD from the University of Michigan, had served in an Office of Strategic Services (the precursor to the Central Intelligence Agency) intelligence unit when World War II prevented him from taking up a Rhodes scholarship. Nine years my senior, Roosa was already respected as an articulate economic analyst and a strong voice in systemwide policy debates. While my memory is dim, Roosa made a point in later years of claiming that he himself had arranged my employment at the New York Fed. There is no doubt that he became my mentor.

At first my assignments were mostly typical for a midlevel economist—analysis of the banking statistics, some economic forecasting, responses to questions about legislation, preparation of background material for meetings of the policy-setting Federal Open Market Committee (FOMC). (As Roosa's general handyman, I was once

---

*Madeline McWhinney became a trailblazer in other ways. In 1960 she was the first female Federal Reserve officer and managed the New York Fed's newly established market statistics department. In the 1970s she helped found and became president of the First Women's Bank.

asked to write a poem in honor of a senior vice president who was retiring. I vaguely recall basing my verses on the unique meter of Rudyard Kipling's "Danny Deever," which described a death march for a British soldier about to be hanged. Fortunately, neither Roosa nor Senior Vice President Roelse were very familiar with Kipling.)

After a couple of years, Roosa somehow arranged for me to attend a meeting of the FOMC in Washington. It was a rare privilege to watch Chairman Martin in action. He let all the other committee members talk, then concluded with a comment along the lines of "Well, I'm so glad we are close to a consensus. And here's the consensus." For me, that first FOMC meeting was an interesting lesson in one way of exerting mastery.

I later came to understand that Martin, for all his friendly manner and personal modesty, had an iron backbone when it came to policy and the defense of Federal Reserve independence. He was one of my heroes. Decades later, Catherine Mallardi, the longtime assistant to a succession of Fed chairmen, would encourage me to visit Martin for solace if she thought the pressure of the job was getting to me.

Even more surprising during my time at the New York Fed was that Roosa convinced the Fed hierarchy to allow me to sit on the trading desk as part of my education.

The trading desk was the holy of holies. That was where the Fed bought or sold Treasury securities, in the process expanding or contracting the reserves of the commercial banks held at the Federal Reserve Banks. (Buying Treasuries meant the Fed paid into the banks' reserve account, while selling Treasuries subtracted reserve funds.*) The total of those reserves influenced both the supply of money in the economy and interest rates, the variables that in turn impacted economic activity. To put it simply, the trading desk was where policy met the market.

---

*Banks are required to keep a set percentage of their deposits on reserve at their regional Federal Reserve Bank (or as cash in a bank vault). By adding to or subtracting from reserve accounts, the Fed influences expansion or contraction of bank deposits and, therefore, the money supply. That indirectly affects short-term interest rates. As an operational matter, the Fed's objective was to influence short-term interest rates.

Entry to the trading room was forbidden to all but a favored few: the officers directing the activity, a few traders, limited clerical help, and, eventually, me. Market prices of each Treasury security, ascertained by means of constant phone calls from the key government bond dealers, were updated throughout the day on a large chalkboard.

Literally months went by before I was permitted to talk to a dealer and then to actually make a trade. The concern was that the words we used or the tone of our voice might inadvertently tip off our counterparties to a change in the direction of monetary policy.

The dealers themselves were a trusted group of professionals, mostly small, independent companies such as C.J. Devine & Company, C.F. Childs & Company, Salomon Brothers, and Discount Corporation. They met individually with Fed officials to discuss market trends and activity and were important partners in helping us execute policy. After I was allowed to talk to market participants, I remember the chief trading officer of one of the big primary dealers called to coach me on how I should more precisely, or perhaps more obscurely, communicate with the market. So far as I know, they maintained confidentiality about Fed operations.

One thing impressed itself on me. I came to sense that, in contrast to the later fashion for econometrics and its dependence on mathematic "regressions," market prices and trading activity hinged on inherently volatile human expectations about what might or might not happen—the next day, next month, or next year. Bob Roosa described the trading desk procedure and its interactions with the dealers in great detail in what became known as his "little red book." He dictated, I edited.

The method of conducting and communicating monetary policy at that time gave the trading desk in New York more leeway to react to the market. These days, the instructions to the desk are more direct: simply maintain, day by day, the overnight market rate set out by the FOMC.*

---

*In those days, and for years thereafter, the Federal Open Market Committee's instructions to the New York Fed's trading desk focused on maintaining a certain level of bank reserves: free reserves, nonborrowed reserves, or some variant thereof. That would in turn influence the Federal Funds interest rate—the rate at which

The government bond market was the dominant financial market. Commercial banks held large portfolios of debt issued by the US Treasury—ranging from three-month Treasury bills (T-bills) to longer-term Treasury notes and bonds. Fluctuations in the price of those securities might be small by today's standards but could strongly influence banks' willingness to buy or sell. The interest rate on Treasuries established a benchmark for borrowing costs that helped determine whether banks would aggressively lend or would hold back.

In those days, market participants and policy makers alike spoke of the importance of fiscal, monetary, and debt management policies. Only recently has debt management—the purchase and sale of Treasury securities of different maturities—come back into fashion as a way to influence markets and economic activity. Inevitably, the responsibility is shared between the Treasury as issuer and the Federal Reserve as buyer or seller, a sensitive matter with respect to Federal Reserve independence.

The New York Fed has a long history, tracing back to the 1920s, of exercising a strong voice in both the framing and implementation of Federal Reserve policies. In the Fed's early days, the Washington-based Board of Governors had weak leadership. Chairmen didn't exercise a strong hand and the board members were little known. The New York Federal Reserve Bank, with its operating responsibilities and a widely respected leader in Benjamin Strong, emerged as the focal point for monetary policy, both domestic and international.

That pattern continued for a time after Strong died in 1928 but without the same degree of respect for the leadership. The following year's stock market crash, the severe banking crisis, and the ensuing Great Depression inevitably raised questions about the effectiveness of Federal Reserve policy. A strong new chairman of the

---

banks would buy or sell reserves to each other overnight. The purpose was to establish short-term interest rates within a target range set by the committee. Deviations from the intended rate were thought to convey useful information about market pressures and economic activity. While it was recognized that changes in reserves also affected growth in the money supply, the money supply was not a prime policy target.

Today the trading desk is a computer. I'm not convinced this is an improvement.

Washington-based board, Marriner Eccles, eventually succeeded with President Roosevelt's support in convincing Congress to rewrite key sections of the Federal Reserve Act in 1935. The Board of Governors, independent of Treasury participation,* was placed more clearly in charge. The New York arm, still responsible for open market operations and maintaining close ties with foreign central banks, was in effect placed on a short leash.

One reflection of that leash was the extreme detail of the New York Fed's weekly reports to the FOMC, setting out the rationale for every purchase or sale. I spent long Wednesday evenings at home drafting the highly confidential reports. (Barbara was always amused that I wasn't senior enough to be on the list of officials qualified to receive the "confidential" report I had just written.)

Through the years of the Depression and war, with interest rates pegged at historically low levels, the Fed had little discretion in monetary policy. That changed after the Accord in 1951.

The Federal Reserve could, and did, begin to exercise its autonomy. Before long a full-scale bureaucratic battle ensued over the basic approach toward policy implementation. My close association with Bob Roosa gave me a front-row seat.

Fed chairman Martin, with strong support from his Washington staff, took the position that it was an abuse of the Federal Reserve's power for it to buy or sell securities that weren't directly related to conducting monetary policy (that is, anything longer term than three-month Treasury bills or overnight "repurchase agreements"). In other words, intervention in the bond market should cease; the Federal Reserve shouldn't seek to influence interest rates on debt maturing in more than three months because that arguably verged upon influencing the allocation of credit among different sectors of the economy.

Martin's view became known as the "bills-only doctrine" because it limited the Fed to trading in three-month Treasury bills or even shorter repurchase agreements. The New York Fed, wanting more

---

*Previously the Treasury secretary and the comptroller of the currency had been included among the members of the Federal Reserve Board.

flexibility, resisted as best it could. I recall writing and even delivering speeches bewailing the bills-only doctrine as causing an unnecessary loss of options for policy execution and effectiveness. But Washington was adamant. The Federal Reserve should confine itself to controlling the banks' reserves, and indirectly the money supply. Debt management was the preserve of the Treasury.

Ultimately, the authority lay in Washington. The respected New York Fed president, Allan Sproul, resigned in 1956. Chairman Martin apparently dominated* the choice of Sproul's replacement: Alfred Hayes, a Yale classmate of Martin's and a mild-mannered vice president of a New York commercial bank without known policy views.

Nineteen years later, in 1975, I succeeded Hayes in office.

The term "bills only" long ago fell out of common use, but its practical application remained in force for decades and the Fed rarely traded securities with longer maturities. Only the massive interventions in the securities markets during and after the 2008 financial crisis—operations in which the Fed purchased long-term government debt and mortgage-backed securities in extremely large multiples of anything contemplated in the 1950s—confirmed its demise. Under the rubric of "quantitative easing," debt management seems to be back in a more exaggerated style.

Few tears have been shed. But what hasn't disappeared is the basic underlying question: How far should a central bank—shielded from political pressures—go in indirectly financing budgetary deficits and influencing the distribution of credit broadly in the economy?

A New Job, a New Family

Late in 1957 I got a call from John Wilson, the head of a newly reorganized Chase Manhattan Bank economics department. Would I like to join Chase as chief financial economist?

---

*While Reserve Bank presidents are selected by their bank's own board of directors, the choice must be approved by the board in Washington. That effectively gives the Federal Reserve Board veto power over anyone the New York Bank's board might appoint.

It caught me at a vulnerable time. I had become bored with the routine of the Fed trading desk—the long periods of inaction, highly detailed reporting, and no clear path ahead. An idle conversation with a colleague reminded me of the lacuna in my education: no PhD, a serious failing if I had any academic pretensions. He reminded me that Harvard's policy called for a dissertation within five years of the general examination. Almost six had lapsed.

I hastily sent off a note to the School of Public Administration pleading for an extension and got an equally speedy reply. For my particular degree, there was no time limit. Procrastination, and a lack of strong incentive, took over. The thesis could wait. It has waited, indefinitely.

Meanwhile, Barbara and I had moved from Brooklyn Heights, where our windowsill (and, more importantly, our baby's forehead) was covered with soot from the nearby port, to a bigger home and cleaner air in Plainfield, New Jersey. That took us away from Ebbets Field, but our beloved 1955 World Series champion Brooklyn Dodgers were moving to Los Angeles anyway. I later transferred my loyalty to the New York Mets, but it is never the same.

Our baby daughter, Janice, had been born more than a year earlier and our son, Jimmy, was soon on the way. A boost in salary would help, so I was willing to talk to Chase. It turned out to be an important career decision.

The Chase National Bank, focused on serving business customers, had recently merged with the Bank of Manhattan Company (founded by Alexander Hamilton's rival, Aaron Burr) to gain a citywide retail branch network. The combined Chase Manhattan Bank was competing head to head with First National City Bank (which eventually became Citibank after several mergers of its own) for the title of largest commercial bank in the United States.

The newly organized Chase research department had ample strength in economic analysis. It could help with customer relationships and produce relevant reports for the public. But there was clearly a hole. Weak financial analysis wasn't sustainable for a bank that saw itself as an intellectual as well as a business leader.

In those days, commercial banks were still tied down by laws and regulations imposed after the financial debacle of the early 1930s. Interest rates on deposits were capped (at zero for demand deposits). The Banking Act of 1933, known as the Glass-Steagall Act for the senator and congressman who sponsored it, forbid banks from underwriting and trading corporate stocks and bonds (effectively separating "deposit-taking" banks from engaging in "investment banking"). Foreign operations were subject to restraints. Branching across state lines was prohibited by federal law and had long been limited within most states, even in New York State.

Management had to anticipate the flow of customer deposits and the strength of loan demand, which in turn depended on changes in economic activity and the prevailing level of interest rates. As a financial economist with Federal Reserve experience, I was presumed to have some insight into those matters. Loan committee meetings were central to management, and I was sometimes admitted even though I hadn't passed through the rigorous Chase credit training program required of all recruits deemed to have management potential.

I soon learned that Chase, big as it was in relative terms, was not as bureaucratic as the New York Fed. I still recall finding myself early on in President George Champion's office to discuss a note I had written for him. He had larger questions on his mind:

Did I think US industry was losing competitive position vis-à-vis a recovering Europe?

Was the dollar in jeopardy at its fixed gold price of $35 an ounce embedded in the Bretton Woods agreement?

I wasn't prepared. I parroted the conventional view: Europe and Japan, our main trading partners, still had a long way to go to recover from the war even if their industries were becoming more competitive. They still needed to import from the United States. There was a chronic dollar shortage outside the United States. The fixed foreign exchange rates established at the end of the war were here to stay. There was no danger to America's promise at the 1944 Bretton Woods monetary conference that it would convert dollars held by foreign governments to gold on demand. Don't worry.

Not my proudest moment. Those very concerns, arguably a bit premature at the time, would become central to my life a few years later.

David Rockefeller, the bank's vice chairman, provided me with a different kind of education. He had been asked to join other leading business figures on the newly formed Commission on Money and Credit, sponsored by the then influential private Committee for Economic Development. Given the limited time David had for the project, he urged me to work on his behalf with the commission staff.

The commission's task was broad. It included a review of the international monetary system, the structure and responsibilities of the Federal Reserve, and the scope of banking regulations. For me, it was a first-class ticket to a high-level discussion of issues that came to dominate my career. I could be introduced to former Fed Board chairman Eccles and, more importantly, to active, influential economists ranging from Milton Friedman to Paul Samuelson. Several members of the commission staff, especially Eli Shapiro of MIT and Larry Ritter of New York University's Stern School of Business, became close friends. The comprehensive commission report has been lost in the mists of time. It did, however, help bolster the case for Federal Reserve independence, which had come into question in parts of the Congress. (At the time, after the turmoil of World War II, a number of leading central banks had lost their independence.)

Within Chase, I was also given the responsibility (and privilege) of preparing a summary of the weekly briefing of the twenty or so most senior Chase officers. While my formal status wasn't high, I became known by top management, even John J. McCloy, the esteemed former public servant and US high commissioner for Germany who was then serving as Chase chairman. For years, we worked together to strengthen the American Council on Germany, an institution of some importance in German-American relations in the early postwar years. In 1989 I felt honored to be a pallbearer at his funeral.

I also became particularly close to Chase's principal outside counsel, Roy Haberkern, through our work together on banking regulation. Roy was a proud and loyal Moravian from Winston-Salem. My wife, Barbara, was descended from one Bishop Bahnson, the founder of North Carolina's tight-knit Moravian community. No doubt that helped begin a lifetime friendship.

In that context, I learned about a critically important contrast between the rival banks, Chase and Citibank. Confronted with any new law or regulation, the Champion/Rockefeller/Haberkern approach was, essentially, to conform. The Citibank view, under its aggressive leader George Moore and later Walter Wriston, always seemed to be to fight and find a way around it.

The 1950s saw the rise of bank holding companies that owned multiple banks and sometimes "nonbank" activities, financial or otherwise. While the 1956 Bank Holding Company Act established Fed oversight of these entities and sought to curb some nonbank investments, there were loopholes. Citibank didn't hesitate to seek ways to expand its activities. But at Chase, I remember there was real debate, with one of the old-time bankers saying, "No, we don't want to become a holding company and get into other things and take our eye off commercial banking."

He also said creating an "incentive" compensation plan for individuals, that is bonuses, would be the end of responsible commercial banking and the understanding that the customer always should be put first.

He may have been premature in his concerns, but he was prescient. The multimillion-dollar bonuses we see today surely twist the incentives for bank officials, not necessarily in the customers' interest. (In contrast, the Chase profit-sharing plan at the time was effectively a 15 percent bonus for every employee, every year that the bank made its conservative profit goals.)

I could hardly have been exposed to more relevant training for my future career, but at that point it wasn't clear what that would be. I wasn't a graduate of the vaunted Chase credit-training program, which over time provided a reservoir of leadership talent not only for Chase but for several regional banks. The economic research department had co-leaders who were unlikely to move for years. A vague possibility might have been eventually managing the Chase investment division, but that wasn't where my heart lay.

The doubts ended when I got a call near the end of 1961 from Bob Roosa, by then under secretary of the Treasury for monetary affairs in the new Kennedy administration.

"Come down and help us."

Within days I was there, excited to be part of the new and highly energized administration.

I remember my closing talk with George Champion, a dyed-in-the-wool Republican.

"You are doing the right thing, Paul. Go down there and help the country. Then come back here. You will have a place."

Five years later, I did return to a new and enhanced position as director of forward planning.

chapter 4

OFF TO WASHINGTON

O*ur young new* Democratic president John F. Kennedy attracted enormous enthusiasm and a sense of a fresh start after eight years of the seemingly staid war-hero Republican president Dwight D. Eisenhower. But the concerns that George Champion had expressed to me about the United States' competitive position in world trade and its potential effects on the dollar were spreading. The country was running a balance-of-payments deficit—spending more money abroad than it was getting back—and foreign governments were increasingly demanding that some of their dollars be converted into gold.

Financial markets and business interests were uneasy about our untested president and his willingness to defend the dollar, reflected in a sudden jump in the market price of gold days before the election. Kennedy promptly insisted that, if elected, he would not devalue the dollar. After the election, he sought to further reassure the financial world by naming Eisenhower's under secretary of state, Douglas Dillon from the Dillon, Read & Co. investment bank, as Treasury secretary.

The US Treasury

Bob Roosa sold the position in Treasury as an opportunity for long-term thinking. I would oversee a new unit, the Office of Financial Analysis, that soon attracted several highly regarded economists. They had interesting projects. I moved my family down to Washington after buying a $35,000 home in Chevy Chase, Maryland—twice the cost (and comfort) of our Plainfield house. I worried whether I could afford it on my $18,500 salary in a job with no tenure, but that was secondary to my Washington opportunity.

It soon became apparent that the top officials, especially Bob Roosa himself, had little time for new research. Too much was pressing. I became "operational"—thrown straight into daily policy implementation.

At the time I joined, the big question for the administration was tax reform and reduction—how much, how soon, how comprehensive? The Treasury, led by Dillon, urged caution. The responsible approach would combine tax cuts with thorough reform to eliminate loopholes and special provisions, keeping the budget balanced. It would take time.

The White House's Council of Economic Advisers (CEA), manned by Keynesians influential with the president, wanted to move fast to keep campaign promises (such as a 5 percent economic growth target) and forestall a feared recession.

The battle for the president's approval was way above my pay grade. But I did play a bit part. One of my responsibilities was economic forecasting, which I had done at the New York Fed. Looking ahead with the help of longtime civil servant and practical economist Herman Liebling, I concluded we would narrowly avoid recession in 1962, contrary to the CEA's concerns. That supported the Treasury view: don't rush the tax bill; do it right. Slow and careful won the day. Happily for the country (and for me), we did avoid recession. The tax program the president outlined in a mid-1962 press conference, days after the worst stock market dive since 1929, looked toward extensive reform.

I recall producing a lengthy analysis of the economic impact of the proposed tax program for Under Secretary Henry "Joe" Fowler. He eagerly advocated for the plan in Congress and to the public. My analysis suggested that, in the then prevailing circumstances (some unemployment and no inflation), the tax reduction could not only provide a direct boost to consumption but also produce a "multiplier" effect—a surge in investment. Conceivably, I naïvely speculated, new investment might generate enough additional economic growth that tax receipts would rise, effectively offsetting much or even all of the lost revenue from cutting the top tax rates. Shades of Alvin Hansen! A precursor of supply-side economics! (Alternatively, a sign of the enthusiasm of a young economist smelling the roses in a big new Washington job.)

As it turned out, Secretary Dillon's initial presentation on the tax bill to Congress early in 1963 turned out to be, if not a disaster, disappointing. There was little or no support for the reform elements, and not much momentum for quick tax cuts either. Fortunately for me, I had no involvement in the failed reform proposals, which Secretary Dillon promptly and only half jokingly labeled as "Harvey's bill" (after Office of Tax Analysis director Harvey Brazer) on his return from testifying.

My direct superiors in the Treasury were Roosa and his deputy, J. Dewey Daane, both Michigan natives and longtime Federal Reserve officials who were primarily concerned with international finance. When Kennedy appointed Daane to the Federal Reserve Board in late 1963, I inherited the role of deputy under secretary with its grand office right across the hall from Roosa.

Kennedy was assassinated just one week before Daane was sworn in. The country was in turmoil. Roosa and I remained preoccupied with the defense of the dollar in international markets. As George Champion had feared, foreign industry had become more competitive. American exports, while still strong, couldn't fully offset the combination of rising imports, foreign aid, military spending, and surging capital outflows. As a result, the US balance of payments had turned negative—the postwar overseas "dollar shortage" was turning into a "dollar glut."

From time to time, European countries with dollar surpluses began to request that some of those reserves be converted into gold. This was a fundamental right established in the Bretton Woods agreement. At the end of 1945 our gold stock was $20 billion, about 70 percent of the total amount of gold held by central banks and governments worldwide and a multiple of all foreign official dollar holdings. By the end of 1961 our gold had declined to $17 billion, while our liabilities to foreigners had surged to $23 billion. Our gold no longer covered the amount of foreign dollar holdings entitled to "convertibility." Year by year, the discrepancy grew.

General Charles de Gaulle, proudly returned to the presidency of France, was preoccupied with restoring his nation's grandeur and resented American corporate takeovers of French companies. He accelerated French purchases of gold. His finance minister, Valéry Giscard d'Estaing, protested America's "exorbitant privilege" of easily financing its balance-of-payment deficits, and particularly US direct investments, by means of its trading partners' willingness to hold dollars.

Roosa's career at the Treasury was consumed by defending the Bretton Woods system of fixed exchange rates and its central premise that foreign central banks and governments could, on demand, convert dollars to gold at $35 an ounce. To Roosa this was as much a moral issue, an obligation taken on by the United States as the leader of the free world, as a matter of economic policy. In his office any consideration of devaluing the dollar or ending the convertibility of the dollar was taboo. The possibility that the dollar was chronically overvalued and that our gold stock might be depleted was simply not recognized in Treasury circles. American honor was at stake. Or so it seemed to those of us in Roosa's ambit.

In taking this view, the Treasury had practical support from President Kennedy, who (reportedly warned by his father) viewed the balance-of-payments deficits as one of the biggest potential threats to his presidency.

Roosa was, of course, highly sophisticated. He was well aware of Belgian economist Robert Triffin and the immutable logic of his "Triffin dilemma": over time, gold (the most trusted store of value) couldn't be produced fast enough to keep up with a growing world economy's need for international reserves. So, as a substitute, foreign central banks were willing to hold dollars for a while.

But to maintain growth in those dollar reserves, the United States would be forced to print more and to keep running balance-of-payments deficits, inexorably producing inflation and undermining the dollar's ability to be converted to gold on demand at the fixed $35 price. As a solution, Triffin proposed creating some kind of new reserve unit that would be globally accepted as a substitute for gold or the dollar.

Supported by his close relationships with key European central bankers, Roosa, in a burst of creative energy over two or three years, found extraordinary means to diffuse the potential pressures. The International Monetary Fund's ability to borrow from and lend to an inner group of member countries (eventually labeled the "Group of Ten," or G-10) was enlarged, arguably reducing the need for reserve growth. Legal grounds were found to allow the Treasury and the Federal Reserve to absorb excess foreign dollar holdings by engaging in so-called foreign currency swaps (in effect, short-term reciprocal borrowing arrangements among central banks). The Treasury broke tradition with some (then small-scale) borrowing in foreign currencies, promptly called "Roosa bonds." The Treasury and Federal Reserve worked together on Operation Twist, an effort to allow short-term interest rates to rise (to lure back investors who had put money abroad in search of higher returns) while keeping long-term interest rates steady (so the cost of mortgages and other loans wouldn't jump).*

Fifty years later these approaches became, consciously or not, precedents for the much more massive Federal Reserve/Treasury interventions to supply needed dollars to foreign central banks and to

---

*As a result, Treasury in mid-1963 was eager for the Fed to push short-term rates higher than was desired by Fed chairman Martin. I remember being instructed to attend the Fed's July 16 announcement of a discount rate increase to "make sure Martin gets his story straight." He can't have appreciated having a junior Treasury official seemingly monitoring his remarks.

stabilize credit markets and the economy during and after the 2008 financial crisis.

When this financial maneuvering seemed to reach its limits, the Treasury called for legislation taxing US capital exports. The intellectual rationale was to "equalize" the low American interest rates at the time with the higher rates prevailing in Europe, reducing incentives for American business to lend and invest abroad. The interest equalization tax would, we hoped, reduce the outflow of dollars.

I was asked to help draft the specifics with the help of Internal Revenue Service (IRS) experts. It was an eye-opener for me. I learned that an approach of seeming intellectual beauty, simple in concept, would be terribly difficult to apply in practice.

My IRS counterpart immediately wanted to know whether ordinary, short-term trade finance would be taxed or exempted. What about direct investment by American companies abroad? And, if exempted, precisely how would direct investment or trade finance be defined? Should the tax apply to Canada, which was furious at the prospect of interrupting the smooth functioning of a closely integrated financial system?

In the end, short-term capital was exempted. So was Canada and direct investment. It all required pages of elaborate definitions.

In one important respect, however, the legal drafting became irrelevant. At least for a time, the markets that might be affected responded as if the law was already in force.

I soon came to understand how one intervention led to another. If bonds were taxed, shouldn't bank loans abroad also be reduced? So "voluntary" restraints on bank lending were soon introduced and reinforced from time to time.

As those controls took effect, it wasn't long before market ingenuity developed what became known as the "Eurodollar market." In effect, dollar deposits ordinarily kept in New York were increasingly placed in London. Complex problems for regulation, competition, and monetary policy were raised and never fully resolved.

In November 1964, after Lyndon Johnson won reelection, Bob Roosa surprised me by deciding to leave for a comfortable partnership in the private bank Brown Brothers Harriman. Whether he was motivated by personal financial concerns (an under secretary's annual salary at the time was $28,500), by family pressures, or by sheer fatigue, I never knew.

I saw no signs that he was losing faith in the Bretton Woods order. However, by that time, our gold reserves had dropped to about half of our foreign liabilities. So the possibility intrigues me. Years later, when I decided the game was up, and acted on that premise, I wondered whether he felt I helped betray his legacy and all of his efforts to maintain the United States' post–World War II monetary leadership. Never in words or manner did he suggest that was so. To the contrary, he was supportive in public and private.

The battle over the dollar was not, of course, one for the Treasury alone. The respected economists appointed to the Council of Economic Advisers were primarily concerned about whether dollar policy would call for higher interest rates. The State Department, particularly Under Secretary George Ball, saw the Treasury's efforts as a potential threat to the dollar outflows needed to pay for overseas troops and foreign aid.

At times, the disagreements could become rather heated. My little insider joke was that part of the official oath of office, "to protect against all enemies foreign and domestic," were actually code words for the State Department and the CEA.

A gold committee, chaired by Secretary Dillon, was created to debate if not resolve the issues. My direct involvement was very limited, but I well remember one meeting in the Treasury conference room. The top foreign policy advisor to the president, the self-assured McGeorge Bundy, Under Secretary of State Ball, and Fed chairman Martin were among those in attendance. I was briefing Dillon when he was called away, leaving me with instructions to start the discussion.

The annoyance of the members over a mere deputy under secretary taking the chair was palpable. Bundy promptly announced that if the meeting was to discuss reducing troop expenditures in Germany to stem the dollar outflow, he would immediately leave. To my everlasting relief, Fed chairman Bill Martin swiftly intervened: "The stability of the dollar and our commitment to maintain the gold price is far more important than how many troops we have in Germany." I was happy to leave as Secretary Dillon reappeared.

Politics and Policy

After Roosa's departure, more and more of my time was spent as a kind of personal economic assistant to Secretary Dillon. I learned a lot from a man with a quick and disciplined mind, confident in his position and authority. I spent days drafting speeches that he edited in minutes. Many mornings I was presented with a request for analysis of one issue or another, often raised by the secretary's reading of the *New York Times* as his limousine passed me on my drive to work on Rock Creek Parkway.*

One particular incident grates to this day as too typical of government. New York governor Nelson Rockefeller, Dillon told me, was planning to build the World Trade Center in downtown New York. He needed help from the Treasury to make it economically viable. US Customs, a large Treasury agency, needed a lot of space in New York. Could it commit to taking many thousands of square feet in the planned buildings? More importantly, the Trade Center would be funded and owned by the New York–New Jersey Port Authority, the bistate agency that Rockefeller pretty much controlled. The Port Authority needed to know that the bonds it offered would be tax exempt, assuring lower interest rates and viable financing.

A couple of days later I delivered a short memo to the secretary.

1. Customs indeed needed new space. Lease negotiations for Canal Street space a few blocks north of the proposed World Trade Center were well advanced and promised a much lower rent.

---

*My old Nash Rambler had a broken front seat propped up by a chair in the back. Given the pressures on the dollar, I told Barbara that any replacement must be American made. We ended up with an inexpensive little red roadster. By contrast, I remember Dillon somewhat unhappily realizing he should replace his Bentley with a Cadillac.

2. There was clearly a considerable excess of downtown office space. Tax exemption for what would essentially be private commercial offices couldn't be justified under established Treasury guidelines.

The secretary quickly read through the memo, looked up, and pronounced:

"That's all fine, Paul. But what Nelson wants, Nelson will get."

In a similar vein, I was asked during the Johnson administration to lead an interagency study to propose how the federal government might encourage access to low-cost student loans. It was a hot issue and a number of approaches were being tested by state and local governments and private entities. We proposed waiting to "let a thousand flowers bloom," and determine later what justified intervention from the federal government. I remember the response from the White House assistant assigned to oversee our study: "Forget about this. There is an election ahead. We're going to have a program, it's going to be a federal program, and President Johnson is going to get credit for it."

Neither incident ended my Treasury days. I stayed on for some interesting months with Joe Fowler, the former under secretary appointed by Johnson to succeed Dillon in 1965.

Secretary Fowler was close to Johnson and extremely loyal. My first private visit to the Oval Office took place because the president wanted a briefing on how to deal with a supermarket chain that was raising prices. By the time Fowler and I arrived, the only thing on the president's mind was his decision a few days earlier to send marines into the Dominican Republic, which had captured the headlines. He delivered a monologue of self-justification. He never uttered a word about supermarket inflation. I was transfixed by the rocker on the president's chair inching closer and closer to his sleeping dog's tail as Johnson spoke and rocked. (Predictably, the tail moved away just in time.)

Fowler put me to a larger test soon after he took office. Returning from an extended "vacation" in Cape Cod, he gave me a draft of a long speech (he specialized in speaking at length) calling for an international conference on monetary reform that he planned to deliver to, of all groups, the Virginia Bar Association. While he didn't detail it there, the ultimate objective was clear enough: to create a new international reserve asset to complement, and eventually substitute, for gold and thus reduce pressure on the dollar. It would be the official answer to the Triffin dilemma.

What did I think?

Well, the frank answer was "Not much." Hadn't Bob Roosa warned repeatedly that initiating such a negotiation would inevitably spark concern about the dollar and the gold price? Shouldn't he at least first quietly assess the feelings of our foreign friends?

No, he said. With President Johnson's approval, he wanted to get a discussion started. He would simply test out the idea as a form of "contingency planning."

It took time but, three years after I left the Treasury, he pulled it off. It would fall to me to activate the new official reserve assets (with the awkward name of "special drawing rights") when, as under secretary for monetary affairs, I faced a deepening dollar crisis.

Later in the fall of 1965, Fowler became deeply concerned about a warning he had received from Fed chairman Martin. The Fed planned to raise its discount rate, the rate the Fed charges banks for short-term loans, with the presumed effect of raising all market rates. Martin's clear aim was to forestall inflationary pressures as Vietnam War spending rose in an already fully employed economy. A spirited internal debate developed. The Council of Economic Advisers and the Bureau of the Budget lined up with Fowler in pleading for delay. Privately, I was sympathetic to Martin's argument and hoped to persuade the secretary into a compromise: perhaps a quarter percentage point increase instead of the planned half point.

The unfortunate result for me was a four-man ad hoc committee to examine the issue. The composition was odd. Although I was the Treasury's representative, I was eager to compromise. Dan Brill, the Fed's research chief, was strongly opposed to any rate hike despite his boss's view. So were, in varying degrees, representatives from the CEA and the Bureau of the Budget (now the Office of Management and Budget). Predictably, we concluded that the decision could wait until January so it could be coordinated with the new budget.

Martin persisted. A Quadriad* meeting of "principals only" with President Johnson was scheduled for October 6. Secretary Fowler brought me along. He laid out the issue. The president recoiled at the idea of raising interest rates. It would, he said with an arm outstretched and fingers clenched, "amount to squeezing blood from the American working man in the interest of Wall Street."

Chairman Martin was unyielding. As he saw it, the restraint was needed and it was his responsibility. "Bill," the president finally said, "I have to have my gall bladder taken out tomorrow. You won't do this while I'm in the hospital, will you?"

"No, Mr. President, we'll wait until you get out."

And so it was done. In early December 1965, soon after I left the Treasury, the Fed did act, voting to raise the discount rate to 4.5 percent from 4 percent. Johnson, down in Texas, released a disappointed statement. Martin was called down to the "Ranch" to be given a mental, and by some reports a physical, trip to the proverbial woodshed.

I don't know the full story but it was a lesson for me. Over time two things did become clear. The Fed was slow to take further restrictive actions as Vietnam expenditures and the economy heated up. The president overruled his economic advisors' private pleas for a tax increase. My guess is that he understood that a tax vote in Congress would simply become a referendum on the unpopular Vietnam War—a referendum he would be bound to lose.

Whatever the reason at the time, some trace the beginning of the crippling Great Inflation of the 1970s, which led to my appointment as Fed chairman, to those failures.

I took up George Champion's offer and returned to the private sector just in time to see that inflationary process get under way.

---

*The Quadriad had been established in the Kennedy years as an informal but influential grouping of the four top economics agency heads: Treasury, Budget, CEA, and the Fed.

Chase Manhattan Redux: 1965–1968

I initially met David Rockefeller in 1957 when I first joined Chase. We were both wandering down the executive floor with new jobs, he as vice chairman of the board, I as the newly hired financial economist several layers of bureaucracy down, feeling rather lost. My years in the Treasury raised my profile when I returned to Chase, as did my new title of director of forward planning. But David and I remained, of course, at entirely different levels, in both the bank and in society.

I was reminded of the contrast once in his office in the dramatic new Chase skyscraper that he rightly hoped would help reinvigorate the downtown economy. It was late on a spring Friday and David graciously asked what I would be doing over the weekend. I responded that I was planning to visit the local nursery to buy some shrubs for planting around our house in New Jersey.* He responded that it was a coincidence; he would be on the same mission—in his case, flying to Florida to acquire some exotic tropical plants for his home and the extensive Rockefeller estates in Pocantico Hills, New York.

My Princeton art class proved useful when I could immediately identify the Cézanne in his office restroom. More visible around the new building were the large number of abstract art masterpieces he had commissioned.

Over the years David regularly traveled around the world, greeted as visiting royalty while meeting business and national leaders of all political stripes. The few trips I made with him were typically much closer to his home in Pocantico. From time to time, I prepared him for some now long-forgotten testimony before congressional committees. Members from both parties invariably welcomed him with respect.

---

*On my new $35,000 Chase salary I'd purchased a big old house on almost an acre of property in Montclair. Large houses were out of fashion at the time, so we got it for a relative bargain of $60,000. I loved that century-old house and its extensive landscaping.

I joined him regularly in the advisory committee meetings that Secretary Fowler had developed to advise, or at least support, the new international agreement creating special drawing rights (SDRs). Over the years, David led important nongovernmental institutions, notably the prestigious Council on Foreign Relations in New York, and the Trilateral Commission, which he essentially founded in the early 1970s (and to which I return in a later chapter). It was not a coincidence that I became active in both organizations.

Within Chase Manhattan itself, sometimes referred to as the "Rockefeller Bank" because of his family's long-standing ties, he shared leadership responsibilities. Over time, it became increasingly clear that the leaders' visions for the future of the bank differed.

George Champion, who rose through the Chase ranks from modest circumstances in Illinois, had become a strong chairman of the board. He was all domestic commercial banker, dedicated to maintaining the deeply ingrained credit culture for which the bank was known. In addition to corporate lending, his priority was to maintain close relationships with big businesses and other "correspondent" banks across the country.*

Chase was his all-consuming occupation. He knew the business and had nurtured the senior staff. Organizationally, Champion was in charge of the "line" operations.

David was a decade younger and hadn't been required to go through the ropes of credit training or to move step by step through the ranks. By instinct and experience, he had a broader international vision, less tied to Chase's traditions. He had the "staff" functions, including the economics unit and planning, the home of one Paul Volcker.

The net result was that over the years Chase, strong in domestic lending and relations with regional banks, fell well behind Citibank in Latin America, Asia, and the rest of the developing world. With domestic competition growing, and legal restrictions on interstate

---

*A correspondent bank carries out functions for another bank in a different location, which in those days before interstate branching was an important activity.

banking eroding, foreign expansion seemed necessary for Chase to catch up.

I was called back to the Treasury just a few years later and lost touch with George Champion and many Chase colleagues.* But from a distance, Chase seemed to lose momentum. It fell well behind the more aggressive Citibank and the new Citicorp holding company. The prestigious Morgan Bank in New York and the big Chicago and California banks were winning market share in what was Chase's home ground.

---

*As chairman of the Trilateral Commission and a member of the committee overseeing the Rockefeller trusts, I remained close to David until his death in 2017 at age 101. By coincidence, my office for many years has been in Rockefeller Center.

chapter 5

"THE BEST JOB IN THE WORLD"

There I was on January 20, 1969, watching President Richard Nixon's inaugural parade from the large office I was about to occupy as the incoming under secretary for monetary affairs in the US Treasury Department. To my south was the statue of Alexander Hamilton, the first and surely the most important secretary of the Treasury. He was also the founding father I most admired for the clarity of his view that good government is dependent on good administration.

Not long after noon, a sealed envelope arrived with the "secret" National Security Study Memorandum 7, signed by Henry Kissinger. A marvel of bureaucratic one-upmanship, the memo (dated January 21) arrived before the president's entourage even reached my vantage point above Fifteenth Street. Henry and his staff were already at work, setting the outer limits of his jurisdiction!

The memo was straightforward. A working group with participants from multiple agencies would be established to consider and recommend international monetary policies. As under secretary of the Treasury for monetary affairs I would chair that group. The fact that my nomination had not yet been publicly announced was beside the point. The study memorandum was indeed a succinct statement of what would occupy most of my attention in the rest of my Treasury career.

I came to play an almost unique role within the US government, granted responsibilities for both domestic and international finance—matters that over the years increasingly overlapped. Those policy areas had become familiar to me.

It was, for me, the best job in the world.

It began with a call from Charls Walker, newly designated as the other (and principal) Treasury under secretary. He asked me to come to Washington to visit with David Kennedy, who was about to become Nixon's Treasury secretary.

I knew "Charly" from his days as the Dallas Federal Reserve Bank's research vice president. Occasionally, he visited when I worked at the New York Fed's trading desk. I got to know him even better when he became president of the American Bankers Association, then located in New York, where he occasionally leaned on me for organizational help.

By contrast, I barely knew David Kennedy, a dedicated Mormon who had been chairman of the Continental Illinois Bank in Chicago. I was aware he'd had some early Federal Reserve experience and was considered a senior statesman in banking circles. Physically he looked the part: white haired, immaculately dressed, with a calm demeanor. Why had he chosen me to be under secretary for monetary affairs, the very position that my mentor, Bob Roosa, had held with such great distinction?

After all, I had served in 1960 as president of the Plainfield, New Jersey, John F. Kennedy for President Club. We won; Nixon lost.

There must have been something of a battle with the White House, where I was later identified as one of the Nixon administration's two Democrats (along with Daniel Patrick Moynihan).

My responsibilities consisted of economic analysis, debt management, oversight of federal credit program financing, dollar policy, and relationships with the IMF and World Bank. As time passed, Secretary Kennedy seemed content to give his team leeway and support: he was not inclined to micromanage. That reinforced my self-confidence (which Miss Palmer had astutely first called into question back when I was in kindergarten).

Charly Walker was satisfied managing most of the rest of Treasury: congressional relations, taxation, shepherding banking legislation, and the wide assortment of Treasury bureaus ranging at that time from Customs and Alcohol, Tobacco and Firearms to the IRS, Secret Service, and even the Coast Guard.

Our strong team included general counsel Bob Knight, economist Murray Weidenbaum, and assistant secretaries Eddie Cohen for taxes, John Petty for international affairs, Gene Rossides for customs, and John Carlock for fiscal affairs. We soon became close friends.

I felt well prepared by my earlier experience at the Federal Reserve, at Chase, and with Bob Roosa, Douglas Dillon, and Joe Fowler in my previous Treasury stint. The dollar problems were all too familiar to me, and my acquaintance (and in some cases working relationships) with a number of foreign financial officials helped.

For all the camaraderie, there was a sense of foreboding in the air. US gold reserves had dropped below $11 billion, while liabilities to foreigners were almost four times that amount. The inflation rate was above 4 percent. What was at stake was nothing less than the survival of the international monetary system established at Bretton Woods twenty-five years earlier to help the world economy heal after the war. We had no way of knowing the consequences—on trade, on unemployment, on peace—if the system collapsed. There was no time to waste.

It was in that context that Secretary Kennedy and his two under secretaries were granted an introductory meeting in the Oval Office. Both Charly and I warned that inflationary forces were gaining hold. The president might find it advantageous to take action early in his administration rather than face a more intractable inflation later.

I don't think President Nixon particularly appreciated our political advice. The conversation was not prolonged.

Two events in 1968 had disturbed already unsettled international monetary affairs. Strong public market demand for gold had required intervention by the major central banks, which sold gold from their reserves to prevent the price from rising above the long-established

$35 an ounce. That was part of an agreement between a "pool" of countries* established early in the Kennedy administration to defend the gold price. As official reserves of gold seeped away, France in 1968 decided to cease its share of the sales. At an emergency meeting in Washington led by Federal Reserve chairman Martin, the remaining pool members agreed to stop intervening to support the $35 price in the public market but to maintain that established price for official intergovernmental transactions. Gold's "market" price and "official" price soon diverged, raising obvious doubts about the dollar's gold value and its future stability.

Later in the year, an emergency meeting of the Group of Ten countries† was called in Bonn to deal with increasing strains among European exchange rates. As the West German economy recovered and its exporters became increasingly competitive, it had built up a big trade surplus, while France was importing more than it was exporting and had experienced a drain on its gold reserves. Economic logic required a lift in the value of Germany's mark (to make German exports more expensive) and a symmetrical devaluation of the French franc (to make French exports cheaper).

After much fruitless negotiation, neither proved politically acceptable. In particular, President Charles de Gaulle, ever devoted to France's honor, instead imposed internal policy restraints including currency controls, budget cuts, and a freeze of wages and prices. He blamed the franc's weakness on the student and worker demonstrations earlier in the year. The result was to encourage political opposition within France. Five months later, the seventy-eight-year-old De Gaulle would resign after losing a referendum.

The uncertainty in monetary affairs was reinforced by escalating calls among academics, and some of my new counterparts over at the White House's Council of Economic Advisers, to allow more fluctuation between currencies. Suggestions included wider trading

---

*Belgium, Britain, France, West Germany, Italy, the Netherlands, Switzerland, and the United States.

†The Group of Ten actually includes eleven major economies that consult on international financial and economic matters.

margins and "crawling" or "sliding" pegs that would permit or encourage currencies to make some small depreciations or appreciations. Milton Friedman, openly and loudly, had been advocating much more radical action: a system of freely floating exchange rates which, in his view, would let the markets rapidly and efficiently correct international payment imbalances and better reconcile differences in national monetary policies. In effect, he was proposing to discard a major part of the Bretton Woods agreement and leave currencies to the whim of the (in his view, perfectly rational) market, without any concern for other countries' wishes.

His principal intellectual opponent was Bob Roosa, who argued that the 1930s experience amply demonstrated the instability that floating exchange rates could create, the very antithesis of the order embodied in the Bretton Woods agreement.

In the United States and abroad there was still little support for simply abandoning fixed exchange rates. It was on my first visit as under secretary to a Working Party III meeting of the Organization for Economic Cooperation and Development (OECD)* in Paris that this point was made forcefully by one of my European counterparts.

In those days, the custom after the official meeting (itself confidential) was for the principal members to retreat to a suburban hideaway, in this case the residence of the Dutch ambassador. The idea was to encourage a frank exchange of views around the dinner table away from our staff and the press. In fact, I was soon verbally (and almost physically) assaulted by the Belgian central bank governor, who came waving his finger in my face: "If you go out and encourage all this talk about flexible exchange rates, speculation will bring down the system. The blood will be on your American head!"

I knew he had a point. The rather technical changes being discussed could not significantly alter our balance-of-payments deficit

---

*The OECD is a forum for international economic cooperation and the Working Party III was a subgroup of the OECD that met privately to address balance-of-payment dislocations.

and would only amplify uncertainty about the future of the dollar. So, after the meeting, when asked at a press conference for my views on flexible exchange rates, I tried to stay aloof. There had been "a lot of discussion [of these ideas] in academic circles and that's where they can stay."

A currency system underpinned by $35 gold remained at risk to speculative pressures. As things turned out, rising US interest rates through most of 1969—reflecting a seemingly determined effort to deal with the inflationary pressure—supported confidence in the dollar. But that couldn't last. Devising solutions to a possible crisis remained a priority for the "Volcker Group" established by Henry Kissinger's Study Memorandum 7. Working harmoniously with many colleagues I knew from my earlier Treasury days, we prepared recommendations for the president.

None of us were ready to simply abandon the Bretton Woods framework of fixed exchange rates and convertibility of the dollar into gold. Our analysis did, however, reinforce the need for change. Our remaining gold reserves in mid-1969 were only 25 percent of foreign-dollar liabilities, down from almost 80 percent at the beginning of the Kennedy administration eight years earlier. The Triffin dilemma was apparent for all to see.

More immediately, we concluded that a probable French devaluation would stir further uncertainty. Indeed, the French did devalue in August 1969, more than three months after De Gaulle resigned.

One obvious idea was to massively increase the official gold price of $35, instantly doubling or tripling the dollar value of our diminished gold reserves. But that would mainly benefit South Africa and the Soviet Union, two politically unfriendly gold-producing countries, as well as rewarding the few European nations like France that had been demanding gold for their dollars. There was no guarantee that it would accomplish our real objectives: reducing the dollar's value relative to other currencies (like the German mark and the Japanese yen) to help boost our exports, reduce our imports, and narrow our balance-of-payments deficit.

To achieve those goals, a small change in the gold price along the lines of 10 or 15 percent might facilitate depreciation of the dollar, but in practice other countries would probably quickly follow with their own devaluations relative to gold. In any case, the United States would be abandoning its long-standing commitment to the fixed dollar price of gold, the lynchpin of the Bretton Woods system, a basic element in cooperative world leadership. That would be especially damaging to our closest allies who had refrained from converting their dollars into gold. Nor would it resolve the Triffin dilemma. Dependence on the dollar at a fixed gold price to meet the growing reserve needs of an expanding world economy was approaching its natural limit.

The remaining option was step-by-step evolutionary change. Creating more officially acceptable international reserve assets to supplement gold and the dollar. Encouraging currency appreciation by economically strong allies—Germany and especially Japan—to help restore balance-of-payments equilibrium. Restoring domestic price stability. All of these approaches would be critical to maintaining confidence in the dollar.

It made for a rather long and complicated presentation to the president in the Cabinet Room of the White House. When Nixon eventually called the meeting to a close, Secretary Kennedy remarked to me, "Paul, he didn't say no. You have a green light." So I was on my way. (Only later did I learn that it was typical for Mr. Nixon to end meetings without comment, only to give his decision in a later memo.)

One hopeful confidence-building step was a tough negotiation to force South Africa to sell its new gold production at market prices instead of to central banks at the official government price, a question that had been left open in 1968 when the two-tier gold market was formed. The result was that, at least temporarily, the market price dropped to (or slightly below) the official price. That could not last for long.

Another, more systematic, step we could take was to propose activation of the recently agreed special drawing rights, the culmination of Joe Fowler's contingency planning speech to the Virginia

Bar. Even that seemingly modest step was questioned by continental Europeans, habitually concerned that the United States was trying by one device or another to escape monetary discipline.

I promptly set off to sell the idea of activating these new special drawing rights, traveling right around the world. We succeeded, but with a reduced amount: $3.5 billion of the "paper gold" in year one and $3 billion in each of the next two. Tiny by today's standards and well short of the boost in confidence that we sought.

Finally, Fed chairman Martin, whose restrictive monetary policy Nixon (advised by then professor Arthur Burns) had blamed for his 1960 election defeat, retired from the Fed in early 1970. Burns then became the new chairman. He was a highly respected business cycle expert and certainly close to the president. But to me the new Fed leadership seemed almost perversely willing to ease policy, reducing money market interest rates, even when the dollar was under pressure. More than once I pleaded with my longtime associate and friend, Fed governor Dewey Daane, to encourage the chairman not to ease when I was scheduled to meet with my foreign counterparts.

In the end, none of those measures—South African gold sales, activating SDRs, or even a mildly restrained monetary policy—would be enough to save the dollar or address the underlying payments deficits. The competitive position of the United States, reflected in a declining trade surplus, was simply not strong enough to offset the large government expenditures abroad and chronic capital outflows. A more fundamental approach would be necessary.

I had great respect for Arthur Burns as a student of business cycles. And I know he also felt strongly, even emotionally, that the independence of the Federal Reserve was critically important—he would often compare it to the Supreme Court. It has since become clear that he was under persistent pressure from the White House. The extent to which that influenced his policies remains unknown to me. After all, central bankers have been congenitally reluctant to "take away the punchbowl" and begin restrictive action when the inflation process is still nascent. In any event, the Fed wasn't going to save the dollar.

We endlessly debated options for reform in the Volcker Group. Every member had ample opportunity to express their ideas. The oldest and wisest, George Willis, led the Treasury's international staff. He was the only one of us who held an official position at the time of the 1944 conference in Bretton Woods. He took endless notes at our meetings. When asked to comment on a proposal, he consistently answered in his deep, gravelly voice: "It won't work."

Exasperated at one meeting, I finally asked, "Okay, George, what will work?"

"Nothing" was the even more gruff answer.

Well, I wasn't ready to surrender. Instead, I came to feel that sooner or later we would have to suspend our promise to convert dollars into gold as a means to an end: the only way of forcing an adequate exchange-rate realignment and serious reform. Rather than waiting until we faced escalating demands for gold, impossible to meet, we needed to find the right time to take the initiative.

To prepare, I asked a careful and discreet senior staff economist, John Auten, to (very confidentially) estimate how much the dollar's market value would have to fall to help balance our external payments. A few weeks later the answer came back: at least 15 percent if the dollar was devalued against just the European and Japanese currencies, 10 percent if (unrealistically) the whole world would accept the change.

That was enough to get me started on a long memo outlining the proposed approach: "suspension" (of gold convertibility), negotiation of new exchange values, and "reform," in that order, all intended to "reinvigorate" the Bretton Woods system.

Just at that time a powerful new political force arrived at the Treasury. John Connally, the former Democratic governor of Texas, had become nationally famous when he was wounded while accompanying President Kennedy in Dallas on the day of the assassination. After seeing the forceful and articulate Connally in action at the White House as a member of the so-called Ash Council to reorganize the government, Nixon became enamored and recruited him to replace David Kennedy at Treasury in early 1971.

Assuming change was in order, I prepared a resignation letter. Connally, the lone Democrat cabinet member in the administration, brushed it aside at our first meeting. His only demand, he told me and other Treasury officials, would be loyalty.

Our personalities could hardly have been more different: a brazen Texas political animal paired with a cautious Ivy League economic advisor. Somehow, opposites attracted; we got along. Living by himself during his early days in Washington, he sometimes invited me to accompany him to dinner with high-ranking friends in the business community.

Without economic training, Connally instead was guided by his instinct that the United States was in economic trouble and needed a weaker dollar, particularly against the Japanese yen, to reduce import competition and to help our exporters. A World War II veteran who served in the Pacific, he became known for blunt lines like "If they aren't willing to accept Iowa beef and Florida citrus and Rhode Island manufactured goods, they had better be prepared to sit on the docks of Yokohama in their Toyotas, watching their own Sonys." Not exactly a cautious diplomatic approach respectful of "the well-manicured playing fields of international finance"—a line I had inserted in one of his speeches. In essence, he had no patience for some of the technical reform ideas discussed by economists and some administration advisors. On that we agreed.

The force of his personality made a mark on the White House as well as on the Treasury. Secretary Kennedy had lost clout and access to the president. Nixon, by contrast, seemed to want Connally's advice on almost every issue. Presidential staff, formerly disdainful of the Treasury and in the habit of giving orders, suddenly were told to check almost everything with the Treasury. Even the White House's resident economic advisors—George Shultz, Paul McCracken, Pete Peterson—suddenly were forced unhappily to play second fiddle. Arthur Burns's own diaries provide a vivid account of the confusion and uncertainty that John Connally's arrival created in the White House.

All of the other demands on his time couldn't distract the new secretary from the growing crisis in the international financial system. One day he wandered into my office and raised the question, "What should we do?" My memorandum on that very subject wasn't yet final. I handed him a draft.

I never saw that text again, but there were signs that he took its recommendations to heart. He made it clear that this was an area in which he (and the Treasury) would lead the charge.

In early May, Germany stopped defending the dollar (stopped buying dollars to combat speculators selling dollars and buying marks) and allowed its currency to float temporarily. By the end of that month, Connally was in Munich for his first official meeting with his foreign counterparts and leading bankers. The annual International Banking Conference was comprised of chief executive officers of the fifty largest international banks and invited official guests.

Connally was the final speaker. We had prepared a draft with an unsurprising conclusion about the need for reform and currency adjustments; that is, appreciation for chronic surplus countries, as Germany had already acted. He replaced it with a firm declaration: "Helpful to the solution of any problem is the understanding there are necessarily some unalterable positions of any participant. Believing this, I want without any arrogance or defiance to make it abundantly clear that we are not going to devalue, we are not going to change the price of gold, we are going to control inflation."

That was one way to fend off the speculators betting against the dollar.

I asked if he really wanted to be so firm given that, realistically, our position very likely needed to change. His reply remains etched in my memory: "That's my unalterable position today. I don't know what it will be this summer."

He delivered the speech with great force, perhaps amplified by the fact that he had a slight fever. The world of finance quickly understood there was a new American leader to be reckoned with.

Complicating the situation further, the US economy had begun to struggle. Unemployment topped 6 percent and the inflation rate remained stubbornly at around 4 percent, neither so bad in light of subsequent developments but not near what the administration had promised. At the Munich conference, Arthur Burns had reiterated his own call for an "incomes policy" to curb increases in wages and prices.

After a lot of internal debate, Connally was designated as the administration's official spokesman for economic policy on June 29 and announced what became known as the "four nos": no mandatory wage and price controls, no wage-and-price review board, no tax cut, no increased federal spending. All were soon to be violated but, temporarily, concerns about the monetary system seemed shoved aside.

Behind the scenes, however, the secretary had privately begun raising with the president the need to suspend gold convertibility as our reserves slid toward $10 billion. He reported to me by early August that the president was pretty convinced. Perhaps I could brief George Shultz, director of the Office of Management and Budget, and Paul McCracken, chair of the Council of Economic Advisers, about our thinking. But the president wanted to defer action until Congress returned from its August recess.

I had earlier assembled a team of three or four people in Treasury that included Assistant General Counsel Michael Bradfield and Bill Dale, the United States' executive director at the IMF, to develop a proposed approach: (1) announce the suspension of gold convertibility and the logic behind it; (2) explain the need for substantial exchange-rate changes after a "transitional" float; (3) impose a three-month wage and price freeze to forestall an immediate inflationary reaction; and (4) clarify that only after the exchange-rate negotiations could we consider a more suitably reformed system. The supporting details went so far as to set out when and whom to notify among our closest foreign colleagues. But, to my subsequent regret, we didn't place front and center the need for restrictive anti-inflationary monetary policies—after all, that was the Fed's business.

Secretary Connally, without reviewing the details, insisted on including a surcharge on imports, aimed particularly at Japan. I disliked the idea, which seemed to be a return to the "economic weapons" that the Bretton Woods agreement was designed to outlaw, and repeatedly dropped it from drafts of the "action" paper. Connally always insisted on restoring it. He was convinced that the monetary negotiations would need to be accompanied by an opening of foreign markets and a better allocation of NATO expenditures. (As I write this in the midst of the Trump administration, *plus ça change, plus c'est la même chose.*)

With action postponed until after the summer recess, Connally retreated to his Texas ranch with instructions to "call me if needed." He didn't have long to wait.

The activist and ambitious Henry Reuss, chairman of the House Banking Committee, issued a report on Saturday, August 7, nominally on behalf of a joint House-Senate subcommittee demanding changes in the dollar exchange rates, especially against the yen. Two months earlier, Reuss had urged the United States to close the gold window and temporarily let the dollar float. He could have been reading our playbook.

Within days, market speculation began in force. The dollar came under selling pressure and much larger gold demands seemed likely, confirmed by a request from the UK at the end of the week. I called Connally to let him know that we couldn't wait. He rushed back and went to see Nixon. They agreed to take action that weekend. The day I had long anticipated, but also long feared, was about to be here. The structure of the international monetary system that I spent years defending would be torn apart.

Camp David

Perhaps twenty of us were called to Camp David, mainly presidential assistants, CEA members, and Budget Director George Shultz. To ensure that our deliberations remained secret, we were prohibited from any communication with the outside world. But I will always recall CEA member Herb Stein's instinctive response to a casual question from a young naval officer who wondered what the sense of excitement was all about:

"This is an historic day."

My feeling precisely.

Shortly after we arrived, sitting in the Aspen Cottage, the president set out the framework for the meeting, and turned it over to Connally, who laid out the plan:

• Suspend dollar-gold convertibility.
• The official gold price is unchanged.
• A ninety-day wage and price freeze.

Nixon and Connally added several elements that hadn't been in my version of the plan. The 10 percent surcharge on imports, a package of tax cuts and credits, some specific trade restrictions, and a vague proposal to extend price controls after the initial freeze. Very little was said about working with our foreign counterparts toward reform.

Arthur Burns dissented. He argued essentially (to me, totally unrealistically) that he could quickly negotiate a satisfactory exchange-rate relationship with his "friends," French finance minister Valéry Giscard d'Estaing and Jelle Zijlstra at the Bank for International Settlements. The president gave him a private hearing but the decision stood.

All of the discussion was later reported in great detail in Nixon speechwriter Bill Safire's 1975 memoir *Before the Fall: An Inside View of the Pre-Watergate White House*. Decades later, I'm still impressed at how insightful he was about what the weekend meant to me:

> Even as we kidded around, the men in the room knew that Volcker was undergoing an especially searing experience. He was schooled in the international monetary system, almost bred to defend it; the Bretton Woods Agreement was sacrosanct to him; all the men he grew up with and dealt with throughout the world trusted each other in crisis to respect the rules and cling to the few constants like the convertibility of gold. Yet here he was participating in the overthrow of all he held permanent; it was not a happy weekend for him.

We spent Saturday putting the pieces together, justifying the import surcharge by executive order with the sweeping, if little used, Tariff Act of 1930 and Trade Expansion Act of 1962. Treasury's assistant general counsel Mike Bradfield, essentially my lawyer, played a crucial role in developing and defending our legal strategy; the Secret Service, at my request, roused him out of bed to get to Camp David. The draft speech I had been asked to prepare on short notice was (appropriately) discarded, and the president himself worked with Bill Safire on preparing for a Sunday evening announcement.

The State Department wasn't represented, apparently reflecting the president's lack of trust that it would adequately defend the new policies to foreign governments. I was told National Security advisor Henry Kissinger was in Europe and that my counterpart at the State Department was on vacation and need not be disturbed. Nor did the IMF receive notice and a request for approval, as called for in its articles of agreement. As a poor substitute I invited the IMF's managing director, Pierre-Paul Schweitzer, to the secretary's office to watch the president's 9 p.m. Sunday broadcast on television. He was not happy about the substance of the program or about learning the news after the fact in this way.

Neither was the State Department assistant secretary whom I'd invited to review the draft press release. He was particularly upset by one addition that had been proposed by Connally: the United States would be notifying Canada of our intent to end a long-established bilateral agreement that ended tariffs on trade in autos and auto parts. "The Canadians will be furious!" he burst out, inadvertently bearing out the president's concerns about the department's loyalties.

It so happened that provision stood alone on the very last page of the press release, which was being printed at that very moment. I suggested he go down to the Treasury printing office and tear off the last page of each release, which he did. So far as I know, no one really cared too much about the omission.

I also violated strict instructions against notifying any of my international colleagues by making a single call to my Japanese counterpart, Yusuke Kashiwagi. Japan's financial market would be opening just as Nixon spoke and I wanted him to be warned.

I don't know whether that call made it any easier for the Japanese to deal with the crisis they would call the "Nixon shokku" coming shortly after the first "Nixon shock" of the opening to China. They pleaded that they had no intention of converting their rapidly growing dollar holdings into gold in any event. I do know that my gesture was greatly appreciated by Japanese officials. Yusuke Kashiwagi, and even now his wife and sons and daughter, have remained friends for fifty years.

chapter 6

MONETARY REFORM

FRUSTRATED

Nixon's August 15 speech was a stark contrast to the plea for cooperation and vaguely apologetic "we have sinned and will do better" draft I had hastily written. He was instead taking "bold leadership" to "create a new prosperity without war."

It worked. Media coverage led with the wage and price controls and the benefits for businesses. Stocks soared, with the Dow Jones Industrial Average posting what was then its biggest one-day gain on record.

Abroad, people were stunned. Currency exchanges were temporarily shut. American tourists discovered their dollars, at least temporarily, were suddenly no longer accepted in many places. The president's decision to suddenly—unilaterally—stop honoring his country's decades-long official commitment to exchange $35 into an ounce of gold cast uncertainty over the international financial order the United States had itself developed and defended.

I set out overnight with Governor Daane and Sam Cross to London, courtesy of the US Air Force, to meet with my European counterparts (and, by chance, two from Japan) and explain why our action was urgently required. We would need a significant realignment of currency rates. Full reform of the system was important but could wait.

The sense of shock, even of betrayal, was palpable, even though market participants had been calling urgently for action to reduce our balance-of-payments deficit. The European press was decidedly mixed. In Paris, where I met with a surprisingly serene Giscard d'Estaing, the media was trumpeting the end of American leadership. I had a chance to see my daughter, who was passing through Paris as part of a summer exchange program. Photographed smiling in the back of a limousine, we were accused in the press of treating ourselves to a family holiday.

Connally shared my view that the "interim" float could and should be maintained for some time, testing our trading partners' appetite for an adequate dollar depreciation that would enable our exports to be more competitive on the world markets. We held firm on our refusal to raise the price of gold. An emergency Group of Ten meeting in London in September only reached agreement that we should meet again later. That was where Connally called for a $13 billion swing in our balance of payments, making the point that a serious adjustment was needed to allow the United States to achieve a minimum surplus in our current account to balance capital and official outflows. He famously responded to critical questions from foreign officials by saying, "The dollar is our currency but your problem." My own counterparts abroad came to recognize the logic of a transitional float and the necessary suspension of gold convertibility. They were eager to reach a quick settlement, but still resistant to the trade and monetary measures we deemed necessary.

By late November, attitudes softened on both sides. A little too much on our side in my view.

President Nixon, presumably concerned with his forthcoming historic trip to China and encouraged by Henry Kissinger, had scheduled visits in December with French president Georges Pompidou and British prime minister Edward Heath. He wanted the monetary issue resolved to smooth the political way. On the eve of a scheduled G-10 meeting in Rome, Connally told me the president was willing to accept a change in the dollar price of gold to facilitate agreement with the French.

The result was the strangest official meeting I have experienced. In a preliminary meeting with my counterparts, I suggested that, for the first time, we were looking toward an 11 percent drop in the value of the dollar, on average, against all of the other industrialized countries' currencies. That offer, we explained, would be enough to enable us to end the import tax, but not to reopen the gold window.

By the order of the alphabet, Connally happened to be G-10 chairman at that time. Somewhat artificially, I was left to be the US spokesperson at the closed-door ministerial meeting at the Palazzo Corsini the next morning. As anticipated, it started with our counterparts insisting that the United States needed to offer more—most insistently, a change in the price of gold to ease their acceptance of a relative appreciation of their currency.

After a whispered consultation with Connally, I raised the hypothetical question of a 10 percent or 15 percent dollar devaluation against gold. Connally immediately responded, "Let's assume 10 percent" and asked for the ministers' responses.

There was silence for nearly an hour. Finally, Karl Schiller, the rather freewheeling German academic who had become economic minister, spoke. Germany could accept a 10 percent dollar devaluation and would be willing to "add some percentage to it." What did "some" mean? Schiller replied that in his language "some" was quite clear; it "doesn't mean one, it means two." So that potentially got us to 12 percent depreciation of the dollar against the mark. After more silence, the request was made to adjourn the meeting until after lunch, with the unstated condition of consultation by the finance ministers with their heads of state.

Definitive responses would have to wait until another day. Connally reminded the group that the United States also would be demanding that their countries increase their own defense spending and reduce trade restrictions with the US. The finance ministers promptly pleaded lack of authority. In particular, trade was within the jurisdiction of the European Commission.

Connally asked, "Does the relevant commissioner happen to be here?"

"Yes, he is in the anteroom."

"Bring him in."

Raymond Barre, put on the spot and ignorant of the background, was understandably helpless to respond to Connally's demands. (Five years later, he would become prime minister of France.)

The meeting ended. The embarrassed ministers demanded that any tapes be destroyed. Connally affirmed that he would take that responsibility, and briefed the press, quite accurately, that progress had been made but no agreement could be reached in Rome.

That evening, I learned something more about the power of Connally's political instincts. After a formal dinner in a grand palazzo at the top of one of Rome's seven hills, he stood and, seemingly extemporaneously, extolled the triumphant achievements of ancient Rome, of Italy, of modern European civilization. We ministers of finance bore responsibility for bringing the world's monetary affairs, and indeed humanity itself, into greater harmony.

The impact was electric. Once viewed as a crude Texas bully insensitive to the need for international cooperation, Connally seemed to reveal himself as an erudite, if forceful, global statesman.

Within four weeks, an agreement was reached.

The terms were pretty well settled in mid-December as part of a meeting between Nixon and Pompidou at, of all places, an American military base in the Azores. Nixon, preparing to visit China, was eager to discuss geopolitics. Pompidou, a former banker at the Rothschild investment firm, instead lectured Nixon on the gold price. He explained that the French had historically cherished gold as a bulwark against turmoil. It was a politically sensitive subject for him. A potential change in the gold price had already been broached in Rome. Pompidou insisted it be raised to precisely $38 an ounce and that the French franc's gold price remain unchanged. That would depreciate the dollar against the franc, but not enough to make me happy.

As Pompidou and Nixon moved on to other topics, the remaining monetary issues were delegated to a parallel meeting between Connally and Giscard d'Estaing, accompanied by their deputies—me and Jacques de Larosière. Although the French had won a somewhat smaller increase in the gold price than the 10 percent discussed in Rome, Giscard acknowledged that dollar convertibility into gold could not and would not be restored until we'd achieved full reform of the international monetary system. Japan would be required to appreciate the yen much more sharply. Substantially wider trading bands would be set around the new "central" values, allowing more currency fluctuation.

Our discussions took a bit longer than those between Nixon and Pompidou, making the leaders impatient. When we eventually reached an agreement, we realized that we lacked secretarial help and that none of us men knew how to type. We called on the wife of an army sergeant stationed at the base to find a typewriter. She turned my barely legible notes into an official document, with me reading over her shoulder. Somewhere, I still have a signed carbon copy.

The Smithsonian agreement that followed in Washington just before Christmas was, for me, something of an anticlimax. Most members of the G-10 accepted that they would follow the agreed adjustment in the gold price with an equivalent appreciation of their own domestic currencies against the dollar. Germany, as promised, did "some" more. Japan was pressed hard to lift the yen by almost twice as much. But the overall result remained well below the 10 to 15 percent dollar devaluation that, in my own mind, seemed the minimum necessary. Still, I know of no precedent for realigning so many currencies in a single meeting.

Connally asked Nixon to appear and put his blessing on the agreement. He did so in grand style, praising it as "the most significant monetary agreement in the history of the world." I turned to one of my assistants and whispered, "I hope it lasts three months."

Floating Forever?

The first cracks appeared just six months later when British inflation and a deteriorating balance of trade led to speculation against the pound. The British stopped defending the pound's official price

and let it float in late June. Late in the year and into 1973, speculative flows out of Italian lira and into Swiss francs gathered strength,
challenging the staying power of the Smithsonian agreement. More
broadly, by February 1973 exchange markets were disturbed to the
point that some official intervention was required to stabilize the
dollar.

Why not seize the moment, I reasoned, and press for the additional dollar depreciation that was needed to strengthen the United
States' competitive position?

Secretary Connally had resigned in mid-May after a dramatic
eighteen months in his Treasury role. It was his successor, George
Shultz, who would need to be convinced of my idea, simple to state
but obviously difficult to implement. The United States would raise
the dollar price of gold by another 10 percent. Japan would be asked
to appreciate the yen 20 percent against the dollar. The Europeans
and, I hoped, some developing countries positioned to benefit from
the Japanese appreciation would permit their currencies to appreciate by 10 percent against the dollar.

Perhaps surprisingly, the idea quickly took hold. The president,
having won a second term in office, authorized me to initiate negotiations. A busy weekend in early February 1973 started with a secret
trip on an air force plane to meet with Japanese finance minister
Kiichi Aichi at his home in Tokyo on Friday night. Understandably, he was taken aback by the scope of my proposals. He couldn't
immediately agree to a 20 percent appreciation. Being a brave and
cooperative man, he proposed to let the yen float upward, even close
to 20 percent higher, provided the Europeans in turn allowed their
currencies to rise by 10 percent vis-à-vis the dollar.

I decided that was good enough and prepared to head to Bonn to
meet with German finance minister Helmut Schmidt, who I thought
was most likely to help in reaching agreement. Unfortunately, the air
force crew was required to get more rest before another overnight
flight; the alternate crew had been left in Anchorage, Alaska. My
deputy in Washington, Jack Bennett, negotiated with the secretary
of defense to get the rule waived.

Given the delay, I landed in Bonn just in time to see Schmidt's plane take off for Paris. Forewarned of my arrival, he wanted to prepare a common position with the French. I stayed overnight in Bonn, and saw Schmidt and the Bundesbank president the next day. I got enough encouragement to travel to Paris and London and even Rome, where the currency market disturbances had originated.

Finally, at a Sunday midnight meeting at Giscard d'Estaing's apartment in Paris, a consensus was reached. The proposals with respect to exchange rates were agreed.

Moreover, there was no objection to George Shultz's position that, with a big adjustment in exchange rates, the United States could safely lift its controls on foreign investment and bank loans. (Our domestic wage and price controls and the 10 percent import surcharge had already been ended.)

I was disappointed by another point. The newly agreed exchange rates and gold price ($42.22), in my view, would be highly vulnerable to renewed speculation. To convey a sense of confidence, we should be prepared to intervene collectively to stabilize the gold market: in effect create a new gold pool. That, unfortunately, was not agreed.

The Japanese had shadowed my trip to Bonn by sending a former vice finance minister who was well known to me. Once the Europeans confirmed the agreement, Japan did as well. My four-day odyssey spanning some thirty thousand miles was over. Secretary Shultz unveiled the changes, including an end to the interest equalization tax that I once helped write, on the evening of Monday, February 12, in Washington.

Most foreign exchange markets in Western Europe and Japan were closed on the day after the announcement. As they reopened, the price of gold held steady at first but soon jumped sharply higher without official resistance. By early March, speculative pressures against the dollar had grown strong enough to lead Japan and Western European countries to close their exchange markets once again.

The major European nations invited the United States to an emergency meeting in Paris on Friday, March 9. It turned out to be momentous. The morning session was spent largely by ministers expressing their individual frustrations about the lack of practical options. Finally, temporary floating seemed the only reasonable avenue.

Shultz, ideologically in favor of floating exchange rates and free markets in general, had been among the Nixon advisors who wanted to adopt that approach when the gold window was closed in 1971. At that point, he had been overruled by Connally and Burns and eventually the president. I wasn't sure how he would react once he had the full responsibilities of Treasury secretary.

Less well known to the rest of the group in Paris, Shultz had remained mute all morning. Eventually, the chair asked Shultz if a resort to floating for the time being would be acceptable. His answer was that, yes, he could accept that result if it was the consensus of the group.

That "temporary" arrangement essentially remains in place fifty years later. The world has been operating without an agreed monetary standard, with varying degrees of "floating" and "fixing," and with the dollar still the global reserve currency.

As I look back, the coda for the Bretton Woods composition was silently expressed at a private lunch in Paris one week later. Arthur Burns pleaded with George Shultz once again to work toward restoring a fixed exchange rate for the dollar. My instinctive comment, given that the dollar couldn't possibly be stabilized unless we tackled our inflation problem, was "Then, you'd better get back to Washington and tighten money."

He didn't go.

At a press conference in Paris, a reporter asked how the agreement would affect US monetary policy. Burns seized the microphone to declare: "Whatever happens to the discount rate is decided in Washington, not in Europe."

Reform

During the year after the Smithsonian agreement but before the decision on the temporary float, the groundwork had been laid for a thoroughgoing reform of the international monetary system. Shortly after he became Treasury secretary in 1972, George Shultz had asked me a perfectly reasonable question. What plans did we have for a reformed monetary system? The honest answer was very little. With the annual meeting of the International Monetary Fund looming on the horizon, that was an unacceptable position—we needed to be better prepared.

I got to work and within a few weeks the Volcker Group had a framework for reform. It provided Secretary Shultz with a forward-looking speech at the annual meeting of the IMF, specifically calling for monetary discussions within a newly created negotiating forum. We suggested that the group remain at an arm's length from the IMF's managing director and board. The heavy weighting of European countries within the G-10, and within the IMF itself, meant that it would be helpful to bring in representatives from some of the larger developing nations as a counterweight. Not so incidentally, they could help resist the European efforts, unrealistic to me, to strictly limit the role of the dollar in the international monetary system.

There was, of course, some irony that the US government, having led the Bretton Woods conference that created the IMF almost forty years earlier, was now creating a new negotiating forum to get around the IMF. But the world had changed in both economic and political dimensions. The small European countries had lost influence relative to Japan and the big developing nations. The latter group, not so incidentally from our point of view, would be likely to accept a less rigid exchange-rate system.

The result was a new Committee of Twenty, comprised of finance officials and central bankers from twenty countries. The number of voices threatened, as one new member soon described it, to descend into a multilateral monologue with no common ground. At times, it seemed to me a dialogue of the world against the United States.*

---

*The following year, Shultz created the precursor to the Group of Five when he invited finance ministers from France, Germany, and the UK to an informal meeting in the White House library. Japan was added to that library group soon afterward.

This was particularly true in September 1972, when, shortly before the IMF annual meeting in Washington, I took it upon myself to address the lingering dissatisfaction among US officials with IMF managing director Pierre-Paul Schweitzer.

Personally, I admired Schweitzer, who had fought in the French resistance during World War II, had been liberated from a concentration camp, and had a Nobel Prize–winning uncle, Albert Schweitzer. But Pierre-Paul had made himself close to persona non grata with Connally and Shultz, and with Secretary Kennedy earlier, by repeatedly trying to seize control of monetary negotiations, by lecturing the United States, and by sometimes even insulting its representatives.

Finally, in an effort to clear the air, I suggested we inform Schweitzer that the United States would support his reappointment on the condition that he agree to serve for only a year or two.

Schweitzer recognized that for what it was—a vote of no confidence—and told the press he did not expect reappointment. It made for a testy beginning to the IMF meeting that year when, at the outset, members gave Schweitzer a standing ovation. The point was, I believe, to criticize the heavy-handed United States as much as to express admiration for the man himself. Secretary Shultz's constructive speech helped to save the day by laying out his desire to advance the reform discussions in the Committee of Twenty.

From the start of those discussions, the Europeans, with Schweitzer's evident support, pressed hard for a system of "asset settlement." The goal was to rule out the wide use of the dollar as a reserve currency and prevent the United States, as they saw it, from exploiting the "exorbitant privilege" that the French had denounced years earlier. Put simply, all nations would be required to settle their balance-of-payments accounts in an agreed neutral asset—presumably gold, SDRs, or some combination thereof. Existing dollar balances would be transformed into an IMF "substitution account," in effect providing a guarantee of its exchange-rate value. The United States should no longer be able to run painless deficits, easily financed by a willingness of surplus countries to hold dollars. Without the discipline of asset settlement, the US would breed inflation—or so the argument went.

Our counterargument was that for decades the United States had in fact had little or no inflation—a better record than most of its trading partners. Unfortunately, at the time, the US was just beginning a pervasive inflationary process. Floating seemed to end any concern about maintaining the value of the dollar on world markets. In fact, a steep decline in the dollar exchange rate was itself inflationary by raising the cost of imports.

Nevertheless, a tightly controlled system of asset settlement seemed to me (and to many others) to be unrealistically rigid for both surplus and deficit nations. Even with a massive increase in the gold price or allocation of the new SDRs, the proposed system would break down for lack of adequate flexibility, forcing more, not less, exchange-rate instability and the heavy use of controls.

We developed an alternative system of "reserve indicators." The basic idea was that a large loss of defined reserve assets would encourage, and potentially force, reduction or elimination of deficits (if necessary, by devaluation). Similarly, a large accumulation of reserve assets would signal a need to reduce or eliminate the surpluses over time. Some convertibility could be restored but the dollar (or other currencies) could remain a useful reserve asset and provide an element of elasticity. Margins around established "central values" would be widened. Floating would remain as a last resort for certain countries.

Shultz had made his mark in the academic world as a labor negotiator and as dean of the University of Chicago business school, known for its spirited economics department. As I worked with him I learned he was by instinct a collaborator and conciliator. He patiently tested my ideas for creating a reformed monetary system with a presumption of specified central exchange-rate values with his cabinet colleagues.

While I had the sense of some progress in our extended debate, the Committee of Twenty could not reach an agreement in time for the September 1973 IMF annual meeting in Nairobi. An oil crisis was brewing, further stoking inflationary pressures. The Watergate scandal added to uncertainty. Giscard d'Estaing, who in my judgment was willing to make a real attempt to find common ground, called for a one-year suspension of the effort.

It never resumed. That was, of course, a disappointing result. I had spent the major part of the job I loved trying, and ultimately failing, to stabilize and reform the international monetary system.

The Impossible Triad

Looking back today from a long perspective, I can sense that I paid too little attention to two larger lessons.

First, international monetary reform faces inherently conflicting objectives; objectives beyond what a mere Treasury under secretary and his foreign counterparts, responsible to national governments, can reconcile.

Sovereign nations typically want (1) full control of their own monetary and fiscal policies; (2) the benefits of a free flow of capital across national boundaries; and (3) stable, predictable foreign exchange rates.

Conceptually, they can achieve and sustain the first two objectives if they are willing to permit their exchange rate to float relatively freely. (Countries that do this include the United States, Canada, Japan, and the United Kingdom.)

They can have the last two—free capital flows and stable exchange rates—if they are willing to sacrifice control over monetary policy. (The extreme example is the euro, in which national currencies are eliminated and a central bank sets monetary policy for the whole area.)

Or they can retain a fixed exchange rate and monetary policy independence if they are willing to close the economy to international flows of money and capital. (The United States itself moved in that direction in the 1960s. Today China is struggling with this question.)

But not all three for any length of time. George Willis was right, back in those Volcker Group discussions: "Nothing will work." It's an impossible triad.

Moreover, an organized international monetary system requires a fixed point of reference—a "numeraire" like gold or a widely accepted national currency, or possibly some combination of the two. But as Professor Triffin taught us back in the Bretton Woods era, it is next to impossible to maintain over time a fixed gold price or even convertibility between gold and a single reserve currency in the context of expanding trade and economic growth. Eventually the sense of trust upon which any currency rests will be eroded if its use is overextended.

Adding to the difficulty is the fact that an exchange-rate decision (or a decision about controls on capital or even monetary policy) can never be an entirely unilateral matter. Most clearly, every exchange-rate change affects the currency value of its trading partners. The riddle can be resolved by an agreement or custom to measure a national currency value against a common numeraire: once upon a time gold, now more commonly these days the dollar. But then the dollar becomes the "nth currency," unable to alter its exchange rate without the agreement of others, precisely the point of the Smithsonian effort.

Looked at from the present vantage point, it is clear the necessary national compromises and discipline inherent in maintaining an orderly international monetary system have been absent. This "nonsystem" has prevailed for almost fifty years.

My second lesson was not a matter of logic or economic theory but of political reality. President Nixon's electoral priorities in 1971 and 1972 easily overrode the need to sustain a stable currency. (As the Watergate break-in and cover-up later proved, those electoral priorities also overrode other important considerations.) With the loss of international discipline and strong fiscal and monetary policies, an inflationary process took hold.

By the accidents of fortune, I was destined a few years later to lead the effort to deal with the Great Inflation and the related Latin American banking crisis.

A Useful Treasury Legacy

Before leaving the Treasury, I did have the opportunity to put in place some useful reforms in how the US government borrows money. In this area, we could make most of the changes on our own, without legislation or international agreement.

For decades, the Treasury Department's standard practice in selling notes and bonds (debt securities maturing in more than a year) was to announce to potential buyers an offering date for a certain dollar amount at a stated maturity and a fixed interest rate. The process involved some uncertainty for the Treasury. Would there be enough investor demand to complete the sale? From the standpoint of the market, there was also risk as investors and traders awaited the timing and terms of the offering.

To minimize those concerns, the Federal Reserve felt compelled to ensure that prevailing market interest rates were steady before, during, and after the offering. As the size and frequency of the offerings increased, the Fed's need to maintain that so-called even-keel approach became increasingly awkward.

We found a remedy by adopting the auction process that had long been used for offerings of Treasury bills—securities that now mature in a year or less. In that process, potential buyers receive notice of the size and maturity of the new security, but not the price or interest rate. Interested buyers then can submit bids specifying the price they are willing to pay and the amount they are willing to purchase. Then the Treasury sets a cut-off price at the level that ensures enough buyers for the new securities.

Despite doubts persisting over the years, the auctions worked well even when they were used for bonds with maturities extending out to thirty years, where the risk of market price changes was greatest. The Fed no longer had to worry about keeping market rates at an even keel over an extended period.

I also oversaw the first sale of a consolidated security by the new Federal Financing Bank. This was designed to replace the array of separate sales that had been historically conducted by special government agencies ranging from the Farmers Home Administration to the Tennessee Valley Authority. Legally, as federal government obligations, the securities offered by each of those entities had the same standing as US Treasuries. But because each agency borrowed in relatively small amounts, the trading activity in those securities was limited and investors demanded significantly higher interest rates than for the more liquid Treasuries.

We persuaded the Congress to require that the agencies' borrowing be combined and that the newly consolidated debt securities, now of a much larger size, be sold alongside Treasuries. In part, the objective was to shed light on the aggregate volume of the scattered agency financing. Today, the Federal Financing Bank securities are sold directly to the Treasury, financed by regular Treasury debt.

The huge mortgage buyers and underwriters Fannie Mae and Freddie Mac,* nominally private government agencies (itself an oxymoron) designed to help finance home ownership, continued to issue their own debt—technically without a government guarantee—into the market. However, Treasury approval was required for the terms and timing of their offerings. With interest rates rising as inflation took hold toward the end of my time in the Treasury, Fannie Mae grew concerned about increasing borrowing costs. Its executives pleaded that they should be allowed to initiate a limited sale of very short-term debt, like private commercial paper. The entire rationale was to save a bit on interest cost, which was lower for short-term debt than for longer-dated securities. I refused on the basis that the temptation to expand the "limited" sale would be hard to resist and it would be risky to become too reliant on volatile short-term funding.

A few years later, after I'd assumed the chairmanship of the Federal Reserve, I was visited by David Maxwell, the new Fannie Mae chairman. He explained that the now very large "agency" was teetering on the edge of bankruptcy. They had sold a lot of short-term debt and the rise in interest rates was difficult to meet.

My successors at Treasury clearly had not heeded my caution!

---

* More formally known as the Federal National Mortgage Association and the Federal Home Loan Mortgage Corporation.

Fannie Mae squeaked through with a big loss at the time, but the whole incident was emblematic of a politically motivated structural weakness that later would contribute to the 2008 financial crisis. Fannie was created as a full-fledged government agency in the 1930s with authority to support the long-term residential mortgage market. It was "privatized" in the late 1960s, purely to remove it as an expense line on the federal budget. But the government agency aura remained, which, among other things, made its debt obligations eligible for purchase by the Federal Reserve (which, by law, can buy federal "agency" securities).

Not entirely coincidentally, Fannie approached me years later, when I was in my new role of investment banker, and asked me to vouch for the adequacy of its capital planning. I signed off on a conditional plan, but a sense of discipline was soon lost.

Fannie Mae and its newly authorized competitor, Freddie Mac, became highly profitable. Both were active buyers of residential mortgages, including many of questionable quality, in the run-up to the 2008 crisis. In the frantic early days of that crisis, government support was needed and provided. The agencies remain under Treasury control to this day—a large piece of unfinished business with respect to financial regulation.

An Interlude

I decided to leave the Treasury in early 1974. The Nixon administration was in turmoil, consumed with the Watergate scandal that was transfixing the public. George Shultz himself had had enough. In May he left to join the renowned Bechtel Corporation. The ambitious Bill Simon, who served as Shultz's deputy secretary and ran the Federal Energy Administration (making him Nixon's "energy czar"), took over as Treasury secretary. Only later did I discover there had been some discussion of my possible appointment, for which I had no ambition at all in so highly politicized and, at that point, dysfunctional an administration. I was also overdue to pay more attention to my family.

There was no shortage of attractive opportunities in the private sector, some offering six- or seven-figure compensation. But before I could decide, an appeal to my Princeton loyalties and commitment to public service lured me into rejoining the Woodrow Wilson School of Public and International Affairs for a semester or two of teaching.

My family, with Barbara carrying most of the burden, had enjoyed Washington life during both of my Treasury sojourns. We had no shortage of good friends from the Treasury, the Fed, and elsewhere—all at similar levels—including the Daanes, the Weidenbaums, the Brills, the Okuns, the Rossides, the Cohens, the Wallichs, and Bob Solomon's family. Barbara had an acerbic view of politics and Washington and a compelling way of expressing it that made her particularly popular. Our daughter, Janice, showed signs of following in that tradition when she affixed an "Impeach Nixon" bumper sticker on the car she used.

Janice had attended a fine elementary school near our house in Chevy Chase, Maryland, during my first stint in Treasury, and then Sidwell Friends, the more liberal of the prime DC private schools, when we moved to Cleveland Avenue in central Washington in 1969.

My son, Jimmy, had a specific challenge. Born with cerebral palsy, it took years and a series of operations before he could walk. But there was nothing wrong with his head.

Barbara, who had fought her own lifetime battle with diabetes, was determined that Jimmy should have a normal education in a regular school. Fortunately, she was put in touch with a dedicated young man, Robert Barros, who was just starting Mater Dei, a new Catholic elementary school. He agreed to accept Jimmy until high school. After that Barbara urged, really demanded, that the revered Canon Martin, headmaster of the prominent St. Albans School, open its doors to a physically challenged student.

I recall apologizing to Janice when I left Treasury that I had deprived her of a hometown. "What do you mean?" she rightly replied "Washington is my hometown."

It was a different place in the 1960s and 1970s. While divided racially (when I went job hunting in 1949 it was still de facto segregated), it was otherwise a comfortable, convenient medium-sized city with the advantage of world-class museums and other cultural institutions. Mostly populated by middle-class professionals, including families of civil servants and members of Congress, there wasn't great wealth. I remember very few top restaurants and only one new four-star hotel.

The prestigious law firms were entirely local and small, occupying maybe a floor or two in a K Street office building. Lobbying had yet to become an all-pervasive local industry. Apart from the chamber of commerce and the AFL-CIO, few special interest groups had offices in the city. Influence peddling, by today's standards, was discreet.

That was then. Decades later, it has become to me a very different, unpleasant, place, dominated by wealth and lobbyists who are joined at the hip with the Congress and too many officials.

I stay away.

chapter 7

BACK TO THE BEGINNING

N *earing* *fifty*, I wasn't sure where I wanted to spend the rest of my working life. (I still wonder about that at age ninety.)

Joe Fowler, my former boss at Treasury, was firmly ensconced at investment bank Goldman Sachs. He loved the (then) partnership culture and urged me to join as his presumed successor.* Bob Roosa tried to recruit me to a senior role at the private bank Brown Brothers Harriman. I'd also held a brief discussion with Tom Clausen, who offered me what he vowed was the second-highest salary at San Francisco–based Bank of America. (At the time just $110,000!) Barbara promptly vetoed a move to San Francisco. More serious was the conversation with Bankers Trust, where my friend Charlie Sanford, even long before he was chief executive, was shaking up a company that had been known as especially conservative.

But from the minute I left Treasury, Arthur Burns had been after me to return to my old home at the New York Fed and replace its president, Al Hayes. I was more than a little suspicious of his motives. Why me? We had clashed often. It had become obvious that he was in almost open warfare with Hayes, who among other

---

*He would stay on as a limited partner until Goldman Sachs went public in 1999. He died less than a year later at age ninety-one.

perceived transgressions consistently opposed Burns in Open Market Committee meetings.

The New York Fed was not my great ambition. While the promised salary was two and a half times what I earned at Treasury, the role lacked the breadth of policy influence to which I had become accustomed. And I knew the chance of a broadly warm welcome was nil; on too many occasions we had been on different sides of international monetary issues.

But, in a sense, it was home. It certainly ranked as public service, shielded somewhat from the cruder forces of politics. It was important. So, on my way to go salmon fishing in a remote part of Canada during the summer of 1974, I used the last available public telephone to call Burns and deliver my somewhat reluctant message: "Okay."

Only later did I become fully acquainted with the intensity of the animosity that had grown up between Burns and some of the New York Fed's directors, who were themselves leaders in the city's legal, business, and philanthropic communities. They were by law responsible for appointing the president. But Burns could control the vote of the Federal Reserve Board, which was necessary to confirm any appointment. Hayes insisted on serving out the rest of his term, so I couldn't take over until August 1975.

Princeton Sojourn

I spent the interlude as a fellow at Princeton's Woodrow Wilson School. I felt strongly that the heavily endowed school was not nearly active enough in teaching and encouraging interest in public management. Spending time there could help kindle interest.

I was soon reminded that teaching was challenging. Leading a conference or task force of highly qualified juniors and seniors took work. What did I know about syllabuses and other professorial tools? I knew enough to corral graduate student assistants. I could correct bad English in student papers. I could certainly invite stimulating guest lecturers. Then, and when I assumed a tenured professorship more than a decade later, I learned how satisfying it can be to mentor bright students and present them with a challenge. Some of them I still occasionally see today.

Barbara and I also had plenty of time to choose a large, well-situated Manhattan apartment from the many available in the midst of New York City's credit crisis. We closed the deal in the very month that co-op apartment price indices set a new decades-long low. It has proven to be a good home and, as things turned out, my best financial asset.

Leading the New York Fed

I vividly recall my first day as president of the New York Fed, the institution that had provided my first job as an economist. In my new office on the executive floor, which had been closed to me in my earlier incarnation, I investigated the elaborate desk. One hidden shelf revealed a surprise: a handwritten list of the pros and cons that former New York Fed president Allan Sproul had weighed after being offered the World Bank presidency (the cons won out). My curiosity led me to press a button concealed in the desk. It was the emergency alarm and instantly closed down the bank. The doors shut and all the bells went off. An inauspicious first day on the job!

I also soon threatened to quit. Chairman Burns sent a Federal Reserve Board member to demand, because of political sensitivities, that I back out of an agreed arrangement to supplement my government pension if I served at least five years. I had already consented to his plea to accept a lower salary than he'd originally promised. As a matter of principle, I decided the pension was nonnegotiable. In the end, my short tenure as New York Fed president added $300 or so to the government pension check I now receive every month.

Given my experience in both Washington and New York, I thought somewhat innocently that I could help bridge the gap that had long characterized the relationship between the board and the bank. I succeeded to a considerable degree, even if I found later in reading Burns's diaries that he found ample grounds for criticizing me, adding my dissents as vice chairman of the Open Market Committee to his earlier complaints about my role in ending the gold convertibility of the dollar.

I've always believed the New York Fed, because of its primary role in executing operations and its oversight of the big banks in the financial center, has a special role within the system, providing expertise and insight into banking and financial market behavior for the Washington-based board, the FOMC, and its chairman. But on the policy side, I found myself increasingly frustrated by Burns's apparent reluctance to combat inflation head-on.

In New York, I got along well with most of the key officials. That was especially true of Dick Debs, the highly qualified first vice president who might himself have had the top job. He faithfully helped ease the transition before he left for a Morgan Stanley partnership. He and his wife, Barbara, became valued friends. Alan Holmes, who oversaw the domestic and international trading desks, was a longtime colleague, commanding real respect throughout the system. The pressures on Holmes were great; being accountable both to the New York president and to the Board of Governors in Washington with its controlling chairman no doubt led to sleepless nights.

I soon learned that the Fed's formidable bureaucracy hadn't let up much since my early experience there. In the first few days, I asked my assistant to dispose of a large plant sitting just outside my office that appeared to be dying. A week or so later, I asked why it was still there. Her dispiriting answer: policy dictated that if I didn't have the plant, none of the officers could have one. It would have to be a group decision.

In those days, the departments with the highest status at the New York Fed were domestic and foreign operations, research, and legal. The low priority given to operational functions posed a challenge. I set about trying to do something about it.

My pathfinder was a young Gerald "Jerry" Corrigan. Drawn from the economic research department, he had been assigned to the administrative side of the bank and before my arrival was appointed secretary to the board of directors.

A blunt Irish American with an economics PhD from Fordham University, Jerry's strong point was not theorizing. He was dedicated to the institution, had a strong sense of its strengths and weaknesses, and a take-no-prisoners style of management. With his help, I devoted a lot of attention to the internal operations of the bank. Jerry, acutely aware of what needed to be done and with good judgment in doing it, rapidly advanced through the ranks.

The New York Fed, like other Reserve Banks, was responsible for bank examinations, check clearing, wire transfers, and maintaining the currency in circulation for its region. I soon discovered that we lagged way behind in most measures of efficiency on the more routine operations. I was determined to do better, to set ambitious targets, and where necessary to import some technological talent. We didn't reach anywhere near the top of the chart, but we made progress. In my last annual report I could brag a bit about the operational improvements we made, including a reduction in total staff from a 1974 peak near 5,300 to about 4,350 at the end of 1979.

Burns and I did agree on one thing. We shared concern about the growing volume of bank lending to Latin American countries. The largest institutions, commercial banks flush with deposits from the newly rich Middle East oil-producing countries, were recycling those funds into seemingly lucrative loans to less developed countries, particularly those in Latin America such as Mexico, Argentina, and Brazil. As time passed, smaller regional banks—even community banks—with no international experience joined in. The process of trying to restrain that lending taught me an important lesson about regulation.

Burns agreed with me on a schematic approach, a stoplight system for indicating which banks and countries were most at risk. To simplify, the signal would be red when banks seemed overcommitted to a high-risk country, green when the danger was low, and of course yellow in between. In principle, the signals would be managed by the individual Reserve Banks as a regular part of the supervisory process. In practice, the supervisors and the banks did not or could not implement the signals with firm discipline and vigor. Ambiguities were an excuse for inaction, I soon learned—a familiar difficulty in enforcing discipline.

Even those of us in government were susceptible. John Heimann, the highly experienced comptroller of the currency at the time, consulted with me one day about Mexico. Nationally chartered US banks by law could not lend more than 10 percent of their capital to a single borrower. The Mexican government, considered as a single entity, was approaching the limit at some banks. But arguably its individual "independent" agencies were separate entities.

Should the lending be cut off? Not if the State Department had anything to say about it! Not if we wanted to avoid calumny for bringing down the "necessary" recycling effort.

As it happened, the most aggressive lender was Citibank, whose leader, Walter Wriston, visited me for an educational meeting early in my new job. He explained that Citi had been consistently making profits. With that record, and what he saw as a relatively placid financial environment, he thought the bank had no need for capital.* He would keep Citi's actual capital as low as his directors would tolerate. And as a leader in Latin American lending, his basic approach was that—and I am not making this up—countries did not and could not go bankrupt.

In fact, the Fed at that point in time had no formal control over bank capital. This was made even clearer to me a few years later when I was chairman of the Federal Reserve Board and executives at both the Continental Illinois Bank and the First Chicago Bank in effect told me to get lost when I encouraged them to raise capital. Little could they know that that attitude forced me to put capital adequacy higher among the Federal Reserve's priorities.

In the event, compromises continued, lending went on. It all landed on my desk as Federal Reserve chairman a couple of years later.

---

* Almost all of the money that banks use to make loans or buy securities is actually borrowed from someone else—depositors, bondholders, other lenders. Capital is the other part, the bank shareholders' own money. The capital needs to be sufficient to take the loss if the bank's loans sour or securities lose value.

Citibank, with a leadership that was contemptuous of authority, provided me several other important lessons in regulation during this time. Early in my New York tenure, I received complaints from a leading foreign central bank that Citibank was dodging taxes on their profits from currency trading. The accusation was that when the tax examiner came along, profits could be moved to another country. I made the mistake of requiring that Citibank conduct an internal investigation. That internal investigation, largely by their own law firm, found no cause for concern. The Securities and Exchange Commission (SEC) investigated but declined to bring any action. Several European authorities eventually recouped back taxes and imposed fines.

A few years later, after I became Fed chairman, a message came from the comptroller of the currency that Citibank was breaking a rule that prohibited banks from offering gifts worth more than $30 for opening a checking or savings account—"free toasters" used to entice new depositors in that era of official interest-rate caps. Not long after imposing an order to cease the practice, the comptroller discovered Citibank was again doing it, but now seemed to be disguising the cost of the gifts in their internal accounts. That was a potentially serious matter: falsifying the bank's books.

Once again, we decided to demand an internal investigation. A branch manager in the Bronx was fired, but somehow no one else could be found to bear any responsibility. The Fed staff recommended a fine of a million dollars, which was a lot in the late 1970s. It would have been our biggest ever fine. Maybe too much—the board thought a $500,000 fine would get plenty of attention. We were wrong; the only mention was a small item in a trade publication.

No one cared about toasters. But what about the bank's culture?

Monetary Policy

Those years in New York, following the sizeable 1973–1975 recession, were when "stagflation" seemed to get a stranglehold on the economy. In retrospect, it is easy to see that the board was indecisive about whether to focus on inflation or on recovery from that mid-1970s economic slump. From my point of view, we clearly kept monetary policy too easy for too long. The growing sense of frustration and political concerns about the lack of full employment were reflected in new legislation.

In 1977 the Federal Reserve Act was amended to require that the central bank "maintain long run growth of the monetary and credit aggregates commensurate with the economy's long run potential to increase production, so as to promote the goals of maximum employment, stable prices, and moderate long-term interest rates." Reasonable enough as an aspiration, but here we have the origin of what has since been interpreted as the "dual mandate."

The following year, Congress passed the Full Employment and Balanced Growth Act, known more widely as the "Humphrey-Hawkins Act" for the senator and congressman who sponsored the legislation. The new law had more than a bit of a monetarist flavor. It required the Federal Reserve chairman to report to the Congress twice a year on plans for monetary policy, setting out the board's targets for the growth in money and credit. That indeed was a specific mandate. It also went on to incorporate the previous less specific language about the "goals" of maximum employment, stable prices, and the now conveniently forgotten moderate long-term interest rates. A key issue for monetary policy is the degree to which that so-called dual mandate leads to clarity or confusion in the operating decisions of the Federal Reserve Board and Open Market Committee. I fear the latter.

In practice, I became increasingly concerned about monetary policy being overly easy during my time in New York. Some bank presidents pressed me to voice my concerns more strongly, in effect to force a policy change.

I did, in fact, begin to dissent more forcefully after Burns was replaced in early 1978 by G. William Miller, a businessman appointed by the newly elected Democratic president Jimmy Carter. "Bill" Miller was an intelligent, capable corporate leader. He did not believe in imposing his personal views on the committee. He found himself outvoted in at least one discount rate decision, which didn't seem to concern him but inevitably undermined his "market" credibility. Frustrated as I was, I was not in a mood to lead an open revolt. In the last analysis, it is the Federal Reserve Board in Washington, not the regional banks, that ultimately carries the heaviest policy responsibility. And, ordinarily, a united front is important.

In late 1978 we also discovered, if we really needed the lesson, that floating currency rates didn't end currency crises. Doubts about the US inflationary process and Federal Reserve policy led to a run on the dollar, which hit record lows in October. I played only a supporting role in helping Carter's Treasury secretary, Michael Blumenthal, and his under secretary for monetary affairs, Tony Solomon, to design a series of emergency measures. A full percentage point increase in the discount rate was initiated by the New York Fed and the sale of foreign currency–denominated Treasury securities (Carter bonds) to foreign central banks made an impact. Heavy intervention in the currency markets by the United States and our main trading partners continued for months.

So that was indeed a strong attack, initially successful. But, by spring and summer, the value of the measures seemed to wear off. A more fundamental change in direction would be required.

chapter 8

ATTACKING INFLATION

P *resident* *Jimmy* *Carter* was up against it. "It" was high, rising, and seemingly intractable inflation. And by 1979 it seemed to be complicating, even blocking, every policy initiative.

Price measures were rising 13 percent a year, driven in part by the oil crisis (the second in a decade) that followed the early 1979 Iranian revolution in which Grand Ayatollah Khomeini replaced the US-supported shah. A gasoline shortage led to long lines and rationing, dominating the news. New budget programs were politically, even economically, nonstarters. The forceful effort to stabilize the dollar in late 1978 had not produced lasting results.

To put it mildly, the public was growing restive. The president retreated to Camp David. For more than a week he consulted with advisors, titans of business, politicians, teachers, clergy, labor leaders, and even some private citizens. Notably, not the Federal Reserve.

On July 15 he descended from the mountain and made a speech. I thought it was a good speech, rightly recognizing the sour and divisive mood in the country, its "crisis of confidence." It came to be famous as the "malaise" speech. He never used that word but it encapsulated the message.

Days later he accepted the resignations of some cabinet secretaries including Michael Blumenthal at Treasury. Carter liked Bill Miller, who had been chairman of conglomerate Textron before succeeding Burns at the Fed less than two years earlier. So Miller became Treasury secretary.

That left a vacancy at the Fed. Given that the Fed chairman is often considered the most important economic policy official, that vacancy was not confidence building.

The White House Calls

Two or three days later, Bill Miller called. Would I be willing to come to Washington and meet the president?

It was not a call I expected. I had never met the president. I had voted against Miller in Open Market Committee meetings. But, of course, I got on the shuttle.

When you're cleaning out old files to write a memoir, long-forgotten things show up. I found a note scribbled on a prescription pad that listed three points I wanted to make to the president: I felt strongly about the independence of the Federal Reserve; the Fed would have to deal head-on with inflation; and I would advocate tighter policies than Miller had.

They were simple points. I followed that script in the Oval Office, even pointing a (friendly) finger at Miller, sitting nearby and still the Fed chairman. It was a short meeting, as it was often accurately described later, including by the president himself.

I got back on the plane and called Bob Kavesh and Larry Ritter, two of my closest friends, to join me for dinner at Parma, a new neighborhood Italian restaurant. "I just blew any chance of becoming Fed chair," I told them.

That didn't disappoint Barbara one bit. Increasingly suffering from her own health problems, including a complicated combination of diabetes and rheumatoid arthritis, she wanted to stay in New York, close to doctors, friends, and Jimmy (then living at home and studying at New York University).

The next day I got a call from the president himself. It was seven-thirty in the morning. I was still in bed. I managed to say yes, I would agree to become the chairman of the Federal Reserve Board. Later I wondered whether the early-rising Georgia peanut farmer would have called if he knew I was still in bed.

Barbara was understanding. She knew this was one job I couldn't turn down. Her final verdict was succinct: "You go, I stay." We agreed I would try to return on weekends.

Malaise may have been the mood of the country in 1979, but the governing process in Washington moved far more efficiently than it does today. Less than a week after my July 25 nomination I had a Senate hearing, days later I was unanimously confirmed, and on August 6 I was sworn in.

Due to a quirk in the Federal Reserve system, the chairman was paid just $57,500, much lower than the $110,000 I received as New York Fed president. I rented a $400-a-month one-bedroom apartment in easy walking distance from the Fed. The building was full of George Washington University students. I furnished the place— in effect, a dormitory room with a kitchen—with little more than a bed, table, and a couple of chairs. Janice, by this point living in nearby Northern Virginia and learning the world of hospitals and nursing, took to inviting me for a weekly dinner and agreed to do my laundry.

The debate in the White House over my appointment, which had essentially pitted the economists (who supported me) against the politicians (uneasy about naming an overly independent Fed chairman) was over. I could get to work with the board and the Federal Open Market Committee that I knew well, with a mutual sense of mission to salvage an economy nearing the end of its inflationary rope. The board's new vice chairman was Fred Schultz, an investment banker from Florida with a talent for politics. He had been confirmed just weeks before I became chairman. He became an essential partner, running interference with members of Congress and taking on difficult assignments. I brought Jerry Corrigan down from New York to be my chief of staff.

Ten days into my term, and less than a month since the previous increase, the board took action to raise the discount rate half a percentage point, to 10 ½ percent, a record.

Market interest rates were already high by historical standards, but inflation was still higher, growing by then at an annual rate of close to 15 percent, the fastest ever in the United States during peacetime. The Fed staff, running their models and "regressions," concluded that, of all things, a recession was likely, and soon.

The next time I led the board in voting to raise the discount rate, on September 18, it presented a problem of credibility. The vote was split 4-3. Three rate increases in little more than a month, without much to show for it and recession risks looming, was a little too much for some of my colleagues to swallow.

At first I saw little cause for concern. The three members who backed me—Fred Schultz, Henry Wallich, Philip Coldwell—could be counted on to maintain an anti-inflation crusade. So, in my view, I had a solid majority.

But the market saw it differently. In their eyes, this split vote was the latest sign that the Fed was losing its nerve and would fail to maintain a disciplined stance against inflation. We would flinch against further increases in interest rates even if the prevailing rates were still below the rising inflation rate. The dollar came under pressure and the price of gold hit a new record.

The Fed was losing credibility. Our long-established pattern of adjusting short-term market interest rates by small increments—either by means of a discount rate change or by direct intervention in the government securities market—tended to be too little, too late to influence expectations. We needed a new approach.

To have more direct impact, we could strictly limit growth in the reserves that commercial banks held at the Federal Reserve against their deposits. That would effectively curb growth in deposits and the overall money supply. Put simply, we would control the quantity of money (the money supply) rather than the price of money (interest rates). The widely quoted adage that inflation is a matter of "too much money chasing too few goods" promised a clear, if overly simplified, rationale.

I knew that a number of Reserve Bank presidents years earlier had been pushing for such a monetarist approach, emphasizing greater attention to the money supply. I myself, some years ago, had raised a question as to whether the Fed should pay more attention to growth in the money supply with an approach later labeled "practical monetarism" (in contrast with the more extreme and mechanistic monetarism that Milton Friedman had advocated).

Now, after years of compromise and flinching from a head-on attack on inflation, it was time to act—to send a convincing message to the markets and to the public. The dollar's ties to gold, and to the Bretton Woods fixed exchange-rate system, were long gone. There was widespread understanding that the dollar's value now depended on the Fed's ability to control the money supply and end the inflationary process.

Then, as now, we could not escape the fact that price stability is the ultimate responsibility of the Federal Reserve—in my judgment of all central banks.

Before leaving for the IMF's annual meeting in Belgrade, I charged two Fed officials—Peter Sternlight, who then ran the trading desk in New York, and Stephen Axilrod, who managed the execution of monetary policy in Washington—to prepare a new approach. It should be directed emphatically toward restraining the growth of money rather than toward setting some perceived appropriate level of interest rates.

Joining Bill Miller and Charlie Shultze, chairman of the Council of Economic Advisers, on a government plane to Belgrade, I filled them in on my thinking. They understood the need to reinforce our inflation-fighting credibility but urged caution in adopting such a radical change in approach. They recognized that interest rates might climb sharply higher and worried about the effects on economic growth.

Our trip included a short stopover in Hamburg at the request of German Chancellor Helmut Schmidt. I knew Schmidt, and his blunt manner, well from his days as finance minister. Generally sympathetic to the United States, he had become disenchanted with what he perceived as American policy inconsistencies and ineffectiveness, including, if not confined to, monetary affairs.

For almost an hour he harangued us about how waffling American policy makers had let inflation run amok and undermined confidence in the dollar and Europe's efforts to restore exchange-rate stability.

I sat there quietly. There could be no more persuasive argument for why I had to act. I invited Bundesbank president Otmar Emminger, who had accompanied Schmidt and long been an interlocutor of mine, to fly with us to Belgrade.

I used the opportunity to hint at the new approach I was considering. Predictably, Emminger was supportive. I became impatient to get back home and to work. I stayed long enough to hear Arthur Burns deliver his Per Jacobsson Lecture, "The Anguish of Central Banking," in which he (infamously) expressed doubt that central banks were even capable of controlling inflation anymore. I left Belgrade before the formal IMF proceedings were over, hoping but failing to escape notice in a nearly empty airport.

By Thursday, October 4, I reviewed the options with the board. Even the "doves" who had opposed our last discount-rate increase were broadly supportive, having been taken aback by the market's violent reaction to the split vote. A special meeting of the Open Market Committee was scheduled for Saturday. Helped by the distraction of Pope John Paul II's visit to Washington, there were no leaks. There were, however, plenty of rumors adding to the turmoil, including that I had resigned or died.

I have had the patience to read carefully only one Open Market Committee meeting transcript, but some years ago I did read this one. It misses the nuance and tone of voice. To an uninformed reader it would appear that I was reluctant about, even opposed to, the proposed program of targeting the money supply directly with the implicit loss of influence over interest rates. I was simply making sure that each member was aware of the risks and of the opposing views of key administrative officials, conscious of the potential recessionary force from sharply higher interest rates. President Carter, aware of those concerns, had also quite properly said to them that he would not intervene with his new appointee.

My objective, of course, was to achieve unanimity and forestall second-guessing and finger pointing. In that I succeeded. Late that Saturday afternoon, on short notice, the media were called from their homes or from their papal coverage. Joe Coyne, our Fed press officer and a good Catholic, convinced them that the pope would understand.

We aimed the whole range of Federal Reserve ammunition at the market: a full percentage point increase in the discount rate to 12 percent, a requirement that banks set aside more of their deposits as reserves, a call for an end to lending for "speculative" activities, and, the heart of the matter, a commitment to restrain growth in the money supply whatever the implications might be for interest rates.

We knew that the immediate market reaction would be higher short-term interest rates. The committee agreed to meet again if those rates rose beyond a tentatively set "upper limit." We (or at least I) hoped that long-term rates would not rise, reflecting market expectations that we would succeed in bringing inflation down.

No such luck. Long-term rates mirrored the short-term rise. And the short rates soon reached our so-called upper limit. After some discussion, we didn't intervene. Neither did we when subsequent upper limits, set in each meeting, were breached. The rate on three-month Treasury bills eventually exceeded 17 percent, the commercial bank prime lending rate peaked at 21.5 percent, and, most sensitively, mortgage rates surpassed 18 percent. Those rates had never been seen before in our financial history.

Perhaps more surprising: right into the new year there was no recession. The mood, and the continuing upward momentum of prices, was reflected at a lunch I had with a cross-section of small business owners and Arthur Levitt, then president of the American Stock Exchange. They listened patiently to my carefully polished analysis: times were tough, money was tight, but relief was on the way. Inflation would soon come down. A businessman sitting to my right was the first to respond. "That's all fine, Mr. Chairman, but I have just arrived from a meeting with my union where I happily agreed to wage increases of 13 percent over each of the next three years."

It was suggestive of the skeptical mood. But I have often wondered whether his firm remained in business.

There were, of course, many complaints. Farmers once surrounded the Fed's Washington building with tractors. Home builders, forced to shut down, sent sawed-off two-by-fours with messages to the board. (I was intrigued by one that read: "Get the interest rates down, cut the money supply.") Economists predictably squabbled. The monetarists, led by Milton Friedman, instead of claiming victory that the Fed was finally adopting a more monetarist approach, insisted we weren't doing it just right, in a manner that somehow more painlessly could eliminate any negative effects on economic growth. Mainstream economists had the opposite complaint: whether we had sufficiently considered the risk of increasing unemployment, which in fact did not rise for months.

Community groups protested at our headquarters on more than one occasion. In April 1980 a group of about five hundred, led by Gale Cincotta of the National People's Action Group, marched outside our building and demanded a meeting with me.

I told Joe Coyne to invite a couple of the leaders to my office to meet after the regular board meeting. It was a hot and rainy day, and when I got there I found more than a dozen people camped out in varying degrees of dishabille. For half an hour we exchanged views. I talked about the need to contain inflation; they asked for interest-rate breaks for community housing projects. I agreed that Fed staff would help explain our policies by attending their regional meetings. On that basis, we walked out to the steps of the Fed and Gale praised our willingness to meet and our agreement to stay in contact. Applause followed, all happily recorded on every evening TV broadcast. Sometimes you get lucky. (Staff members who attended subsequent meetings were aggressively heckled.)

Not all of the disagreements were resolved so harmoniously. By December 1980 the Fed insisted I agree to "personal security escort protection." A year later an armed man somehow entered the Federal Reserve, threatening to take the board hostage. My speeches were occasionally interrupted by screaming protestors, once by rats let loose in the audience, typically organized by the far-right radical Lyndon LaRouche and his supporters.

Credit Controls

In early 1980 the Federal Reserve, and more importantly President Carter, couldn't show much progress. Inflation and interest rates remained sky high. The absence of recession and practically no increase in the already high unemployment rate were small comfort.

The president's initial budget, some $16 billion in deficit and with no major cuts to social programs, was deemed unacceptable even to some members of his own party as interest rates surged. He decided to redo it and asked if I would join his staff in consulting with the Congress. This was not really any of my business as Fed chairman, but I did end up sitting in as an observer at the internal White House session where he agreed on the final cuts. One by one, tentative cuts were presented to him. Time and again he would agree to them, only to have a staff member demur, telling the president that one pressure group or another would object. In the end, the message of restraint was diluted. President Carter's instincts, as I saw them, were more conservative than those of his staff and the Democratic Party.

The president had another request. He had the ability, enacted by the Congress years earlier in an effort to pressure President Nixon, to "trigger" credit controls. The Fed would then have the authority to administer those controls.

It was a transparently political ploy. We didn't want to do it. Excessive credit wasn't the problem. The president clearly felt he could help by providing political and moral support for our highly restrictive monetary policies. Adding credit controls to a package of budgetary and monetary restraint would forestall any doubts about our common purpose in fighting inflation and speeding a decline in interest rates.

In the circumstances we could hardly object. We quickly designed "controls" that we hoped would lack real teeth. Lending for auto or home purchases was exempt. Credit card lending wouldn't be restrained until it reached the previous peak, which was unlikely to happen until the Christmas season, nine or ten months off. The remaining forms of consumer credit didn't amount to much.

The president's anti-inflation program of budget cuts and credit controls, designed to support Fed policy, was announced in a big East Room ceremony on the afternoon of March 14.

Within weeks, we began getting unanticipated reports. The money supply dropped sharply. There was scattered evidence that orders for manufactured goods were falling. The long-predicted recession seemed to have started.

The picture became clearer when we learned that the White House was being deluged by cut-up credit cards sent in by supportive citizens. "Mr. President, we are with you" was the refrain. The immediate consequence of so many Americans paying off their credit cards was a sharp drop in bank deposits and the money supply.

Given our commitment to target the money supply, we had to backpedal fast. Interest rates plunged. We eased the credit controls, such as they were, in June. The controls were lifted entirely in July and in August the economy and the money supply began a strong recovery. By late September we felt we had no choice but to tighten policy and to signal restraint by raising the discount rate to 11 percent from 10 percent. It was uncomfortably close to the presidential election. Mr. Carter couldn't resist a mildly critical comment at a Philadelphia garden party, calling the Fed's decision to focus on the money supply "ill-advised."*

The National Bureau of Economics later placed that short-lived downturn on its widely respected list of recessions. To me, it should be labeled with an asterisk as an artificial construct. It was, for sure, another lesson, a serious lesson, of the unanticipated consequences that regulatory "controls," even weak ones, could have on the economy.

As I look back, that mistake cost us six months. The delay in the attack on inflation certainly didn't help President Carter's campaign

---

*Years later, on a fishing trip with Carter, I asked him if he thought Federal Reserve monetary policy had cost him the 1980 election, which he lost to Ronald Reagan. A wry smile spread over his face as he said, "I think there were a few other factors as well." I have become a strong admirer of the man.

for a second term. To his credit, only once did he express concern about our tightening of policy.

Ronald Reagan: A New President

By the beginning of 1981, with a new Republican president in office, we were back in the trenches, fighting to restrain monetary growth. The much predicted recession finally arrived in full force. But it was hard to see progress on the inflation front. Interest rates and the money supply, while increasing at a slower rate, remained stubbornly high. The Fed board remained determined to carry on.

There had been, of course, much speculation about President Ronald Reagan, a former Hollywood actor and California governor, and his new administration's attitude toward economic policy. Arthur Burns, almost apoplectic, had urgently returned to Washington to warn me about a meeting he had attended where efforts were under way, supported by Milton Friedman, Walter Wriston, Bill Simon, and others, to rein in the Fed, not just in monetary policy but as an institution. More openly, there was another small group asked to consider a return to the gold standard in one form or another.

Against that background, I was more than a little concerned when I received a message that President Reagan would like to visit me at the Fed just days after the inauguration.

So far as I knew, apart from a visit by President Franklin Roosevelt at the dedication of the new building in 1937, it was unprecedented for a president to come to the Federal Reserve. Given the attitudes of some of his advisors toward the Fed, it would be sure to raise questions. I suggested it would be more appropriate for me to visit the White House, following the time-honored practice. Somehow, a strange compromise was arranged. We would meet in the Treasury with the new Treasury secretary, Donald Regan, and several advisors.

At the meeting I found myself sitting next to the new president, wondering what would happen when he opened the conversation.

"There's good news that the gold price is way down. We may be getting inflation under control," he said. I don't kiss men, but I was tempted.

The president did raise a question or two he had received about the role of the Federal Reserve. But the conversation drifted off into my area of concern: the importance of getting the deficit under control.

There's no doubt there were times over the next few years when the president, preparing for press conferences or otherwise, was urged by his staff to take on the Fed. He never did so publicly. He once explained to me that a professor at his small college in Illinois had impressed upon him the dangers of inflation. He understood the importance of our mission.

Reagan also made one important but little-recognized contribution to the fight against inflation. In August 1981 he fired thousands of striking air traffic controllers. While the strike was aimed at working conditions more than wages, the union defeat sent a powerful psychological message that there would be limits on wage demands.

Still, relationships with the Treasury were uncomfortable. Secretary Regan, the former Merrill Lynch & Co. chief executive officer, was not experienced in the ways of Washington. He had been saddled with a staff of strong-minded monetarists and supply siders, both highly critical of the Federal Reserve for their own reasons. Fortunately for me, they were even more critical of each other. The result was an absence of mutual trust. I avoided discussions of specific near-term policy action; Don didn't welcome my "wisdom" on tactics with respect to budgetary or other financial policies. We had a common interest, but not always agreement, on matters of financial regulation.

There was a good deal of carping from Treasury officials, including Regan himself, about the Federal Reserve's seeming inability to assure, week by week, confidence-building control of the money supply, something that we learned is technically impossible to do. At one point, I sent Don, an avid golfer, an elaborate panorama showing a golfer hitting into the rough, right or left, sometimes into a sand trap, but finally ending up with the ball in the hole after a par round. He didn't appreciate the humor of the message.*

Almost from the start, the press reported grumblings about the Fed from the White House staff. But my occasional meetings with the president remained cordial. David Stockman, Reagan's outspoken budget director, shared his anti-inflation instincts and regularly urged me to stick with it. Murray Weidenbaum, my former Treasury colleague, was understanding in his role as CEA chairman, as was his successor, Martin Feldstein.

From time to time, I faced highly skeptical, even hostile, questioning in congressional hearings. I didn't take the threats of impeachment seriously. I knew I had defenders in Senate Banking Committee chairman William Proxmire, as well as certain members of the House Committee on Financial Services. My sense was that the Fed had a well of unspoken or even overt support from the public. There was a willingness to endure some near-term pain to conquer inflation. Even in those groups with the most at stake—farm groups, community activists, and home builders—there was understanding.

One rather dramatic occasion for me was reassuring. In January 1982 I was invited to address the annual meeting of the National Association of Home Builders in, of all places, Las Vegas. On my way to the meeting, I happened to run into a rather sour, unfriendly senator. "What are you doing here? The home builders will kill you."

Well, maybe because I was a bit concerned by his comment, I was more eloquent than usual. I told them I knew they were suffering but that any letup in our inflation fight would mean all of the pain was for nothing. My message boiled down to the concluding words "Stick with us. Inflation and interest rates will come down. There are a lot of homes to be built."

Standing ovation!

In May 1982 I received a particularly poignant one-page typewritten letter from a young man who introduced himself as a recent

---

*Several years later, when Regan was White House chief of staff, he tried to persuade me to leave the Fed to succeed Bank of America's Tom Clausen as president of the World Bank. New York Congressman Barber Conable later took the role instead.

college graduate in a management training program at a small international bank. He said he'd been following my career closely, had read the recent magazine cover stories that described the sacrifices my family and I had been making, and wanted to lend his support and praise in this difficult time as he felt a "curiously strong sense of identification" with me. It was from my son, Jimmy. I responded in the same tone, thanking him for his gift of a crossword puzzle subscription and assuring him that I realized his admirable family upbringing was largely "a reflection of the maternal side."

Impatience is a mild description of my mood in the spring of 1982. The unemployment rate reached a postwar record. Even though the inflation rate had dropped, the money supply remained well above target. I started thinking, "Fifteen percent interest rates and the money supply still high? Good God, come on." But I didn't see how we could overtly ease. We stuck with the program.

Finally, in the summer of 1982, the inflation rate was clearly falling well down into the single digits. The forward indicators seemed to be turning favorable. There were glimmers of slower growth in the money supply, which for technical reasons had become difficult to interpret. Excesses in bank lending to Latin American countries, especially to Mexico, were posing new risks to the financial system and needed urgent attention.

In July we started easing, lowering the discount rate three times in a four-week period. By mid-August the shift was heralded by Wall Street's "Dr. Doom" (my old friend Henry Kaufman) as a sign that the worst was over. The markets took off.

By year's end, the inflation rate had dropped all the way to 4 percent. Short-term interest rates were at half their peak. While the unemployment rate was still close to 10 percent, a recovery had clearly begun.

My Federal Reserve driver, Mr. Peña, provided the conclusive evidence of victory. On the way to speak at a big Washington dinner, I spotted a book on the front seat next to Mr. Peña with the title *How to Live with Inflation*.

Shocking that my own driver had no confidence in me! But, Mr. Peña explained, he'd only bought the book because its price had been marked down to $1.98 from $10.95. The crowd at the dinner appreciated the story.

After much discussion with the Federal Reserve Board, and a good deal of reluctance for fear of losing our hard-won credibility, the decision was taken to abandon priority attention to the money supply. The fact is that institutional developments, most importantly the end of interest-rate controls on bank deposits, had led to a revision of narrow money supply measurements and definitions. The so-called M1a, M1b, M2, and M3 too often diverged as banks took advantage of their new freedom to set deposit interest rates.

In remarks to the annual meeting of the Business Council on October 9, I expressed satisfaction that inflation had come under control. I also noted that the money supply signals were erratic and unreliable. At the same time, I emphasized that our basic anti-inflation policy hadn't changed; it was a matter of tactics. The substantial declines in the inflation rate enabled us to credibly change tactics while maintaining policy. And then we could help to sustain the economic recovery.

By mid-1983 most signals were positive, but one personal issue remained unresolved. Would the chairman be reappointed? There was one strong vote against: Barbara Bahnson Volcker.

Her rheumatoid arthritis was getting worse. The family's financial squeeze had led her to take on a part-time accounting job and, at one point, she rented out our back room. I made a family deal. If the president chose to reappoint me, I'd stay on for only half of the four-year term.

I asked to meet with the president and a bit of serendipity intervened.

A White House garden party was getting under way as I awaited President Reagan in the large hallway off the family quarters that overlooked the back lawn. Unexpectedly, Nancy Reagan appeared in a gorgeous red dress. We had never met. By nature I'm not forthcoming with compliments, but somehow the words spontaneously burst forth: "Mrs. Reagan, you look beautiful!"

After that, my meeting with the smiling president himself was short and amiable. My only plea was that he should decide soon; it was in our mutual interest to quell the inevitable speculation about my possible reappointment. My family deal was that in any event I would not serve a full term, perhaps a couple of years. The president recorded that understanding in his diary.

A few days later, as I was about to leave my New York apartment for a weekend of fishing, I got a call. The president said he would, in the next few minutes, announce my reappointment in his weekly radio broadcast. Barbara cried.

The Senate confirmation vote this time was not unanimous. It split symmetrically: eight right-wing Republicans and eight left-wing Democrats opposed my nomination. The eighty-four senators in the center approved.

Lashed to the Mast

I am sometimes asked whether the October 1979 Saturday night program was deliberately designed to produce a recession.

Deliberately designed? No.

Designed with a clear understanding that sooner or later the accelerating inflation process would culminate in a recession? Certainly, I myself was convinced that the longer the process continued, the greater the risk of a deep recession.

It is an interesting fact that the Fed staff had concluded the economy was at the edge of recession even before the Saturday package was announced. Every month for the rest of the year, the staff position was that the anticipated recession was beginning, even as interest rates rose to high double-digit levels.

I suppose if some Delphic oracle had whispered in my ear that our policy would result in interest rates of 20 percent or more, I might have packed my bags and headed home.

But that option wasn't open. We had a message to deliver, a message to the public and to ourselves.

A relationship between money and the price level is one of the oldest propositions in economics, going back at least to the Scottish philosopher David Hume in the 1750s. Milton Friedman and his acolytes had some success in impressing in the public mind an (overly) simple proposition: "Inflation is always and everywhere a monetary phenomenon."

The simplicity of that thesis helped provide a basis for presenting the new approach to the American public.

At the same time, that approach enforced upon the Federal Reserve an internal discipline that had been lacking: we could not back away from our newfound emphasis on restraining the growth in the money supply without risking a damaging loss of credibility that, once lost, would be hard to restore. To overdramatize a bit, we were doomed to follow through. We were "lashed to the mast" in pursuit of price stability.

Did I realize at the time how high interest rates might go before we could claim success? No. From today's vantage point, was there a better path? Not to my knowledge—not then or now.

An Awkward Meeting

As this memoir makes clear, the Federal Reserve must have and always will have contacts with the administration in power. Some coordination in international affairs is imperative given the overlapping responsibilities with respect to exchange rates and regulation. Sweeping use of "emergency" and "implied" authority requires consultation if for no other reason than to reinforce the effectiveness of the action. But that needs to take place in the context of the Federal Reserve's independence to set monetary policy.

That was challenged only once in my direct experience, in the summer of 1984. I was summoned to a meeting with President Reagan at the White House. Strangely, it didn't take place in the Oval Office, but in the more informal library. As I arrived, the president, sitting there with Chief of Staff Jim Baker, seemed a bit uncomfortable. He didn't say a word. Instead, Baker delivered a message: "The president is ordering you not to raise interest rates before the election."

I was stunned. Not only was the president clearly overstepping his authority by giving an order to the Fed, but also it was disconcerting because I wasn't planning tighter monetary policy at the time. In the aftermath of Continental Illinois's collapse (described in the next chapter), market interest rates had risen and I thought the FOMC might need to calm the market by easing a bit.

What to say? What to do?

I walked out without saying a word.

I later surmised that the library location had been chosen because, unlike the Oval Office, it probably lacked a taping system. The meeting would go unrecorded. If I repeated the incident to the other members of the Federal Reserve Board or to the FOMC—or to Senator Proxmire, as I had promised to do if such a situation arose—the story would have inevitably leaked to nobody's benefit. How could I explain that I was ordered not to do something that at the time I had no intention of doing?

As I considered the incident later, I thought that it was not precisely the right time for a short lecture on the constitutional authority of the Congress to oversee the Federal Reserve and the deliberate insulation of the Fed from direction by the executive branch.

The president's silence, his apparent discomfort, and the meeting locale made me quite sure the White House would keep quiet. It was a matter to be kept between me and Catherine Mallardi, the longtime faithful assistant to Federal Reserve chairmen.

But it was a striking reminder about the pressure that politics can exert on the Fed as elections approach. And it wasn't the last I would see of Jim Baker.

chapter 9

FINANCIAL CRISES, DOMESTIC

AND INTERNATIONAL

*I*n *the early 1960s,* I was sent by the Treasury to hear the remarks of the populist Wright Patman, then chairman of the House Banking Committee, in dedication of the new home of the Federal Deposit Insurance Corporation (FDIC) on Seventeenth Street, across from the White House. He famously complained that for decades there had been too few bank failures, in fact almost none. He saw that as evidence of an unfortunate absence of risk taking.

Well, he had a point. But surely we ended up overdoing it.

The American banking system had a long interlude of slow and orderly growth following the massive failures and regulatory reforms of the Great Depression (including the creation of the FDIC) and the wartime years. Restrictions on foreign banking, caps on interest rates paid on deposits, and seemingly adequate capital (10 percent was once considered the norm) persisted into the 1980s. "Term loans" that extended credit over several years were just emerging. Commercial banks were prohibited from engaging in most forms of investment banking by the 1933 Glass-Steagall legislation. The independent investment banking firms were themselves cautious partnerships without significant trading activity.

The June 1970 bankruptcy of the Penn Central Transportation Company—then the largest bankruptcy in the nation's history—

posed a threat most immediately to the commercial paper market where it was a substantial borrower.* Federal assistance was considered and finally rejected. While the Fed made a point of its willingness to lend to banks if needed and the New York Fed was called upon to exercise oversight, no real danger to banking stability arose.

The sudden shutdown of the German private bank Bankhaus Herstatt in the middle of the US trading day on June 26, 1974, sent shudders through the international payments system, but again with the help of the New York Fed the fallout was quickly managed. So was the failure in October 1974 of the fast-growing Franklin National Bank in Long Island, New York, a victim of fraud.

So it wasn't too long before Chairman Patman, the congressional archenemy of the Fed, got his way. Financial crises became the order of the day.

By the end of the 1970s, the financial world I'd always known was beginning to break down. The unique role of commercial banks was challenged by new rivals. Proliferating money market funds, free of regulation, offered higher yields than bank deposits. Investment banks increasingly began trading to generate revenue and competed to finance ambitious corporate takeovers and leveraged buyouts. Traditionally conservative "thrift" institutions—savings and loans and mutual savings banks—became more aggressive, taking advantage of lax regulation and higher interest-rate ceilings than those enforced on commercial banks. High inflation no doubt contributed to the uncertainties and speculative practices in financial markets.

So the banks themselves, recipients of deposits from Middle Eastern countries wallowing in oil revenue, began lending more enthusiastically, even imprudently, to Latin America and elsewhere.

The implication was clear. Beyond the attack on inflation, the new Federal Reserve chairman would likely have his hands full. The challenges extended beyond domestic finance to the international banking system.

---

*Goldman Sachs, as Penn Central's sole dealer in commercial paper, was able to exit any exposure before the company failed. It was later sued by investors.

Domestic Failure: The Chrysler Bailout

No sooner did I take office in 1979 than I was called upon to help implement the congressional decision to prevent the collapse of an American industrial icon. The Chrysler Corporation was on the brink of bankruptcy. Congress created a three-man committee to oversee a rescue. Senator Proxmire, the Senate Banking Committee chairman, insisted over my protests that the Fed chairman serve on the committee with Treasury Secretary Bill Miller and the long-respected comptroller general of the United States, Elmer Staats. His point was simple: he only trusted the Fed. It was a remarkable point by a leading Democratic senator that I never forgot.

Setting aside the basic question of whether a major corporation should be bailed out, the law calling for government assistance was well written. A "contribution" to the company's survival was demanded from each of the interested parties: the union, the creditor banks, and local municipalities. New management was brought aboard. Dedicated and talented Treasury employees provided staff assistance. The Salomon Brothers investment bank was enlisted to coordinate the participation of creditor banks and to search for a merger partner.

I learned the power of the government in dealing with a crisis once it got its act together. Congress pretty much had laid down the nature of the commitments required from the affected parties. As a result there were limited negotiating options. Even so, dealing with labor unions raised political qualms and it was suggested by my fellow committee members that the nonpolitical Fed might volunteer to negotiate the necessary agreement. I invited United Auto Workers chief Doug Fraser to meet in my office. He later reportedly said I was the toughest negotiating counterparty he ever had. The union agreed to significant cuts in wages and fringe benefits. The simple fact is I had the law on my side.

I needed to be just as tough with the banks that had been unable to reach a consensus right up to the deadline. Finally, I met with the senior bankers and explained that it was now or never: agree to a "haircut" or extension on their loans or go home and write off the existing credits in bankruptcy. They agreed to take the haircut.

Chrysler survived. In my view the Treasury's hard-working staff—general counsel Robert Mundheim and especially Brian Freeman, named executive director of the Chrysler Loan Guarantee Board—did the hard work and deserved the credit. So did my principal aide, Donald Kohn, a relatively new Fed economist with a practical cast of mind that eventually led him to the vice chairmanship of the Board of Governors.

The government's backbone in demanding the sale of Chrysler's executive planes over the persistent complaints of the new chairman, Lee Iacocca, helped resonate with the public.* A well-designed "K-car" was just coming into production and Chrysler became competitive. All of the creditors, including the US Treasury, ultimately could make millions: the new loans extended in the crisis included warrants for new stock. Those warrants (contracts that give the owner the right to buy stock at a set price over a certain time period) surged in value as the company recovered.

Iacocca, a flamboyant master salesman, pleaded with the new Reagan administration to cancel the warrants, arguing that they were essentially an unearned and undue reward. He didn't win. Chrysler ended up paying more than $300 million to buy back and cancel warrants held by the Treasury. My wife sent me a little typewritten note, enclosing an ad for Don Diego cigars featuring a handsome Lee Iacocca, cigar in hand. The note read: "Would you give a loan to this man?" My handwritten reply: "Not willingly!"

Homemade Financial Strains

It was still early in 1980 when, in the midst of a routine board meeting, I got a call from Harry Jacobs, CEO of Bache Halsey Stuart

---

*In 1985 Chrysler got its revenge by buying luxury corporate jet-maker Gulfstream Aerospace. Four years later it sold it back.

Shields, the second-largest brokerage house after Merrill Lynch. He said his company was on the brink of failure.

Huge loans, secured by silver, had been made to Nelson "Bunker" Hunt and his brothers. The billionaires, betting on more inflation, had pretty much cornered the silver market, riding an increase in the price from about $5 to almost $50 an ounce. The price was so high that it induced eager sales of family silverware.

In January 1980 the commodity exchanges had started cracking down on silver futures trading, first imposing position limits and disclosure requirements and then limiting trades to the liquidation of contracts. On March 14 the Fed's new credit controls program explicitly discouraged banks from financing "purely speculative holdings of commodities or precious metals." Rapidly, the silver price fell, reaching the point that the value of silver used as collateral for the Hunt loans and margin purchases had dropped below the loans' stated value.

Jacobs explained in his March 26 call to me that if the price fell any lower, Bache would be technically insolvent and unable to withstand a run by its many short-term creditors.

"Close the market," he pleaded.

Well, the Fed, the Treasury, and the Securities and Exchange Commission, which I had quickly called, had neither the desire nor the authority to step into the commodities market. Instead, we set about determining the facts. The Commodity Futures Trading Commission (CFTC) was the obvious place to begin. At first it refused to provide "confidential" information. However, we soon knew enough to discover that a further sizeable price decline could also cripple Merrill Lynch itself and then First Chicago, a leading midwestern bank, both loaded with substantial Hunt silver loans.

After a sharp decline the following day, which came to be known as "Silver Thursday," the silver price stabilized just enough to get us to the weekend. Then, late on Friday, I learned that the Hunts had also entered large futures contracts with Engelhard Minerals & Chemical Corp. that would require the Hunts to buy large amounts of silver above the market price. Payment was due on Monday and the Hunts didn't have the cash.

As it happened, that weekend I was scheduled to speak at a banking conference in Boca Raton, Florida. The bankers, gathered in the same hotel, promised to keep me informed of the Sunday night negotiations to resolve the issue. At first, that failed. In desperation, I was roused out of bed. Maybe that had some psychological effect. At any rate, early the next morning I learned of a last-minute deal in which certain Hunt oil drilling rights in the Beaufort Sea, north of Alaska, were acquired by Philipp Brothers, a major commodity trading house and subsidiary of Engelhard.

In the following weeks, and on the condition that none of the money be used for further speculation, the Fed allowed the remaining silver loans to be consolidated and secured by Placid Oil Company, by far the strongest Hunt family property. All of the Hunt brothers' assets, including ranches and racehorses, were locked in a trust. The Fed kept an eye on it. No government money was spent, but the Fed's involvement in helping to fend off the fallout inevitably attracted congressional and public attention.

About a month later, the First Pennsylvania Corporation, which owned the state's oldest and second-largest bank, was in crisis. Led by John Bunting, a former economic research official at the Philadelphia Fed, First Pennsylvania had piled into long-term Treasury bonds that lost value as interest rates rose. Encouraged by the Fed, which was providing emergency lending, the FDIC and a group of a couple dozen banks provided a $1.5 billion rescue made up of loans and a line of credit. They also received twenty million warrants to purchase common stock—enough to provide a controlling majority. It would prove to be an important model.

Continental Illinois: Too Big to Fail?

The failure of two minor government securities dealers over the next year or two could be handled without setting off alarm bells. The story was different with respect to the July 1982 bankruptcy of a seemingly innocuous Oklahoma bank called Penn Square with under $500 million in deposits, about half covered by FDIC insurance.

Small it might have been, but it had originated more than $2 billion of loans to speculative oil developers, an object lesson about the trouble that unscrupulous "retail" banks can cause without strong supervisory oversight. The loans were sold on to several large banks around the country, notably to Continental Illinois, one of the two big Chicago banks that I had warned about inadequate capital shortly after I took office.

Continental, limited by Illinois law to one location in Chicago, had become a leading commercial lender with national ambitions. It was a major "correspondent" providing services on behalf of many smaller midwestern banks and relied on "wholesale" deposits (that is, large-scale deposits from those correspondents and other institutions) that were well beyond the FDIC's $100,000 insurance limit. Using those interest rate–sensitive deposits, it had acquired a large amount of "oil patch" loans originated by Penn Square.

Continental chairman Roger Anderson flew out to visit me in midsummer, interrupting my morning on a Wyoming trout stream. He told me that the Penn Square loan portfolio could sink his bank. There were signs of depositor restiveness. Together with the comptroller of the currency and the FDIC, we put his bank under close surveillance. (In fact, the comptroller directly responsible for supervision of both Penn Square and Continental, and maybe the Fed, should have acted much earlier.) I recall contacting Continental's presumed lead director a little later, calling for a management change from the top on down, only to be told that would be a matter for me to discuss with the chairman. Only he could decide. So much for effective board oversight.

As its problems mounted, the bank became a heavy and frequent borrower of emergency loans from the Fed's discount window* as well as relying on financing from a large number of smaller institutions. Management changes were eventually made. But by mid-May

---

*Some credit the Continental Illinois debacle for creating the stigma attached to borrowing at the Fed's discount window, a signal that the bank is in trouble. Previously, such overnight loans were a more routine way for banks to manage occasional reserve shortfalls. It was always a bad sign if any institution relied on it frequently.

1984, the market's confidence was lost. We had a first-class emergency at hand.

With the FDIC, my preferred approach was to replicate the successful First Pennsylvania rescue, calling for a substantial contribution from a group of leading bankers. I arranged a meeting in New York with the six or seven leading banks at a convenient Morgan Guaranty branch, entering through the garage to avoid attention. The bankers, who had already agreed to participate in a $4.5 billion credit line to Continental Illinois earlier in the week, were wary.

With Bill Isaac, the FDIC chair, I made the pitch. The Fed would continue to provide Continental Illinois with full liquidity support through the discount window, counting on it having adequate collateral. The FDIC would provide $2 billion in capital in the form of subordinated debt. Bill pressed the banks to join for $500 million of the debt.

The representative of the largest bank, Citibank, soon announced they had no interest in rescuing a major competitor. But the negotiations continued and progress was made.

I headed off that afternoon to receive an honorary degree at Columbia University, concerned about the signal it would send if I didn't show up. Bill, who was putting the FDIC's funds at risk, stayed behind.

When I returned, I discovered he had decided to go one seemingly small step beyond what I intended by essentially providing all of the bank's—and its holding company's—creditors with an explicit guarantee.* After all, it was the FDIC's capital that was at risk and his point was that he needed to restore full confidence. The banks finally signed up for the $500 million infusion and increased their line of credit to $5.5 billion, now not so brave because the loan was essentially protected by the de facto guarantee of the FDIC.

The immediate sense of crisis receded, but it was clear from the start that the quick fix for Continental was not designed to last.

---

*Continental owed more than $30 billion to uninsured depositors and creditors, compared with just over $3 billion in insured deposits according to the FDIC's 1984 Annual Report.

In July the FDIC negotiated a second rescue that gave it effective control of the company and installed new management. Continental Illinois survived for a while but, amid management turmoil, lost its competitive position. Shareholders never recovered their losses.

This episode has often been credited with popularizing the phrase "too big to fail." Any ambiguity about the willingness of the government to bail out the big banks seemed to be lost when the comptroller of the currency, the supervisor of most of the big banks, went beyond his authority, seeming to commit to such support for the eleven largest in his later congressional testimony.

The Independent Community Bankers of America, representing thousands of small banks (including, for instance, the Penn Square Bank) argued that its constituents were placed at a competitive disadvantage: depositors, perhaps all creditors, of "systematically important" lenders would be protected from losses. In practice, most depositors of small banks tended themselves to be small and had the full protection of FDIC insurance. And it seemed to me, then and now, that Continental Illinois, its management, and its stockholders, did, by any reasonable definition, "fail."

The too-big-to-fail debate resumed loudly during the 2008 financial crisis. It continues to roil the politics of banking legislation and regulation to this day. In my view, the Dodd-Frank legislation signed by President Barack Obama in 2010 goes a long way toward creating an effective resolution process for failing banks. While inherently complicated and necessarily a matter of international concern, it requires removing management of a failing bank and, if necessary, liquidating or reorganizing the bank at the expense of stockholders and creditors instead of taxpayers.

The Savings and Loan Fiasco

The most extensive financial institution failures from that earlier period involved the "thrift" industry: savings and loans (S&Ls) and, to a more limited extent, their sister mutual institutions, savings banks. Encouraged to develop during the New Deal years, later amplified by special tax and regulatory measures (including deposit insurance), thousands of S&Ls came to dominate the small depositor and home mortgage market. Their basic financing model was inherently risky: S&Ls attracted "shares," essentially short-term deposits at interest rates slightly above those permitted for banks, to fund investments in fixed-rate mortgages that typically extended for thirty years and usually came with some form of government or quasi-government insurance.

Through the years of the Depression and war that financial approach worked. However, it wasn't compatible with high inflation and sharply elevated interest rates. By the early 1980s the ceiling on bank deposit interest rates was eliminated. Rising share costs and declining prices of existing mortgages essentially depleted both earnings and capital.

With regulatory "forbearance," which in practice meant the S&Ls could delay recognizing asset price declines on their balance sheets, most managed to survive well into the mid-1980s. But earnings never recovered. Strong political pressure developed to allow thrifts to expand into commercial lending and (inherently risky) real estate development and ownership. It started with some state regulatory authorities, and then the federal government was pressed to ease the lending restrictions as well.

I pleaded with the Congress for restraint at a number of hearings. S&Ls were ill equipped to responsibly manage a broad expansion of lending and investment powers. Real estate development posed obvious conflicts of interest along with market risks. Edwin Gray, the new chairman of the Federal Home Loan Bank (FHLB) board, essentially the S&Ls' Federal Reserve, came to amplify my concerns.

Newly appointed by President Reagan in 1983 after some White House experience, Ed was something of an innocent in the world of finance—a truly honest innocent. He was shocked by what he came to see in the volume of speculative, and even fraudulent, real estate developments sponsored and financed by S&Ls. He quickly came to understand that the regulatory side of the FHLB was weak, in some areas almost nonexistent, in terms of disciplining the dangerous industry practices.

His reward was to become the whipping boy for those in the industry opposed to regulation and their powerful congressional friends. He was accused by some industry leaders of undertaking a personal vendetta. The truly ugly result was congressional resistance to his reform efforts. In the end, five senators, the so-called Keating Five, got caught up in an attempt to browbeat Gray into easing regulatory requirements on the failing S&Ls, particularly Charles Keating's Lincoln Savings and Loan empire.

Utah senator "Jake" Garn, chairman of the Senate Banking Committee, was an intelligent and honest senator. He was also a strong supporter of expanding S&Ls' powers. He took to questioning me in hearings: "Mr. Volcker, can you identify any problems arising from the expanded powers of S&Ls?" "No, not yet" was the only answer I was able to give at the time. It was still too early to present tangible evidence of the problems I sensed would eventually emerge.

It was a case of *après moi, le déluge*. The savings and loan industry essentially collapsed. The ultimate cost to the federal government has been estimated at nearly $150 billion. (More than $250 billion in today's money.) Keating went to jail and some of the senators who had received contributions from Keating were themselves investigated by the Senate Ethics Committee. Some left the Senate. An interesting bit of history in the light of financial industry lobbying today.

For all of his brave and honest effort, the controversial Ed Gray found it hard to get a job after he left the government. He could take some satisfaction that his trusted, loyal, and experienced general counsel, William Black, told the story of his efforts in his book, *The Best Way to Rob a Bank Is to Own One: How Corporate Executives and Politicians Looted the S&L Industry*.

He didn't mince words.

Locked Together: Big Banks and Latin America

Those domestic crises, while symptomatic of deteriorating financial practices, were to me at the time just a sideshow to what became known as the Latin America debt crisis. It was, in fact, an international banking crisis, encompassing virtually all of the industry leaders and many unthinking followers.

A growing flood of loans had been made during the 1970s and early 1980s to virtually all of the Latin American countries and a few other developing nations as well (then collectively known as the "less developed countries" or LDCs). The borrowers needed the money to finance their countries' deficits and the banks were flush with low-cost deposits surging in from the newly oil-rich Middle East. Latin American debt more than doubled to $327 billion in 1982 from $159 billion only three years earlier in 1979. By the end of 1982, the loans averaged more than twice the capital of the eight largest US banks. Some leading foreign banks weren't far behind.

In its early phase, this "petrodollar recycling" had been welcomed as a constructive private market response to the high oil prices and the need for development finance. In actuality, the stage was set for a massive international debt crisis. Both the borrowers and the lenders were at risk of bankruptcy.

It started with Mexico.

At one point in 1981 the radical left-wing president José López Portillo heard a warning from his then finance minister that Mexico was becoming financially overextended. The easy borrowing might stop. He sent his son and friends to check with the banks. Their report was that the banks remained eager to lend. The finance minister was fired, too often the penalty for being right too soon.

In the following months, the relevant Mexican officials, Jesús "Chucho" Silva Herzog and Miguel Mancera, the new finance minister and the central banking chief, respectively, became increasingly concerned. Contrary to past practices, they decided to keep in close touch with the Fed and Treasury, and with IMF managing director Jacques de Larosière as well, anticipating the approach of a crisis. Chucho, a fluent English speaker with a graduate degree in economics from Yale University, later named our monthly meetings in my dining room at the Fed "the lemon meringue lunches" after the favorite dessert I imposed on him.

Pressure began to build in early 1982, when some of the exposed banks did curtail further lending. Mexico was, by tradition, bound to announce the size of its international reserves only rarely, but one of those occasions fell in May 1982. In response to a Mexican request to bolster the amount of their reserves, the Fed agreed to release $600 million overnight as part of an established "swap" arrangement—in effect, a prearranged short-term loan. We later agreed to a larger commitment, now a real loan, designed to last through the summer. It was based on the expectation that President López Portillo, left wing and anti-capitalist, would by early September have stepped aside in favor of the newly elected Miguel de la Madrid, who was more conservative, business friendly, supportive of both Silva Herzog and Mancera, and well prepared to deal with the pending crisis.

Unfortunately, our timing was a bit off. Mexico ran out of money in August, a month earlier than we'd expected. It could not, without help, make its debt payments. By unhappy coincidence, I was notified on the afternoon of the same day that the Continental Illinois chairman visited me in my cabin overlooking the rising trout on the Snake River. I called for all hands on deck, packed my rods, and returned to Washington.

The Mexican officials, meeting with De Larosière, had already been warned about the unacceptable consequences of an outright default, which would touch off a banking crisis throughout Latin America and beyond. The US Treasury, recognizing the huge consequences a Mexican default would have on our own banking system, promptly went to work arranging whatever government funds could be made immediately available. These were essentially advance payments to Mexico for oil imports and financing support for agricultural exports. On the Fed side, we urged our counterparts at European and Japanese central banks to see that it was in their own interest to join our stopgap efforts pending an approach by the new Mexican government to the IMF for continuing financing.

Holed up over the weekend with New York Fed president Tony Solomon, Ted Truman, and Michael Bradfield from the Federal Reserve Board staff and, importantly, Treasury deputy secretary R. T. "Tim" McNamar, we worked with Silva Herzog and the IMF to develop a workable strategy. While fewer than fifty of the international banks really mattered in terms of volume, Mexico began by inviting more than a hundred of its bank creditors to a meeting at the New York Fed. The location was chosen to add a sense of gravity, but no Fed or Treasury officials attended or participated beyond welcoming remarks from Tony Solomon. Silva Herzog reportedly started the meeting with his reassurance that the creditors were in safe hands: "My name is Jesús and my chief assistant is an angel." ("Angel" Gurría, now the longtime head of the OECD in Paris.)

He described the situation bluntly: Mexico had no money to pay off maturing loans. A default was not in Mexico's interest, and presumably not in the interest of the banks either. Mexico would need new loans to refund the maturing debt and to pay interest. He asked the banks to organize a creditors' committee to negotiate a workable arrangement. The IMF would be approached.

Reportedly, a long silence ensued. Very few questions.

Chucho followed his script. He explained to the press that his proposal for a coordinating committee to deal with the bank loans was accepted. After all, no objection had been voiced.

The key American bank was Citibank. Its chairman, Walter Wriston, had long promoted the view that lending to less developed countries was safe: "Countries don't go bankrupt." And now his bank had the most to lose. He soon recommended Bill Rhodes, Citibank's relatively young but experienced Latin America banker, to lead a creditors' committee.

It was a fortunate choice. Bill proved to have a rare knack among bankers of working well with the official community—governments, central banks, and the IMF. In the years immediately ahead, Bill would spend a lot of time in my office and at the IMF. Later, he became well recognized as the go-to man when the developing world faced a damaging financial crisis. That didn't enhance his popularity among many of his Citibank colleagues, but it was critical to managing the continuing crisis.

Just as those discussions got under way, the looming Mexican crisis was further aggravated by López Portillo's parting shot. In a speech delivered right at the same time as an IMF annual meeting in Toronto, he announced that Mexican banks would be nationalized and all payments to foreigners frozen, which would derail any rescue process. Miguel Mancera, the head of the central bank, felt compelled to resign. Silva Herzog was tempted to do the same but was persuaded to hang on until the incoming president, De la Madrid, was officially installed in December.

We got together a quick meeting in Toronto of central bank governors through the Bank for International Settlements (BIS). Fortunately, the highly respected leaders of two key central banks—Gordon Richardson from the Bank of England and Fritz Leutwiler of the Swiss National Bank—carried both understanding and credibility to a request for continuing BIS and central bank support. They were more convincing and eloquent than I alone could have managed. Together with the Fed and Treasury swap lines, we succeeded in finding a way to buy some time.

A formula for success soon emerged. The IMF's De Larosière was in the indispensable role. Support for "rolling over" existing debt and extending any further loans would depend on Mexico, under its new president, agreeing to a stringent program of economic reform. The IMF, in support, could provide medium-term credit, but only if essentially all of the significant creditor banks, De Larosière's now famous "critical mass," agreed to participate. The IMF would, in turn, need to validate the adequacy of Mexico's economic reform program.

The plan came to be replicated in country after country, eventually extending beyond Latin America. As the relatively new managing director of the IMF, De Larosière instinctively moved rapidly to bring his cautious board of directors into agreement, overcoming the procedural handicaps and established precedents all too common in complex international institutions. The key was the borrower's commitment to a satisfactory, fund-approved reform program and near unanimity among the bank lenders.

I became a bit concerned about the Federal Reserve participating so actively, essentially taking the US government lead with the IMF in what was basically Treasury territory. The problems were likely to (and did) spread to other Latin American countries and beyond. Secretary Regan fully participated in our efforts but I could sense he was uneasy. To ensure we had the administration's backing in continuing in a lead role, I agreed to a meeting with Jim Baker, the White House chief of staff. It was the first time I met him.

I handed Baker a short memo outlining the general approach so far and noting the likelihood of more Latin American problems. He immediately indicated support for the efforts. That ensured Treasury's continued full and active cooperation, particularly in the person of Tim McNamar, assigned to the task by Secretary Regan.

Indeed, almost all of the major Latin American countries (Colombia was one exception) did fall like ten pins.* Governments, the international banking system, and major economies were at risk. We had a lot of work to do.

Jim Baker would soon become Treasury secretary himself. His name became attached to a subsequent version of the common effort, known as the "Baker Plan," that was announced at the October 1985 IMF meeting in Seoul. Maintaining the same basic approach, it added the prospect of the World Bank and other international institutions increasing lending to cooperating countries.

Under pressure, and with the incentive of IMF support and lending, the leaders of Mexico, Argentina, Ecuador, and others made a lot of progress in curbing inflation, in disciplining their budgets, and in building more open, competitive economies.

Gradually, a sense of creditworthiness was restored and bank capital positions improved. Beginning with the new Citibank chairman John Reed, the main banks began to write down their loan exposure. I was hopeful that Latin American policies were turning the page from inward looking and protectionist to more competitive and stable.

Before the end of the decade I had left office. A new administration under George H. W. Bush and the new Treasury secretary Nicholas "Nick" Brady drew a line under the crisis. The so-called Brady Plan ingeniously developed means for the borrowers to offer creditors solid guarantees if they opted to accept some combination of lower interest rates, reduced principal, and long-delayed

---

*Eventually nine different Latin American nations had debt restructurings during the decade, virtually all through Bill Rhodes.

maturities. Borrowers and lenders, both in stronger positions than ten years earlier, largely agreed. The crisis was deemed over.

An Afterthought

The 1980s have been described as the "lost decade" for Latin America. My view is different: it was one of lost opportunities.

Mexico, Argentina, Ecuador, and Venezuela all instituted strong reform programs, seemingly successful for a time. It's true that growth was slow, the almost inevitable consequence of years of massive overborrowing and semisocialist, partly closed, authoritarian economies. The approach of bank forbearance and a flow of medium-term and longer-term IMF, World Bank, and Inter-American Bank financing with IMF policy oversight—all internationally agreed—certainly fit the category of tough love. But to me it had the ingredients of an escape from the classic Latin American pattern of closed, socialist economies heavily dependent on external credit.

Was there a viable alternative? Some suggested a debt haircut from the start, of some 10 or 15 percent across the board, might have been preferable. But a one-size-fits-all approach was not practical. New funds would not have been available to meet the continuing deficits. It could only have created expectations of more debt relief to come, with serious consequences for the solvency of some lending banks and without providing a real solution for the borrowers.

How about something more dramatic—just cutting the debt in half or more? But then who would recapitalize the banks and provide any assurance of reform?

The sad story, as I write this memoir, is not the lost decade but the extent of the more recent political and economic relapse in the region.

Venezuela, rich in resources, is a failed democracy in total economic turmoil.

Argentina, suffering from generations of Peronism, ultimately failed in good-faith attempts by successive governments to maintain promising reforms and currency stabilization. It is being tested once again.

Brazil, the largest South American country and with enormous potential, has become embroiled in political corruption and seems unable to sustain once highly promising reform efforts.

Mexico, with an economy closely aligned with the United States and a beneficiary of the North American Free Trade Agreement (NAFTA), has indeed gained strength but is still far short of where it could be. And, ironically, shortly after receiving wide respect and support for its reform efforts over two presidencies, it failed in 1994 to manage effectively a seemingly simple exchange-rate realignment. The result was, in relative terms, a limited crisis, but it turned out to be enough to set off reverberations that were felt later in the decade in Asia, where an ostensibly containable exchange-rate crisis in Thailand evolved into a threat to continent-wide economic development.*

Looking back, I see Latin America today as a sad culmination of hard-fought, constructive efforts to deal with a debt crisis that, aided and abetted by reckless bank lending practices, grew out of a chronic absence of suitably disciplined economic policies. And now, inevitably, it's caught up within the threatened breakdown of the broader post–World War II economic and political order.

---

*Indonesia, the most important Southeast Asian country affected by the crisis, at one point occupied quite a bit of my time as a formal and informal advisor. I was joined there by Singapore's founding father, Lee Kuan Yew, and others.

chapter 10

UNFINISHED BUSINESS

Repairing the Financial System

B y *1984*, in my second term, the major policy challenge of breaking the back of inflation and restoring growth seemed well in hand. The repetitive financial crises, large and small, carried a different message. Long-neglected weaknesses in the American and international financial structures needed attention.

Meanwhile, flourishing cross-border capital flows, aided in part by increasingly aggressive trading and lending, raised once again the question of currency movements.

Exchange-Rate Management

The combination of more stable prices (at one point the consumer price index actually declined for a few months) and a growing economy attracted funds from abroad, helping to finance our large budgetary and balance-of-payment deficits. The days of chronic dollar weakness seemed long over. Conditions in Europe and Japan were less propitious. Despite my entreaties, Germany in particular felt unable to reduce its interest rates to support a stronger economy.

Active discussion among finance ministers and central bankers about the efficacy, or lack thereof, of mutual intervention in foreign exchange markets had produced little concrete action. Suddenly, on the eve of the IMF's September 1984 meeting, the Bundesbank intervened massively, selling the "superdollar" to buy depressed deutsche marks. The effort pushed the mark up and some analysts compared the German effort to the Carter administration's 1978 dollar rescue. The United States stood by passively, despite my appeals to the Don Regan Treasury to join the effort.

Determining and executing exchange-rate policy raises delicate and difficult questions. In the United States, as in most other countries, the Treasury (or finance ministry) customarily takes the lead. But it is the central bank, in its conduct of monetary policy, that inevitably exerts an influence, sometimes a dominant influence, on exchange rates. Moreover, the central bank has the capacity to finance large-scale exchange operations.

In my experience, the operational result is that US intervention takes place only with a meeting of the minds. So the Bundesbank was left alone and the influence of its intervention gradually ended.

The "Baker Treasury," which took over in February 1985, was far more activist, in particular more confident about the potential value of intervening. That became evident early on when the Treasury responded to a plea from British prime minister Margaret Thatcher to President Reagan that the price of one pound sterling not be allowed to fall to one dollar, a politically sensitive level for Britain. After all, for a century before World War II, $4.80 to the pound was normal.

More generally, Baker clearly saw the dollar as too high. Protectionist pressures were rising in the United States as imports flooded in, threatening American companies and jobs. A politician at heart, Baker wasn't in thrall to the radical free-market, laissez-faire economic philosophy influencing others in the administration.

I had the sense that the secretary and his ambitious deputy secretary Dick Darman were becoming intrigued by the increasingly debated idea of establishing "target zones" for the major currencies. It was an idea supported by my old mentor Bob Roosa as a means of agreeing to, and maintaining, a degree of stability among the major currencies consistent with competitive balance.

Going into spring, cooperative intervention did help reduce the dollar exchange rate, but the rate rose again in the summer as the intervention ended. Baker was clearly concerned about the political consequences as the strong dollar led to increasingly forceful complaints by American industry. While I was not consulted, Baker at that point began exploring an explicit agreement with his Group of Five (G-5) finance minister counterparts to actively depreciate the dollar.

Given existing and expected economic conditions, I personally anticipated that the dollar was past its peak and would resume its decline in the fall. I wasn't enthused, to say the least, about giving it a strong, officially sponsored downward shove at the risk of setting off an accelerating speculative slide. So we had an internal negotiation.

Baker well understood the potential role of monetary policy in influencing exchange rates and the need to include the greater Fed resources in any intervention in the markets. He agreed with my insistence that anticipated intervention not be open ended and that we would guard against a "freefall" as speculators reacted.

The G-5 met in late September at the Plaza Hotel in New York, a location chosen, as I well understood, to keep it out of the Fed's territory and any appearance of Fed leadership. The carefully scripted meeting went well. I was puzzled when I was shoved to the front during the ensuing picture taking. The wily Mr. Baker apparently thought I needed to be kept under control and committed to the plan.

The dollar, as anticipated, declined immediately. The initial intervention could shortly be suspended. The drop resumed intermittently and, by the end of the year, I thought it had gone far enough. Baker thought differently. Our views repeatedly differed in emphasis in our separate congressional testimonies, but not so radically as to foment a serious clash.

As I think back, our disagreements may have had more significant consequences.

In January 1986, at the next G-5 meeting in London, I was presented with a draft communiqué to which the finance ministers, certainly led by Baker, had apparently agreed at a private meeting the previous evening. It strongly hinted at intentions for monetary easing, which of course was in the Fed's domain. I objected and would have strongly preferred not to sign any statement, as had been G-5 practice before the Plaza. Bundesbank president Karl Otto Pöhl objected equally strongly. The language was removed.

A front-page story the next day said the five countries agreed they might push down interest rates, citing an unidentified high-level Treasury official. I had an idea who that unnamed official might be.

The Revolt

Perhaps my refusal to accept the proposed communiqué language embarrassed Secretary Baker before his peers. I can't know for sure, but not long afterward I faced an insurrection in my own board.

Preston Martin was a former head of the Federal Home Loan Bank Board and had been somewhat close to then governor Reagan in California. I knew him only slightly when, in 1982, he was appointed to succeed Fred Schultz as Federal Reserve vice chairman. While I had supported another candidate suggested by Vice President Bush, I thought I had an experienced colleague at hand. Martin was surely ambitious.

We worked together pretty well for a couple of years. Then I started to notice some unusual behavior: trips abroad, as well as in the United States, without informing me; no warning before casting dissenting votes at the Fed's Open Market Committee meetings; finally, in June 1985 a public speech second-guessing the Latin American debt strategy that had been firmly supported by me and the entire Fed board. I thought a public reprimand was in order. (I recently learned that, after my statement was released, the Fed's in-house barber Lenny, the "hairman of the board," told Martin: "You and I have something in common—we've gone as far in this organization as we can." Martin laughed, or so I am told.)

At a regular board meeting one Monday, a day that was by tradition reserved for staff presentations and routine business, Martin made an out-of-the-blue proposal to cut the Federal Reserve's discount rate. My immediate request to hold off discussion until our normal "policy" day on Thursday was ignored. Two brand new board members, Manuel Johnson* and Wayne Angell, and one frequent dissenter, Martha Seger, joined with Martin in demanding the rate cut then and there. No debate needed.

I clearly had been ambushed. So I left the meeting, called Barbara, and told her I'd be home for dinner.

By pure coincidence, I had a scheduled lunch in the Fed's dining room with Chucho Silva Herzog and Jim Baker himself. After lunch, I took Baker aside and told him that my resignation would be on its way to the president after I got back to my desk. This was February 1986, after all, close to the time I had committed both to my wife and to the president, in that order, that I would leave.

It wasn't long before my faithful assistant, Catherine Mallardi, visibly upset to be preparing my resignation letter, told me that Wayne Angell, one of the new governors, wanted to see me. He suggested a second vote. Martin appeared soon afterward and agreed. The vote was reversed with my promise that we would go ahead when and if I could reach agreement with the Bundesbank's Karl Otto Pöhl and the Japanese central banker Satoshi Sumita to act together, as I had been urging.

That is what happened in early March, a few weeks later. It was a really remarkable success of central bank coordination, reflecting our mutual trust and also our individual substantive concerns. I had, in fact, been pleading with Karl Otto to reduce German—and by extension, European—interest rates. He understandably had been resistant to going it alone.

Soon afterward, the confrontation inside the Fed's board leaked out. Preston Martin resigned in late March, less than a month after the attempted coup. My relationship with the new governors,

---

*Johnson had notified me of his promise to Baker to vote for easier monetary policy at his first opportunity as a Federal Reserve Board governor. Having not anticipated the surprise vote, I couldn't take his warning into account. He later became an important and responsible vice chairman.

including some who joined afterward, became stronger over time. Mutual respect, for sure, but life was never quite the same.

In the circumstances, it seemed awkward to resign just eighteen months or so before the end of my term. I stayed until the end after all and got no open complaint, either from the White House or from my wife. President Reagan had his hands full with Irangate. Barbara had become resigned to the fate of marriage to a public official.

The Louvre

The idea of target zones for exchange rates, and the implied need for central bank cooperation, advanced beyond the Plaza agreement with a more ambitious effort.

Secretary Baker, apparently satisfied with the level of the dollar by the end of 1986, began exploring with Japan and other G-5 ministers the possibility of creating a framework for stabilizing the exchange rates close to then existing levels. Again, the Fed's position would be critically important in making any commitments.

The objective was entirely compatible with my own thinking. I was, in fact, in the habit of writing speeches calling for renewed interest in exchange-rate stability. My overly simple argument was that in an economically open world, with free flows of capital as well as trade, stable—even fixed—exchange rates were the logical component. I typically concluded that it was not a vision for my lifetime, but the creation of the euro could be a step forward.

Such musings along the lines espoused by Nobel Prize–winner Bob Mundell* were radically at odds with the earlier Reagan administration free-market, anti-interventionist doctrine opposed to any concerted effort at international monetary reform. Nor had the Baker Treasury taken any initiative to bring the Fed into its seemingly new approach.

---

*Mundell, sometimes called the "father of the euro" for his pioneering work on optimum currency areas, also helped lay the foundation for supply-side economics.

Instead, it called for a G-5 meeting in early 1987 at the Palais du Louvre in Paris, which housed the French finance ministry. (Leonardo da Vinci's *Mona Lisa* and the *Winged Victory of Samothrace* occupied the opposite wing.) As a historical note, the Italian finance minister learned of the meeting and appeared at the doorstep demanding entry. After long negotiation he rejected the offer to provide him with a post-decision briefing and left. Then the Canadian minister appeared. He accepted the offer of a briefing. That's how the Group of Five edged momentarily toward a Group of Six. By the next meeting a little later, it became the Group of Seven.

The substance of our discussion took less time than the prolonged attempt at face saving. Secretary Baker had prepared well and an unannounced agreement was reached on rather narrow, and really unrealistic, exchange-rate bands (initially plus or minus 2.5 percent), presumably to be supported by cooperation among the "five" on fiscal and monetary policies. I recall, in particular, the commitment by the United States on budgetary discipline. When I suggested to Baker that the stated goal of a balanced budget seemed clearly beyond our intent or possibility, his response reminded me of Connally's vow fifteen years earlier in his maiden speech before an important international meeting. Baker's budget "commitment" was just as short-lived as Connally's promise that "we are not going to devalue, we are not going to change the price of gold."

For a short while the markets behaved and with some intervention the currencies stayed close to their indicated ranges, but the agreed approach was far too ambitious. By March the dollar was slipping below its band. Given our domestic economic strength, the Fed could have justified a discount rate increase. I decided not to force the issue, keeping our powder dry for stronger action later. So we made just a small nudge to the market toward restraint. It was my last policy move, almost invisible, before the end of my term of office on August 11.

By that time, the narrow exchange-rate bands agreed at the Louvre had essentially become nonoperative. The strong written commitment to complementary fiscal and monetary policy was absent. The essential riddle of international monetary reform remained unresolved.

Still, I remained hopeful that someday a true reform could be enacted. In 1995 I delivered the prestigious Stamp Lecture at the University of London and called for greater attention to exchange rates, including an effort to explicitly recognize the then prevailing rate of a hundred yen to a dollar as a reasonable approximation of equilibrium and make a concerted effort to defend it within some sensible range. The Europeans could join later as they implemented a common currency, perhaps at parity with the dollar. As I returned to my seat, Bank of England governor Eddie George leaned over to me and whispered, "Nice speech, but it won't happen." He was right.

The last time I participated in an attempt to develop an outline for comprehensive monetary reform came much later, after the great financial crisis. Dubbed the "Palais-Royal Initiative," the attempt was led by former IMF managing director Michel Camdessus, Alexandre Lamfalussy, and Tomasso Padoa-Schioppa,* each well-respected European proponents of reform. Little noticed at the time, the report was lost amid the pressing concerns of the European debt crisis in 2011.

Recapitalizing the Banks

As international financial markets were freed from controls and rapidly expanded in the 1970s and 1980s, competition among the major international banks intensified. The big American banks developed active trading operations in European and Asian centers alongside their more traditional lending activities as they followed their commercial customers abroad. The foreign banks, as large or larger, became active in the United States. The natural result was pressure, particularly from American banks that felt heavily disadvantaged, to equalize capital and other regulatory requirements.

Diverse national attitudes and the absence of common statistical definitions made comparisons difficult. Nevertheless, certain outliers

---

*Padoa-Schioppa died suddenly on December 18, 2010. He was a cherished friend and colleague.

stood out. In particular, the huge Japanese banks had extremely low ratios of capital to their assets. Moreover, the computed ratios included sizable equity holdings, potentially highly volatile.

Even then, the banks argued that capital decisions and differences were a reflection of different business models and competitive factors rather than a critical element in risk management. After all, Walter Wriston was willing to deny the need for any capital at all for what was then the largest American bank. My earlier brief encounter with the Chicago bank executives in 1980 reflected those attitudes. Apparently, it was the first time the adequacy of their capital had been questioned by one of their supervisors. They saw no need to worry about such a "suggestion" from a new Fed chair who, after all, had no explicit authority over them.

The travails of First Pennsylvania and Continental Illinois, the massive threat posed by the Latin American crisis, and the obvious strains on the capital of thrift institutions had an impact on thinking over time, but strong action was competitively (and politically) stalled by the absence of an international consensus.

An approach toward dealing with that problem was taken by the G-10 central banking group meeting under the auspices of the Bank for International Settlements,* headquartered in Basel, Switzerland. A new Basel Committee would assess existing standards and practices in a search for an analytic understanding.

Progress was slow. Even within the Fed there was reluctance to move unilaterally, reflecting the inherent difficulty of finding common ground among different US regulatory agencies, each concerned about their own constituents, still a chronic problem.

Eventually, I succeeded in urging my fellow BIS central bank governors to take action, reaching beyond the Basel Committee itself, which had become stymied in its attempt to set out common statistical approaches. The concept of dictating and enforcing common standards seemed beyond its reach.

The issue would not go away, not in the face of the Latin American debt crisis, which demonstrated the capital inadequacy of so many

---

*The BIS, created in 1930, is sometimes called the "central bank for central banks."

lenders, and the clear discrepancies in national practices. There was also some support from American banks and supervisors, concerned in particular about the "unfair" competition from their undercapitalized Japanese rivals. Even in the European banking community interest eventually emerged. But one gaping difference in approach made progress difficult.

The US practice had been to assess capital adequacy by using a simple "leverage" ratio—in other words, the bank's total assets compared with the margin of capital available to absorb any losses on those assets. (Historically, before the 1931 banking collapse, a 10 percent ratio was considered normal.)

The Europeans, as a group, firmly insisted upon a "risk-based" approach, seemingly more sophisticated because it calculated assets based on how risky they seemed to be. They felt it was common sense that certain kinds of assets—certainly including domestic government bonds but also home mortgages and other sovereign debt—shouldn't require much if any capital. Commercial loans, by contrast, would have strict and high capital requirements, whatever the credit rating might be.

Both approaches could claim to have strengths. Each had weaknesses. How to resolve the impasse?

At the end of a European tour in September 1986, I planned to stop in London for an informal dinner with the Bank of England's then governor, Robin Leigh-Pemberton. In that comfortable setting, without a lot of forethought, I suggested to him that if it was necessary to reach agreement, I'd try to sell the risk-based approach to my US colleagues.

He faced practical political difficulties with his European colleagues, some of whom were unenthusiastic about the prospect of any global standard. None of them were eager for a "made in the USA" approach. Robin would have to overrule his own Bank of England subordinate, Peter Cooke, who was then serving as Basel Committee chairman.

Nonetheless, he bravely decided to move forward. The Fed and the Bank of England came to a bilateral understanding, announced in early 1987, just seven months before I left office. That was enough time for Jerry Corrigan, my old assistant who was by then New York Fed president, to take upon himself the challenge of inducing Japanese agreement. At that point, the continental Europeans didn't have much choice but to sign on as well.

The Basel Committee, which was bypassed originally because of its reluctant posture, was delegated the task of writing the final rules later that year. It became known as the "Basel Agreement" then and in all of its later permutations.

Over time, the inherent problems with the risk-based approach became apparent. The assets assigned the lowest risk, for which capital requirements were therefore low or nonexistent, were those that had the most political support: sovereign credits and home mortgages. Ironically, losses on those two types of assets would fuel the global crisis in 2008 and a subsequent European crisis in 2011. The American "overall leverage" approach had a disadvantage as well in the eyes of shareholders and executives focused on return on capital; it seemed to discourage holdings of the safest assets, in particular low-return US government securities.

The Basel Agreement has come under almost constant pressure for revision. Global regulators in December 2017 completed the third iteration. Meanwhile, the United States has legislated its own set of rules. In recent years, a sensible middle approach has emerged, applying both a risk-based measurement and a simple leverage ratio, each helping to offset the weaknesses of the other. Conflict remains, not just in the nature of the approach, but the enforcement of specific ratios internationally and domestically among banks of different sizes and activities. The needed stiffening of the capital requirements in the United States and elsewhere after the 2008 crisis began to be diluted less than a decade later.

Last Days at the Fed

By the time of the Basel Agreement, my commitment to leave office early was well past its sell-by date. After the short-lived revolt and the vice chairman's resignation, the time hadn't seemed quite right.

Relations with both the president, and seemingly with the secretary of the Treasury, had returned to an even keel.

There was clearly unfinished business. Only limited progress had been made in efforts to relax outmoded restrictions on interstate banking. More importantly, leakages in the old Glass-Steagall restrictions on trading and investment banking left open questions about partial or complete repeal. The Federal Reserve itself had begun easing the possibility of trading activities in bank subsidiaries. Long discussions about reform with Don Regan and later Jim Baker did not materialize in legislation.

That unfinished business in no way changed my intention to leave. I ran into Howard Baker, Reagan's new chief of staff, at a New York Times reception in late May. I suggested a meeting. First thing the next morning, he was at my office.

I told him that I didn't want to be reappointed and that the time had come to announce a successor. He protested with some apparent vigor, insisting I should stay. But eventually he asked whom I would suggest.

My answer was twofold. John Whitehead, the highly respected former co-chair of Goldman Sachs, was clearly qualified by experience and temperament. In those days, Goldman was still a partnership and I viewed it as a highly principled, client-driven investment bank. Former Treasury secretary Joe Fowler was a partner and prized the firm's culture. Whitehead was, at that time, serving as George Shultz's deputy secretary of state and seemed to get along very well in Washington. (He later expressed to me with some feeling that his limited Washington years—where he met his new wife, the journalist Nancy Dickerson—were among the most satisfying of his life.)

Alan Greenspan was the other, more obvious choice. I had known him, not well, since the earliest days of our professional lives in New York. He was a superb financial technician, a long-standing Republican, and had strong free-market views.

A few days after I met with Howard Baker, Jim Baker chimed in. He told me that, in effect, it was my responsibility to stay. I must reconsider over the weekend. He would arrange a meeting with the president on Monday, June 1. My overall impression that he would not be personally heartbroken by my decision to leave has since been confirmed: according to one report he thought I would slow the momentum toward freeing the banks from Glass-Steagall, a politically sensitive objective.

I deeply appreciated the unsolicited support for my reappointment from a group of senior senators, led by the majority leader Bob Dole. But I also recalled some advice I'd gotten from Joe Fowler years earlier. When you want to leave a senior government post, put the resignation in writing and present it. That way you can't be talked out of it.

So I dutifully did put my decision not to accept a third term in writing. I handed it to the president as we met. There was no objection.

The next day, Alan and I went out to meet the press. A few weeks later, a dinner was held in my honor at the State Department, co-hosted by Jim Baker, George Shultz, and John Connally, and attended by Douglas Dillon, Joe Fowler, and Ronald and Nancy Reagan. It was a generous send-off by men I respected, and dozens of men and women with whom I had worked.

Alan Greenspan was a well-known and respected figure with good political instincts. He loved the job and became widely revered as the economy grew amid stable prices. He too found a Washington wife in the indefatigable television correspondent Andrea Mitchell. Alan was reappointed five times, serving longer than any other Fed chairman except Bill Martin.

Quite naturally, I have wondered what might have happened if I had walked into that final meeting and said something like "Mr. President, after talking with Howard and Jim, I've changed my mind. I'm up to another term."

Of course, their concern was less about keeping me in place and more about avoiding any market perception that I was being forced out. The stock market did initially drop sharply. But it soon stabilized. In his gracious remarks at our press conference, Alan made it clear that he would see to it that our hard-won gains in fighting inflation were maintained.

And they were.

In 1990 I was able to deliver a traditional Per Jacobsson Lecture at the annual meeting of the IMF with the title "The Triumph of Central Banking?" Its conclusions about central bankers' ability and need to control inflation were sharply different from those in Arthur Burns's memorably pessimistic "The Anguish of Central Banking" Jacobsson Lecture eleven years earlier. I could leave office with a sense of satisfaction that the Federal Reserve was a well-respected institution, capable of providing leadership in a never-ending effort to achieve and maintain financial stability.

Our experience in beating back inflation no doubt helped to restore the credibility of central banks around the world, providing improved insulation from partisan political attacks.

At the same time, the question mark at the end of my title was significant. I was well aware that serious challenges remained ahead.

chapter 11

AFTER THE FED

I left the Federal Reserve with no fixed idea of how I'd return to private life. I was sixty, not far from what was then considered a normal retirement age. Barbara's lifelong diabetes and rheumatoid arthritis were presenting more serious challenges.

At the same time, I knew there were a lot of options. The family financial squeeze was resolved with a few speaking engagements in Europe and Japan. I could take my time.

I was flooded with offers to serve on corporate boards. Two possibilities that really intrigued me were the Washington Post Company and Dow Jones, then the *Wall Street Journal*'s parent company. I had strong relationships with both organizations and, as a result, felt emotionally conflicted about joining either. I did agree to serve on the boards of two large foreign companies: Swiss food giant Nestlé and British chemical manufacturer ICI presented interesting international exposure, free of conflicts.

Bill Bowen, the Princeton University president upon whose board I had briefly served, urged me to return to the Woodrow Wilson School. He suggested appointing me as a tenured professor, even part time and without the requisite PhD. Adding to the allure, the proposed professorship had been created by Fred Shultz, my loyal Fed vice chairman and good friend.

I had no desire to join a financial firm as a director or as some kind of window dressing. (Wisely, no one suggested I join as CEO.) So, once again, I procrastinated.

To meet Barbara's concerns over my inability to make up my mind, I began to consider hanging out a shingle of my own, something as original as "Paul Volcker Advisory Services." Then I happened to run into Jim Wolfensohn, the highly personable and well-connected Australia-born investment banker with extensive experience in London and New York. I knew him a bit from his time as a senior partner at Salomon Brothers, when it had been retained to help out with the negotiations to rescue Chrysler.

Some years earlier he had left Salomon, which remained dominated by big trading operations rather than traditional investment banking. Jim pioneered a very different model, a "boutique" firm that would specialize in advising companies on mergers and acquisitions (M&A) and other strategic business concerns. There would be no trading, no underwriting, no speculation—in short, nothing that might put the firm's interests in conflict with those of its clients. As we talked, by design or chance, the idea arose that I might join Wolfensohn's firm and share leadership responsibility.

Why go to all the trouble of starting my own little firm? I could spend Friday through Monday at Princeton and the rest of the week at Wolfensohn.

Wolfensohn

While Jim was not enthused about the detailed contract that my lawyer friends demanded I negotiate, it effectively granted me veto power over company decisions and certain perks like a car that high government service inures one to. In the event, much of that was ignored. I think it was on the very first day that Jim asked me: "Paul, you don't really need a car, do you?" And the fact was, I didn't. And still don't.

The basic Wolfensohn strategy was to work with a limited number of large international companies that were willing to pay an annual retainer fee, effectively assuring the firm a lead advisory role on their M&A or other strategic transactions.

When I arrived, the firm had, along with Jim, a couple of well-established investment bankers and a small group of young potential partners. "Sandy"White, a veteran of the firm White Weld, and Ray Golden from Salomon Brothers brought a touch of gray. But soon Glen Lewy, Jeffrey Goldstein, and Elliot Slade led the team and grew its senior partnership. Stephen Oxman, straight from the US State Department, brought an international dimension while Bevis Longstreth, whom I had known when he was at the Securities and Exchange Commission, provided professional legal support. The firm also had remarkable success attracting some of the cream of the junior Wall Street analysts and more senior associates. After my arrival, we went on to develop small joint ventures in Tokyo and Paris. Building on Jim's early success, we maintained a solid client base. Naturally, in my case, those came to include some leading international banks like Chase Manhattan, my old employer, the aggressive NationsBank (which eventually bought and renamed itself Bank of America in 1998), the Dutch ING Group, and Britain's HSBC, one of Jim's original clients.

In time, Jim became fixated on another ambition, launching a campaign to become president of the World Bank. In 1995 he got the job and left. I, contentedly, took the proverbial corner office. My partners did the work and kept our standards high. I will never forget one incident—small, taken for granted, but I thought emblematic about our firm and the regular practices of Wall Street.

Glen Lewy, one of our newer senior partners, came into my office to report on a rather singular phone conversation. A former client called to say he was at a new company where he was in the midst of secretly negotiating a path-breaking merger. The aim was to announce it within days. He would pay Wolfensohn for a so-called fairness opinion, a standard piece of Wall Street boilerplate providing assurance that the transaction was fair to the investors of the merging companies.

Glen told the potential client that Wolfensohn couldn't provide such a fairness opinion overnight, without sufficient time to adequately investigate the deal. "Okay," the prospective client responded. "I can get the fairness opinion somewhere else, but I want you with me for the last few days as we seal the agreement."

The deal got done. Glen earned a sizable fee. We stuck to our principles.

Citibank, having survived the Latin American crisis, certainly did not look to me for advice. However, by the early 1990s it found itself once again saddled with bad loans, this time to real estate projects. The bank was being closely monitored by the New York Fed, by then led by Jerry Corrigan, and the FDIC, led by Bill Taylor. During my time at the Fed, Taylor had been in charge of supervision. Visiting my office at Wolfensohn one day, just across the street from Citibank, he remarked that the bank's regulators were considering calling for the resignation of Chief Executive John Reed, who had been my antagonist during the last stages of the Latin American debt crisis.

"Who would you put in his place?" I asked.

His finger pointed at me. I think it was a joke.

Around the same time, I was visited by a Middle Eastern man who said he was representing an investor from Saudi Arabia. Could we advise him on a potentially large investment in Citibank? In consultation with Jim, I decided that dealing with mysterious investors from the Middle East was not our line of work. We let my guest take his business elsewhere. We soon learned he represented Sheikh Al-Waleed of Saudi Arabia, who became the biggest investor in Citibank for years to come, providing capital that helped the bank survive that and subsequent crises. (Somewhat ironically, given his predecessor Walter Wriston's past insistence to me that his bank didn't really need capital, John Reed was quoted at the time of the Al-Waleed investment explaining that "we want to be perceived in the marketplace as strongly capitalized.")

Years later, I was told by a member of the firm that did advise the sheikh that their role was limited and their compensation was low.

Princeton: Education for Public Service

The arrangement with Princeton suited the Volcker family well. At least for a few years.

The university had available a small, prerevolutionary house facing the main road, Nassau Street, on the front and the campus out back, maybe two or three hundred yards from my academic office. There were cracks in some of the floors, no insulation, a dirt floor in the cellar, but a huge fireplace. I could almost imagine that "George Washington slept here." After all, the victorious battle of Princeton was fought only a mile or two away.

Barbara could manage in the house. The first floor had bath facilities. Children and grandchildren could visit and small dinner parties were easy in the dining room with that fine fireplace.

Alas, the idea of an indefinite stay into gentle retirement couldn't last. Barbara's deteriorating health made the frequent New York–Princeton travel burdensome. My greater Wolfensohn responsibilities ultimately forced me to end the dream.

At Princeton, my obligations included two quite different academic assignments: a graduate seminar for one term and a Woodrow Wilson School undergraduate "conference," or "task force," in the other term. In both cases, I could call upon advanced graduate students to help and was able to bring in friends and former colleagues to provide students with a variety of perspectives. That included one year with Toyoo Gyohten, who was retiring from his role as Japan's vice minister of finance. We wrote a book, *Changing Fortunes: The World's Money and the Threat to American Leadership,* together, based on our lectures during one seminar. (I just reread it. It's recommended reading!) Helmut Schlesinger, who retired as Bundesbank president in 1993, happily spent another year teaching with me. Helmut and his students bonded in a sausage, sauerkraut, and beer party.

One evening stands out in my mind. The grad students in the seminar urged me to invite a real, live speculator. George Soros kindly agreed to fill the bill.

Attendance at the seminar doubled when a sizable number of the economics faculty appeared. I don't recall Professor Ben Bernanke (who would go on to succeed Greenspan as Fed chairman) among them. I was well aware that prestige on the Princeton faculty was a matter of testing theories and conducting research, not participating in markets and institutions. I had observed a highly regarded young professor of international finance, an area of potential faculty weakness, turned down flatly as lacking sufficient "theoretical standing." Today, decades later, he stands out as a leader in international monetary analysis—but on the West Coast.

George Soros spoke openly and at some length. The point he insisted upon over and over again was that the concept of "equilibrium" didn't apply to financial markets. Instead, markets tend to move from one extreme to another, passing right through any imagined steady state of equilibrium. If you wanted to win in the markets, you had to observe a developing trend, jump on it, and get off in time. Economic theory wouldn't help.

As the chief interlocutor, I tried my best to defend the notion that, while markets may overshoot and undershoot, there was surely some value in identifying a sustainable balance. I didn't get much help from the more established economic theorists in the room, who seemed unwilling to test their own theories against a brilliant investor, and George had none of it.

The evening concluded after my principal graduate assistant suggested to Mr. Soros that perhaps he wasn't fully aware of the contributions academics were currently making to "chaos theory." I could only think back to how often I had been forced to deal with financial market chaos in real time—and that was before the great crisis of 2008.

Those Princeton years were deeply satisfying in terms of my contacts with students and some of the less theoretical faculty. The conferences provided a unique undergraduate experience. Each required substantial student research, an extensive joint report, and the need to organize and reach consensus on real, live issues. In each case, students were exposed to and asked to report to serving officials or others who had actual responsibility with respect to the issues they were studying.

On one occasion we were asked to visit Puerto Rico to report publicly on the students' conclusions about Puerto Rican governance, an

issue that remains just as relevant today. In another instance, baseball's then commissioner Bud Selig was not entirely pleased with
the students' recommendations about changes in the economic and
competitive structure of Major League Baseball. (That happened to
be a matter I also opined upon as a member of two separate committees asked to review possible changes in professional baseball business practices.) I knew it was an emotional subject.

Amid all the satisfactions, reality sometimes intruded. Not all advanced Princeton undergraduates were capable of writing a succinct,
grammatically correct research paper. I also observed how well the
conferences re-created the bureaucratic processes I'd seen in Treasury and other parts of government. Getting together to make a
report while respecting everyone's point of view wasn't easy. Campus
"political" considerations entered in. And I didn't much like the fact
that, as is the fashion these days, at the end of the course the students
rated their professors.

Training for Public Service

My experience as a Woodrow Wilson School professor only reinforced some of my growing concerns about the school's mission, and
about educating for public service more generally.

In that respect, I felt that Princeton lost an important opportunity. The university had received a $35 million gift in 1961 (almost $300
million in today's dollars) from A&P grocery store heirs Charles
and Marie Robertson to support a new graduate program in what
became the Woodrow Wilson School. The funds, held in a separate
account, were to be directed quite specifically to training students
for public service, emphasizing international affairs. Right down the
Princeton alley, I thought, with its motto "In the Nation's Service."

Princeton's new young president at the time, Robert Goheen,
formally expressed the hope that the gift would enable "Princeton
University to do what it and other universities have long wished to
do: establish professional education for public service at a level of
excellence comparable to the country's best schools of medicine and

law." I don't know just what he had in mind, but he also made clear that Princeton was a university that needed to keep its "attitudes significantly philosophic and liberal." It would not become a training school for "managers or bureaucratic cogs." Harold Dodds, the brash young man's predecessor and professor of public administration, must have quietly shaken his head.

In the end, however conflicted the thought, Princeton accepted the endowment. It grew over time to hundreds of millions of dollars, an important fraction of the university's endowment.

In the early years, a reasonable effort was made to respect the donors' intent. Several senior professors were hired and the first deans did have a sense of mission. Still, as early as 1970 Charles Robertson expressed dismay at how few of the school's graduates entered government service. Donald Stokes, the school's dean during my first sojourn, urged me to help construct a new program and curriculum that would be relevant for the limited number of graduate students, essentially all of whom were attracted by a generous stipend. I failed in his assignment. Developing such a curriculum preoccupies me to this day as a mission of the Volcker Alliance.

Over time, in addition to the income skimmed off the special endowment for university administration, increasing sums were devoted to support the economics and political science departments. Many of their professors were deemed co–Woodrow Wilson School faculty. Some had a continuing interest in public policy, but few cared specifically about training for public service. After Stokes died in 1997, the deans began rotating between the prestigious economics and political science faculty.

During my time on the faculty, there were a few Woodrow Wilson School professors who did value public administration as both an academic discipline and a profession. However, it became clear to them that this was not an institutional priority. Richard Nathan, who had served in the Nixon administration's Office of Management and Budget and was a researcher at the Brookings Institution, left to join SUNY-Albany and serve as director of its Rockefeller Institute of Government. John DiIulio, a young Harvard PhD with a Woodrow Wilson School–Politics Department joint appointment, enthusiastically taught the core public administration course. However, he refused reappointment as he came to sense the school's lack of commitment. DiIulio later joined Donald Kettl, a top public administration scholar, in establishing what lives on today as the Brookings Institution's Center for Effective Public Management, itself undernourished.

Twenty years later, to the best of my knowledge, Princeton has not hired and tenured any scholar who is primarily focused on research on public administration and training for public service.

I recall one of the new deans, a respected economist from another university. Knowing of my interest, he visited me in New York and asked a simple question: "What is public administration all about?" Then: "Should we be hiring psychologists?" (I don't think he had in mind the now fashionable behavioral economics.) A new dean apparently absent any sense of mission or real interest epitomized my concern.

In a memorandum to Harold Shapiro, who succeeded Bill Bowen as Princeton's president in 1988, I objected forcibly to the lack of attention to the core mission of public affairs and management. Whether by coincidence or otherwise, I later learned that Princeton's provost had herself initiated a review of the school—not by the usual accrediting body, but by a special three-man committee of outside experts. In polite academic terms, their report emphasized my point that a strong sense of mission was absent. Princeton, with all its resources, was not providing the leadership that the Robertsons had anticipated. And it was evident that the few professors dedicated to the Woodrow Wilson School alone were retiring or leaving.

Early in the twenty-first century, I wrote again to the new president, Shirley Tilghman, at some length with an even more forceful view. Former Treasury secretary Michael Blumenthal, another Woodrow Wilson graduate, and a few others joined my effort. At the same time, the Robertson family heirs filed a suit claiming that the still-segregated funds, which ultimately grew to more than $900 million, were being misused. Instead of shrugging off the claim, pending a trial, the New Jersey judge properly urged a settlement.

President Tilghman took note. She clearly understood there was a real issue. As a prominent (but still quiet) critic, I was sought out. She promised to make changes. Over faculty resistance she brought in a new dean, Anne-Marie Slaughter, from Harvard Law School. She came with a strong interest in foreign affairs, clearly a priority area for the Robertsons. Together, the new president and new dean began to take some useful steps in keeping with the mission. However, a clear sense of direction consistent with the Robertsons' intent remained elusive. No doubt, with the lawsuit hanging over the university, its counsel advised against making any changes, even constructive changes, that might be construed as an admission of failure to take account of donor intent.

After a few contentious years, the suit was settled in 2008 on the proverbial courthouse steps. The Robertsons were feeling a financial pinch. The university may not have wanted a public debate about donors' rights and presumably did not want to place the matter before a jury composed of Mercer County residents, culturally antagonistic towards the "rich" university. My understanding is that the foundation paid some $40 million for the Robertson family's legal fees and essentially gave back $50 million over seven years to the Robertsons for a new foundation preparing students for careers in government service. The school was allowed substantial leeway in how it uses the income from the remaining hundreds of millions for an effective Woodrow Wilson graduate program.

The clash at Princeton between the objective of professional training for public service and the allure of "policy" education was extreme but is by no means unique. Political science ("politics" at Princeton) and economics faculties have long-established prestige and recognition. They emphasize "theory" and are proud defenders of the "humanities." Training graduates in the arguably more mundane tasks of effective administration doesn't fit their definition of an academic discipline.

The irony for me is that there is today far more practical training at Princeton and elsewhere than when I was a student. The training is in the engineering school, considered a second rate option in my day but now richly rewarded for turning out new financial engineers and data wizards for Wall Street and Silicon Valley. That's where the money is and that's where the talent flows, including two of my grandsons.

The point was driven home to me one evening when, by chance, I was walking with a young economics professor toward the Woodrow Wilson School. I idly remarked that "this university doesn't pay enough attention to public administration."

"Why should it?" he responded. "Public administration is not a real discipline like economics."

Politely, I restrained myself from reminding him of the abject failure of economists to make reliable forecasts, the essence of a "real" science, or to foresee and understand the financial crisis we were then undergoing. But I could not resist telling him that I became a student at Princeton in large part because its president was, in fact, an honored professor of public administration.

"I don't believe it," he replied. "This great university would not have as president a professor of public administration."

I silently thought of Woodrow Wilson, a leading scholar of public administration, president of both Princeton and of the United States, restive in his grave. A great university simply has not risen to the challenge of effective education for public service.

Family

By the mid-1990s, Barbara's health had deteriorated to the point that full-time help was needed. Fortunately, we had a wonderful and capable young woman, Mercedes "Meechy" Dowling, as a housekeeper and organizer. She was able to manage the household pretty much on her own.

Janice had long since graduated from Georgetown University, trained in nursing, and was married in 1981. She never left the medical field or the Washington area. That was convenient for me while I was Fed chairman, living in my small, minimally furnished apartment and dropping off my laundry.

The arrival of three sons interrupted her career (I was, rarely, a babysitter), but she returned to medicine and has now earned a doctorate in nursing. My fine grandsons have followed quite different career paths, two now living in San Francisco with careers in "big data" and fine wines and one, more traditionally, working on Wall Street.

Where else do highly educated young men go these days?

My son is a remarkable story. Conquering his early inability to walk or to safely drive a car, he earned undergraduate and graduate degrees from New York University, trained in a commercial bank for a while, and then married and moved to Boston with a career in facilitating financing for medical research. He and his wife, Martha, adopted a baby girl from China. My granddaughter, Jennifer, is now in college, competing in ice skating and, I trust, in the classroom. At last I have a "name carrier" in a world in which women are counted.

Barbara deserves much of the credit. For more than 40 years she took on the responsibility of raising our children, often with her husband away, preoccupied, or both. She was always determined to show Jimmy, and those around him, that cerebral palsy should not be an excuse for relying on others.

She had overcome her own long odds in a lifetime battle with juvenile diabetes. Dependent on insulin her entire life, she took a real risk as a pioneering diabetic giving birth to two children in the 1950s. She made it to age sixty-eight, a rare feat for diabetics in those days, allowing her to see both Janice and Jimmy happily married and with families of their own.

Cigars

Images from my years as Fed chairman invariably depict me with one of my cheap cigars or enwreathed in a cloud of smoke, often while testifying to Congress in front of a "No Smoking" sign. My father had been a pipe smoker who treated himself to the occasional cigar; indeed, cigars were the one gift he would allow himself to accept while he was Teaneck's town manager. In my early years I smoked cigarettes, but eventually found they often gave me a head-ache. The switch to cigars helped me to relieve tension. And they could be a useful prop during meetings. But, after all, it became an addiction.

As time went on, I began to feel increasingly guilty about sub-jecting colleagues, friends, and family to my fumes. Janice, learn-ing nursing and with three young sons, relentlessly reminded me of the hazards of smoking. Yet it wasn't until I received a stiff warning during a medical exam at the Mayo Clinic, where I was serving on the board of trustees, that I realized the time had come to stop. Even after learning the warning was a false alarm, I decided to kick the habit in my last few months at the Fed. After all, by that time the professional pressure seemed to be off anyway. I haven't smoked a cigar in more than thirty years, even when the mosquitoes gathered on a trout stream.

Fishing

Increasingly at home in the evenings as Barbara's health deterio-rated, I took up a new avocation: learning to tie trout flies. With the children gone, I equipped one room as fishing headquarters.

Years earlier, I'd made a grievous mistake. I took Barbara fishing in the wilds of Maine on our honeymoon. Familiar to me, it was new to her—and it didn't take. Watching the bears sorting through the refuse pile in the nearest tiny village didn't impress her. We hastily retreated to a golf resort.

For a long while, I pretty much stopped fishing. I also gave up golf, using the excuse that I was too tall to hit the ball straight.

When Barbara's parents retired to upstate New York, things changed a bit. They were near trout streams. I had the opportunity to join a couple of trout fishing clubs. Then I was invited to join the Restigouche Salmon Club, the holy of holies for Atlantic salmon. Indeed, as I edit this memoir, I am sitting on the broad porch of In-dian House looking hopefully for rising salmon. No luck. So, about thirty years later, fishing days are rare, but it's been a great privilege, even if I can no longer rely on cigar smoke to keep the bugs away.

Anke

Shortly after I agreed to join Wolfensohn in 1988, I had an unexpected knock on the door. An attractive, fortysomething woman appeared. She had a slight German accent.

She came with the blessing of my former New York Fed assistant, Ann Poniatowski, who was helping me with the transition to Wolfensohn. She had contacted Ann after reading a *New York Times* story about my return to the city. As she was a bit bored with her job, did Ann think I would need a new assistant?

That's how I met Anke Dening. She'd grown up in a German professional family and lived and worked in Italy and France, rounding out her formal education. She had visited New York years earlier, quickly got a job, and eventually rose as a secretarial assistant in the higher reaches of the *Washington Post–Newsweek* organization and CBS. She was fluent in English, German, French, and Italian.

For once I didn't procrastinate. Thirty years later she is still with me. In 2010 she became my wife—and, reversing our roles, the boss.

chapter 12

MR. CHAIRMAN

IN SEVERAL GUISES

*J**ust a few months** after Jim left me in charge of
Wolfensohn, a British bank announced it was acquiring one of
our boutique rivals, Gleacher & Company, for $135 million. My part-
ners immediately realized what that could mean for the value of our
firm; after all, we thought of ourselves as far better established. I was
satisfied with the progress and culture at Wolfensohn and not motivated to do a deal. But I agreed that my colleagues could search for a
suitable partner, provided it met their high financial expectations. In
May 1996 the firm was sold to Bankers Trust, where the new chief
executive officer, Frank Newman, was eager to make his mark in the
world of investment banking.

I was nearing seventy and had no interest in assuming executive
responsibilities, or even a consultative arrangement, at a big bank.
But part of the deal was that I would serve on the Bankers Trust
board for a time. Before long I had a too-large portfolio of board
memberships at corporations, philanthropies, and "policy-oriented"
institutions. It was a chance to learn more about institutional management from the inside.

Lessons from the Private Sector

As a central banker and as an investment banker, weaknesses in the top-level management of banks and other financial institutions were too often exposed to me in times of crisis. The larger, more difficult challenge is to identify the fault lines and act before a crisis. A weak CEO, failures of internal controls, and sloppy auditing practices are symptomatic but hard for an outsider to detect. Alas, too often that is true for board members as well.

That is the reason I have favored the growing, but still far from uniform, American practice of separating the responsibilities of an independent board chairman, who makes sure the entire board is active and informed, from the chief executive officer, who develops and implements policy. My experience in the corporate world also strongly supports the growing consensus in favor of smaller boards. In the much larger boards upon which I have served, an individual director is unlikely to feel a strong sense of influence or responsibility. And, yes, these days retirement ages can reasonably be higher than the old norms of seventy to seventy-two. But seventy-five is probably enough. Without some limit, it's sometimes just too hard to ask "old-timers" to leave when they have outlived their ability to contribute.

Too often board membership is viewed as a kind of sinecure, a reward for prior service, demanding little more than full support for the CEO (who may well have been responsible for your appointment). Whatever their ages or other qualifications, every director should feel a real sense of personal responsibility, not merely for providing strategic vision or some market or technology insights—matters for which consultants can be employed—but for demanding strong operational, accounting, and ethical standards.

For too many years I served on the large board of the well-run Swiss food giant Nestlé. It had a strong and highly competent chairman who consulted with a small group of the Swiss directors about the strategic questions. Fritz Leutwiler, a good friend from our central banking days, was one of those. He pulled me aside after one of my first board meetings.

"It's all right, Paul, to ask questions. But you're not supposed to ask difficult ones." He was only partly joking.

Almost thirty years later, I sense that attitude has changed!

No doubt I've served on boards where I failed adequately to recognize and insist upon executive oversight.

I learned this the hard way as a director at Bankers Trust and Prudential Insurance, two well-respected firms that, over many years, were leaders in responsible banking and life insurance, respectively. I and other experienced directors were caught flat-footed by management miscues and failures to deal promptly with ethical issues. In both instances, we directors were reluctant to act early enough and forcibly enough. The consequence was being left with the possibility of criminal indictments of the companies, only narrowly avoided. Not a pleasant prospect, unsettling management, sapping institutional energy, and running up auditing and legal expenses. I might point out that, in both cases, supervisory efforts could not be relied upon to expose difficulties for which boards had the primary responsibility.

The ensuing years have only amplified my concerns. Almost daily, we read accounts of corporate managers falling short of their now typical written commitments to ethical standards.

Boards of philanthropic institutions are a different affair. Membership is inevitably influenced by past or prospective financial contributions as well as public prominence. For the most prestigious institutions, boards tend to be very large and unwieldy. It is understood that a smaller group within the board will be responsible for actively "minding the store." The commitment and experience of that inner group is essential.

Well into my post-Wolfensohn "retirement," I agreed to chair three nonprofit institutions that conformed with my personal and professional interests. Each was quite different in mission but global in scope.

International House in New York provides both housing and a variety of cultural experiences for about seven hundred graduate students from around the world. Originally created by John D. Rockefeller Jr. and Cleveland H. Dodge, their two families have maintained a strong interest for close to a century, providing a sense of mission and management continuity. The New York International House became the model for "I-Houses" elsewhere in the United States, Europe, and Japan.

In contrast to the 1920s, international education is commonplace today. Hundreds of thousands of foreign students flood into American universities. Nevertheless, I-Houses still have a special role as homes away from home, exposing students, both foreign and American, to diverse cultures and professions on a day-to-day basis. In New York's case, thirty or so board members share a common vision and have long worked together. The finances are mostly but not entirely self-sustaining, largely covered by room charges. The internal management, for years led by Don Cuneo in New York, has been both small and highly disciplined, and from my point of view a little overprotective of the outside chairman.

Much smaller and somewhat self-indulgent is the expansively entitled Consultative Group on International Economic and Monetary Affairs. It is more commonly known as the Group of Thirty, or G-30. Established in the aftermath of the breakdown of the Bretton Woods system, the group's membership is drawn largely from the ranks of retired senior central bankers and finance ministry officials, seasoned by the active participants in financial markets, international business, and academia. The semiannual meetings provide former, and some current, high-level financial officials a greatly valued opportunity for informal debate and discussion.

Potentially more important, from time to time the G-30 sponsors studies of current issues. During the first months of my responsibilities as chairman in 1993, the G-30 published a definitive report on derivatives, the then still-nascent world of financial contracts that derive their value from some other underlying asset.

In July 2008 I myself chaired, with two colleagues, a G-30 steering committee tasked with studying long-term, comprehensive proposals for financial reform. Stephen Thieke, our hard-working project director with both high-level central banking and commercial bank risk-management expertise, succeeded in getting the report published in January 2009, early enough so that it had some influence in shaping financial reform after the crisis. The report's recommendations included consolidating supervision and regulation of the largest, most complex financial institutions under a single regulator, strong capital standards and risk controls (including on proprietary trading by institutions benefiting from the protection of deposit insurance and access to Federal Reserve financing), and emphasis on the effective oversight of all financial markets. I carried the message into discussions with the new Obama administration, as I will describe in a later chapter.

In taking a public position in these and other areas, the G-30, like other self-appointed expert groups, needs to take care that these reports do not lose truly independent stature, free of pleading for the particular interests of its members. There are more than enough professional lobbyists in Washington. Reflecting that responsibility, the G-30 more recently has focused on the need for leaders of financial institutions to make and support a commitment to strong internal controls and cultural values—a commitment that must extend beyond endorsing written statements of corporate values. I recommend the 2015 report, titled "Banking Culture and Conduct: A Call for Sustained and Comprehensive Reform," by a working group co-chaired by Bill Rhodes and Roger Ferguson. The relevance is obvious. Enforcement is difficult.

The Wells Fargo bank is a case in point. Not so long ago hailed as a model of customer-oriented responsible management, it has faced official and public opprobrium about entrenched fraudulent business practices. It is a glaring example of deeply flawed incentive compensation systems, reaching down through the management and employee ranks, overriding the company's prominently stated ethical standards.

The Wells Fargo experience may be unique in the breadth of the wrongdoing, extending down to the teller's window. However, distorted incentives have become widespread. Guided by "independent" consultants and typically related to short-term profit (or stock price performance), a kind of contagion seems to be at work. Stepping back, do the CEOs of today's top banks (or other financial institutions) really contribute five to ten times as much (in price-adjusted terms) to the success of their institutions, or the economy, as their predecessors did forty or so years ago? I have my doubts. At least, it doesn't show up in the economic growth rate, certainly not in the pay of the average worker or, more specifically, in an absence of financial crises.

It's not clear to me that the strong incentives for particular "deals" lead to better management. They certainly can and do lead to conflicts of interest with "relationship" clients. For better or worse, it is a very long way from back in my days at Chase Manhattan when I was lectured by a senior officer that payment of individual bonuses would ruin the conservative customer-oriented approach appropriate for commercial banks. It turns out he had a point.

At the opposite end of my nonprofit spectrum from the small and focused G-30 is the sprawling Trilateral Commission. Conceived in the early 1970s by David Rockefeller, with Professor "Zbig" Brzezinski bringing strong academic and policy credentials, the immediate objective was to draw Japan into closer economic and political cooperation with Western liberal democracies. It quickly drew interest from the academic and think-tank communities as well as from business leaders in North America, Europe, and Japan, all reflecting the rapid expansion of international markets within the context of open, liberal societies.

The invited membership quickly expanded to more than two hundred. Annual (and later regional) meetings attracted high-level policy makers anxious to address the influential membership. Substantial studies were sponsored on geopolitical, economic, and environmental issues of international importance.

I was asked in 1991 to share leadership with Count Otto Lambsdorff, the chairman of Germany's Free Democratic Party, and Akio Morita, the cofounder and chairman of Japan's Sony Corporation, who was succeeded as Asian chairman of the Trilateral

Commission by Kiichi Miyazawa. I took particular satisfaction in the last years of my decade-long chairmanship from our success in extending membership to Mexican participants. After much hesitation, Japan invited South Korea and other Asian democracies to join. From time to time the committee also invited influential policy-oriented individuals from Russia and China.

The clear and overriding message was that liberal democracy and open markets had become the way of the world, seemingly confirmed by the eventual collapse of the Soviet Union and the extension of democratic norms to Eastern Europe. The evidence of some opening of China toward a more capitalist, market-based system during the 1980s and 1990s seemed to confirm that America's leadership since World War II was indeed successful in shaping a constructive new world order.

Alas, that presumed consensus about the value of open, democratic societies and free trade is at risk today. Rampant populism runs right against the grain. Authoritarian governments on the fringes of Europe, in Asia, and in parts of Latin America are attracting attention. The relevance of the Trilateral Commission and like-minded organizations in today's world is surely challenged.

Quite visibly, while the size and breadth of the organization has grown, attention and influence seem to be shrinking. Amid other responsibilities, active business participation has become harder to maintain.

Strengthening America's Public Governance

The clear thread running through my career has been the challenge and satisfaction of public service. I well understand the American government at every level has its share of inefficiency, waste, and short-sighted political gamesmanship. A healthy dose of skepticism about government is built into our collective psyche. Ronald Reagan could always win applause by announcing that "government is the problem."

And, yes, in some ways it is.

It also happens to be a necessary part of our national being and of a successful society. Inescapable, we'd better make it work effectively.

That is why, a couple of weeks before officially leaving the Federal Reserve, I agreed to lead the newly formed and privately funded National Commission on the Public Service.

The unpaid chairmanship wasn't about money or power. While I didn't think about it at the time, my motivation was more personal. Public service is important, and when I hear people denigrating public service my visceral, unspoken reaction is "Goddamn it, my father was a public servant. His pay was limited but he wasn't denigrated."

The concept of the commission and the leadership of its professional staff were a reflection of deeply felt concerns in particular about the declining strength of, and respect for, our federal civil service. Bruce Laingen, recently retired as a senior foreign service officer, was a prime example of the best. As chargé d'affaires of our Iranian embassy in 1979, he was captured and isolated for many months, a very visible part of the hostage crisis that dominated the American psyche, as well as Jimmy Carter's reelection effort, for months on end.

Bruce wasn't discouraged about the value of government service. To the contrary, his long diplomatic experience seemed to reinforce his sense of commitment to the mission of effective government. Recruiting, properly educating, and reasonably rewarding talented young men and women to build the strength of the civil service, and especially the diplomatic service, were personal priorities.

Thirty years ago, we called the growing weaknesses in administrative practices extending across all of government a "quiet crisis." It had developed over many years and was little understood by our public at large or, for that matter, most of the political leadership.

Before I became involved, Bruce and early supporters had already attracted to the commission a cross-section of strong and experienced leaders from government, business, labor, and academia. A broad range of political views were represented, starting with former president Gerald Ford and including prominent ex-cabinet officers from both parties. Business and union experience was brought to bear.

With a small and deeply committed staff* we produced a forceful report, "Leadership for America: Rebuilding the Public Service," drawing both on our collective personal experiences and extensive research.

In March 1989 we proudly presented the report to President George H. W. Bush in the White House Cabinet Room. George Bush had himself spent much of his life in government, both exposed to the political side in Congress and to the need for administrative effectiveness in leading the Central Intelligence Agency and serving as vice president. As president, he was sympathetic to our cause. But I also knew—we all knew—that constructive change would require, as noted in the report itself, "sustained, bi-partisan commitment."

To that end we managed to convince Congress to authorize a small new entity charged specifically with annually reviewing progress toward needed reforms. Bill Scranton, Pennsylvania's widely respected former governor and congressman, agreed to lead the effort. I felt we were accomplishing something.

William Jefferson Clinton, the new US president, soon appeared for his joint first address to the Congress on his administration's priorities. In midstream, as a token of his determination to promote government efficiency and to cut spending, he proposed cutting thousands of federal jobs and freezing salaries, exactly the opposite of the investment in civil service our report had advocated. He also said he planned 150 specific spending cuts. Those turned out to include not only unnecessary programs such as the long-defunct Bicentennial Commission, but also our proposed (and much needed!) Independent Advisory Council that was not yet operational and essentially cost free.

The irony is that his heart was in the right place even if the politics were not. The Clinton administration, seemingly ignoring our

---

*Charles Levine, recognized as the leading scholar of public administration and serving as the deputy director of our commission, died suddenly at age forty-nine in September 1988. We were fortunate that Paul Light, a dedicated young scholar, was able to step in to help complete our report.

efforts, would itself sponsor a significant reform effort: Vice President Al Gore's program for "reinventing government." It helped call attention to the challenge but was of limited effectiveness. Somehow, other priorities interfered.

Our effort did have one directly relevant result. A follow-on commission focused entirely on state and local government, chaired by former Mississippi governor William Winter. Its conclusions complemented those of our national report. Together both stimulated some attention in schools of public administration and policy. But, paralleling my own limited experience with the Woodrow Wilson School at Princeton, the challenge of effective public management seems to be of dwindling academic interest and support.

Stubbornly, I returned to the effort a few years later with another, identically named, National Commission on the Public Service. Much smaller but with an equally distinguished membership, its recommendations were even broader, calling for a sweeping review of the federal administrative structure. Some cabinet departments and other agencies could be eliminated or consolidated. Strong political leadership would be required and career professional management should be emphasized and encouraged.

It was a model that was incorporated, knowingly or not, in the creation of the new Department of Homeland Security, which combined twenty-two federal departments and agencies, during the George W. Bush administration.

Good try, poorly implemented.

It simply had neither the strong political leadership nor the practical administrative strength that is required—demonstrated most dramatically by the failures in responding to 2005's Hurricane Katrina.

chapter 13

THE SEARCH FOR

INTEGRITY

T *o w a r d m y* closing days at Wolfensohn in 1996, I was approached by Curtis Hoxter, an intermediary acting on behalf of both the World Jewish Congress and the Swiss Bankers Association (SBA). Would I consider leading an investigation into how Swiss banks had handled funds placed with them by victims of Nazi persecution?

Clearly this was an emotionally and politically sensitive matter. Previous efforts had been unsuccessful. I sought assurance that both sides were indeed finally committed to an inevitably expensive and contentious investigation with potentially unsettling conclusions.

Fritz Leutwiler, the iconic Swiss central banker and a fellow Nestlé director, urged me to overcome my hesitation. He emphasized the importance to the Swiss people of a fair inquiry; the accusations of wrongdoing strongly pressed by the Jewish community against the Swiss banks were a stain on the country's honor as well as on the banks themselves. Both sides would benefit from a fair and trustworthy investigation.

Fritz had become a close friend. On more than one occasion he played a key role in enrolling European bank support for management of the Latin American debt crisis. He argued that I had little to lose in taking on an investigation. After all, there wouldn't be useful bank records for long-dormant accounts opened fifty or sixty years ago. I was trusted. I could quickly evaluate the competing arguments, negotiate a dollar settlement, and be finished in a few months.

How wrong he was.

Separate class-action lawsuits against the Swiss banks filed in a US federal court in Brooklyn complicated things. They sought billions in cash restitution for the families of Holocaust victims but lacked definitive supporting evidence about individual claimants or the practices of Swiss banks.

Judge Edward Korman consolidated those cases and reserved his decision pending settlement negotiations and the outcome of the Independent Committee of Eminent Persons (ICEP) investigation that I fearfully but finally had agreed to chair. The judge and I were destined to become joined at the hip.*

What soon became known as the "Volcker Commission" consisted of three representatives and two alternates chosen by the World Jewish Restitution Organization (with the World Jewish Congress) and an equal number chosen by the Swiss Bankers Association. Understandably there were deep-seated suspicions on both sides. However, as we got under way it seemed apparent that the Swiss government, at least as insistent as the Swiss Bankers Association, did want to clear the air, however uncomfortable the circumstances. The Swiss banking regulator granted crucial assistance by providing legal authorization to access bank records. In December 1996 the Swiss parliament established a parallel official commission with international membership. The so-called Bergier Commission was charged with investigating broader aspects of the Swiss-Nazi-Jewish relationships and had legal authority to reach beyond the banks.

For all the time it would take, for all the substantial costs and uncertainties and the eventual monetary settlements, it was not the money that was most essential. On the Jewish side, clarity and a

---

*Only as I wrote this memoir did I learn that the last of thousands of payments to Holocaust victims from the class action suits have been made.

sense of justice were at stake. For the Swiss, straightforward recognition of long-denied culpability and restoration of national pride were the issues.

Even with good will on both sides, the ICEP was tough going. The top accounting firms we first approached for help balked at the potential reputational and legal risks. Finally, the five major firms were persuaded that a group effort would ameliorate the business risks, help avoid conflicts of interest, and encourage competition in excellence.*

The strong expectation, set out by the banks themselves, was that very few records would be found—Swiss law permitted destroying dormant account records after ten years. However, prodded by the ICEP staff and contrary to those expectations, millions of scattered records were found, sometimes lodged in alpine caves, that the banks themselves had long forgotten, assumed did not exist, or perhaps wished did not exist.† To be sure, the records that did exist were often fragmentary. Sometimes there was a name with a date, rarely an address, maybe the size of the initial deposit amount, almost never with any updated accounting beyond the first few years.

Nevertheless, we learned that of the 6.8 million Holocaust-era accounts held in Swiss banks‡ there were still some records for 4.1 million. And not all of them were fragmentary. In fact, we initially concluded from the bank files and from other research (including lists of victims) that at least fifty-four thousand of these accounts "probably" or "possibly" belonged to Holocaust victims.

---

*These were Arthur Andersen, Coopers & Lybrand, Deloitte, KPMG, and Price Waterhouse. The teams from Coopers and Price Waterhouse maintained their separate identities throughout the investigation, although their two firms merged in July 1998.

†In one interesting, embarrassing, and meaningful incident, a bank security guard "rescued" relevant records headed for the shredding machine in violation of a ban on destroying wartime records. It was, to put it mildly, hard for the top bank official to explain.

‡The 254 banks that existed between 1933 and 1945 had been reduced through mergers and acquisitions to 59 banks by the time of our inquiry; in fact 141 of the banks had been consolidated into Switzerland's two biggest commercial banks.

In the end, after another round of review, we could and did pub-lish approximately twenty-one thousand accounts that were proba-bly owned by victims, with another fifteen thousand not published but made available for claims analysis. For sure, many potential claimants had died. Their family and heirs had to be identified. In the absence of more precise evidence, we could only estimate ac-count size and lost income. Once the investigation was complete, we established a team in Zurich of lawyers—Swiss and American—to deal with individual claims.

The investigation into the Swiss banks' treatment of Holocaust victims and their families could not be entirely satisfying given the fragmentary evidence of individual accounts, the time that had passed, and the number and ages of the potential claimants.

Our effort was unable to establish concrete evidence for the claim that Swiss banks had knowingly and jointly colluded on a common policy of denying Holocaust survivors and heirs access to their ac-counts. However, there could be no doubt that many banks indi-vidually stalled and effectively denied access to potential claimants. No effort was made to keep adequate records or to accommodate inquiries by victims' relatives. We found clear evidence of question-able and plainly deceitful actions by some individual banks. There were instances in which the SBA itself seemed to counsel limited, and consequently misleading, responses. Claims that Swiss bank se-crecy laws and the passage of time justified inaction seemed hollow, particularly given that the account liabilities came to be erased from the books.

We learned years later that our failure to identify and expose a common agreement among the banks was rectified: the Bergier Commission, with its stronger Swiss government authority, could and finally did uncover some evidence of such concerted efforts and an agreement among the larger banks to deflect inquiries.

In retrospect, I must admit I'm not sure the formula we devised for repayment of accepted claims was fully adequate. The account balances were often estimated. We took the technical approach that claimants were eligible to payments compounded at prevailing Swiss interest rates. Those were very low by international standards. We could have been, and maybe should have been, more generous to the victims who, in concept, could have placed the funds elsewhere. But, of course, that would have been guesswork. Our efforts, and those of the Bergier Commission, to identify accounts opened in the name of Swiss "agents" were not successful, although the amounts involved were likely substantial.

In our report, we concluded with one strong point beyond our strict mandate. The absence of Swiss law about the treatment of long-dormant, unclaimed accounts led to inconsistent practices and the temptation to use them to enhance bank profits. There was a need for uniform escheatment laws.

My own direct involvement ended more than ten years ago. Beyond the agreed final report of the investigation in December 1999, we set out a hard outline for a process of evaluating individual claims and authorizing payments. It was always under the interested eye of Judge Korman in Brooklyn, who still had settlement of the independent class-action matter on his hands. In principle, he reserved funds from that $1.25 billion settlement to assure payment of individual claims.

All in all, a sad bit of history. All the sadder in that I am told a political movement has reappeared in Switzerland seeking to deny the validity of the Volcker and Bergier report conclusions. Fritz Leutwiler, long since dead, would not be happy.

I cannot complete a review of the Holocaust investigation without recognizing one man who played a critical role in the entire effort: Michael Bradfield, a colleague and close friend of mine from our days together in the US Treasury in the 1970s.

From the start, Mike never accepted the notion that individual account records at Swiss banks had been lost or comprehensively destroyed. He pushed the banks and the accountants to find the facts. He designed and implemented the arrangements for identifying the families of claimants. He stuck with it for years after I had moved on, working as a designated "special master" under Judge Korman.

Mike died in 2017. His efforts helped to return more than $720 million from Swiss banks to Holocaust victims and their heirs of the nearly $1.29 billion in total distributions from the class-action settlement. Mike's determination to tell the individual stories of what happened to the accounts and the victims who owned them is his lasting legacy.

Collective Responsibilities

I happen to believe that there is an indispensable role for international organizations in today's world. The simple fact is that much of the apparatus—the United Nations, the International Monetary Fund, the World Trade Organization, the World Bank, and others—is the product of American leadership. Taken together they are an essential link in maintaining the rule of law internationally, in peacekeeping, in dealing with natural disasters and refugee crises, in encouraging development, and in much else.

I have also learned that international institutions have a culture of their own. They provide a kind of cocoon, with a cosmopolitan staff a little insulated from national customs, laws, and procedures but highly sensitive to the internal politics of the organization. Efficiency isn't typically a high priority. Effective oversight, both internal and external, is too often lacking.

I learned all that from direct experience in the first decade of the twenty-first century when much of my attention was drawn to two separate inquiries into the management of international organizations. The first involved accusations of widespread corruption in the United Nations' management of the Iraqi Oil-for-Food program. Those allegations extended all the way to Kofi Annan himself, the generally popular secretary-general.

The second looked into an internal conflict and an uprising at the World Bank over how to deal with corruption in its programs, which at one point seemed to be threatening the effectiveness of the entire organization. The ouster of a new president was just one casualty.

The UN on Trial: The Challenge of Managing
the Oil-for-Food Program

Henceforth, the most comprehensive coercive economic
measures ever devised by the UN were tempered by the
largest humanitarian relief operation in the UN's history.

—PETER VAN WALSUM
Netherlands ambassador to the United Nations

The United Nations' Oil-for-Food program was launched in 1996
with the best of intentions: ensuring that trade sanctions imposed by
the UN against the corrupt and threatening Iraqi regime of Saddam
Hussein wouldn't lead to starvation or other humanitarian threats
to the Iraqi people. The program's design required oversight of commercial transactions between Iraq and thousands of importers and
exporters. Over the seven years of the program, transactions total-
ing more than $64 billion took place with parties in at least eighty-
eight countries. The pricing and shipping specifics for each approved
"humanitarian" transaction—thousands upon thousands—almost
invited corruption. An enormously complex monitoring challenge
came face to face with an inherently loosely managed UN organization. The UN Security Council, to the extent it exercised any oversight, was almost entirely concerned that Iraqi purchases of military
equipment or nuclear material did not slip through the cracks.

It took a lot of persuading by the secretary-general to convince
me to take on the investigation. His strongest argument was that he
had already reached a tentative agreement for two highly qualified
men to join the proposed three-member independent inquiry committee. Justice Richard Goldstone of South Africa was renowned
for his investigation into corruption and brutality by South Africa's
police and army as that country's apartheid regime ended. Mark Pieth, a Swiss lawyer with unequaled expertise in corporate and official
cross-border corruption and money laundering, has been a driving
force in the OECD's efforts to curb corrupt practices in international trade and investment.

I stipulated that, to be successful, our investigation would require adequate staff working for a year or more, assurance of millions of dollars in funding, and the full support of the Security Council. The conclusions and analyses of the investigation would need to be made public.

Kofi Annan, with his own reputation at stake, agreed to all of those terms. So, in 2004, I became chairman of yet another investigation. The Independent Inquiry Committee (IIC) of the United Nations soon became more widely known as the "Volcker Committee."

In essence, our mandate was to address the allegations of mismanagement or faulty administration of the program by the UN itself. More broadly, we investigated whether contractors of the UN, purchasers of Iraqi oil, or providers of humanitarian aid engaged in illicit or corrupt activities.

In most respects it was, for me, a uniquely satisfying experience. Once under way, we had no difficulty recruiting highly able investigators, typically senior lawyers from US attorneys' offices and their equivalents from other countries. Experienced accountants joined, including some I had worked with in identifying Holocaust victims' accounts in Swiss banks. Capable and enthusiastic junior staffers were eager to take part. At its peak, the IIC comprised more than eighty staff from twenty-eight countries.

The greater challenge was to find a recognized and respected leader to manage the complicated international relationships and the highly motivated but not yet organized staff. Several retiring senior US attorneys backed away from the potential controversy. Serendipity solved that problem.

A good Canadian friend, former ambassador to the United States Allan Gotlieb, called me one day with a suspicion that I might be looking for help. He offered a solution: Reid Morden happened to be free. Reid had been the top civil servant and deputy minister in Canada's foreign office. Subsequently, he had led Canada's smaller equivalents to the US intelligence and atomic energy offices. Early in his career he had also been assigned to the UN. Ready and willing, Reid brought just the experience and qualities needed to manage a group of younger men and women operating at the peak of their energy and abilities.

It was an eye-opening experience for me. The cynical reaction of many observers was that without subpoena power or national authority, we couldn't succeed. Neither problem proved insurmountable.

As the experienced investigators on the team knew, those accused or fearing accusation would want to talk. Banks cooperated, even in Switzerland, where, unlike my earlier experience, the authorities stretched to the full extent possible interpretations of its secrecy law. (I suspect that strong cooperation reflected Switzerland's eagerness to show its value as a new member of the UN, which it had just joined in 2002.) We had near total access to Iraqi records, which, despite initial doubts and subsequent claims of misdeeds, were consistently found to be accurate. No doubt the Iraqi clerks and officials wanted to maintain precise records about which of their supervisors had authorized specific transactions.

We could not possibly look into all of the many thousands of transactions, even when there were clear grounds for suspicion of kickbacks, illicit pricing, and other infractions of the rules. Cooperation from other governments varied. Surprisingly, we got little help from British authorities, even when the Scotland-based engineering firm Weir Group in effect voluntarily disclosed their own guilty behavior in July 2004. We were a bit bemused by the fact that Britain's Serious Fraud Office (SFO) did not seem particularly serious so far as identifying Oil-for-Food corruption was concerned.

The UK, which outlawed overseas bribery in 2001, nevertheless in 2006 forced the SFO to shut down a criminal inquiry into large-scale contracts to sell British-made planes to Saudi Arabia. In explaining the decision, Attorney General Lord Goldsmith said in Parliament that the decision to end the investigation reflected the fact that matters of national and international security could outweigh the rule of law. A clear but surprising statement in the mother of parliaments. In any event, amends would be made by authorizing more funds for the SFO to investigate old Oil-for-Food matters. A little late and a little stingy.

A French magistrate, by contrast, seemed intrigued by the possibility of high-level political involvement, later confirmed, and we exchanged some investigatory leads. Russia and China predictably refused to cooperate, but again Iraqi records made their official involvement unambiguously clear. Large shipments of US dollars in Iraqi diplomatic pouches from Moscow to Baghdad each week apparently contained illicit payoffs.

The committee could only itself investigate fully a handful of firms engaged in illicit activity, counting on individual countries to follow through on clear indications of involvement. As it turned out, the largest single violator was the Australian Wheat Board, in those days the government-sponsored monopoly for all Australian wheat exports. As the program's largest humanitarian aid provider, it was discovered to have provided more than $221 million in kickbacks to Saddam Hussein's government that were disguised as trucking fees, and to have engaged in egregious overpricing.

Australia did launch an aggressive internal investigation, essentially confirming and amplifying our findings. But somehow the investigation did not reach a final conclusion with respect to allegations that the activity had been surreptitiously encouraged by the Australian government itself. What we do know is that the Wheat Board, with its monopoly on sales, no longer exists.

One of the inquiry's disclosures gave rise to an unexpected blast of publicity in India. Our final report identified, among many others, a certain Natwar Singh as a probable beneficiary of illicit trades. It turned out that, unknown to us, the particular Mr. Singh identified was India's unpopular foreign minister. His resignation was hailed in the Indian press with headlines crediting the "Volcker Effect" and the "Volcker Report." Hero in India for a day!

The allegations of corruption in the UN inevitably attracted political interest within the US Congress. At one point, five committees of the Congress had the Oil-for-Food issue on their agendas. Congressional investigations with more than a tinge of bias would clearly complicate our work. In the name of our independence and objectivity, I refused to testify formally. However, I was able to convince the key congressional leaders that tensions and competing efforts could only result in a negative impact on our work and on their own work. I did agree to informally brief government bodies of the United States or any other member state of the UN. That approach helped keep our investigation focused and politically neutral.

The central issue in US political terms, but also for the UN itself, was whether Kofi Annan had unduly influenced the program or at least had serious conflicts of interest. That question absorbed much of the committee's attention.

We looked hard. We had experienced investigators with the bit in their teeth. We found no evidence that the secretary-general had benefited from, or in some way illicitly influenced, decisions about particular transactions. Much more questionable was his possible awareness of contracts awarded to a company that at one time employed his son Kojo, who was living with his father in New York some of the time and certainly had knowledge of the Oil-for-Food programs.

We did find conclusive evidence that the UN official who had direct responsibility for administrating the program had himself benefited indirectly from the allocation of some oil-sale contracts. Benon Sevan, who denied the accusations, had had a long and successful record of increasingly important administrative responsibilities within the UN, particularly in managing extensive UN peacekeeping activity. He had advanced through the years to the rank of under-secretary-general.

Sadly, he did not resist the temptation, through a close friend, to accept some illicit payments. Placed on leave from the UN, Sevan avoided prosecution by fleeing to his home country of Cyprus, which didn't extradite him to the United States. The stain on the UN remains.

Our final report determined that the Iraqi regime had benefited from some $1.8 billion in kickbacks and bribes over the life of the program. Moreover, from 1991 until 2003, an estimated $10 billion of Iraqi oil was smuggled, in direct violation of the sanctions, to Jordan, Turkey, and Syria. The United States and other Security Council members must have been aware of these illegal sales. Their failure to do anything undoubtedly colored attitudes about the smaller violations of the sanctions.

The investigation stumbled across another source of internal UN corruption, not in the Oil-for-Food program but in the purchasing department. These two incidents do not suggest widespread corruption in the UN central administration. However, weakness in its internal controls and investigatory staff was blatantly evident. Our report strongly criticized the secretary-general's lack of attention to administrative and anti-corruption controls. He himself came to acknowledge the problem, pleading the difficulty of combining his diplomatic responsibilities with strong administrative oversight.

An important recommendation of the committee was that the UN appoint a strong independent oversight board of recognized accounting and investigation experts to review progress on strengthening internal controls and anti-corruption efforts. My impression is that the proposed body operated effectively for some years and significant progress was made in tightening controls. However, both the oversight board and an intensive internal follow-on investigation of the purchasing department were dropped over time. No doubt management and staff found the oversight overbearing, and member states have not been consistently supportive.

A second recommendation was that the UN was in need of a strong "chief operating officer," appointed by the General Assembly and with direct reporting responsibilities. Earlier attempts to strengthen controls have too often petered out. And, in fact, neither of these two key proposals have been sustained. The organization simply seems to resist strong management discipline. In the end, that laxity can only weaken the political and moral support upon which it depends.

Early in 2018 there was a spontaneous reunion of our Volcker Committee staff in New York. Attendance was high. Members came from a distance to attend. Memories of our common sense of mission, close cooperation, and successful professional effort were balm for my ninety-year-old soul. But that is small recompense for the failure of the UN to maintain the strong administrative oversight that is so clearly required.

Corruption in World Bank Programs

A corruption crisis at the World Bank (officially the International Bank for Reconstruction and Development) started not so much as a question of what goes on inside the building but how its programs perform after the money goes out the door.

The World Bank has long been manned by strong program directors, often former senior officials of member states. There is a sense of professionalism and institutional independence. Success is measured in terms of program development and spending, agreed upon with the client states.

What seems obvious now, but was long routinely neglected, is the failure to effectively execute the programs once they're in place and the money is spent. Safeguards against corruption simply were lacking. That was somehow viewed as a matter for the client governments to supervise, not for the World Bank.

I was exposed to the problem in the midst of a program failure that would become a management crisis. Jim Wolfensohn, more than a year after becoming the World Bank's president, had bravely identified the "cancer of corruption" as a problem that had to be addressed.

Why do I write "bravely"? The World Bank's senior staff wasn't happy that, right in the middle of his speech at the annual IMF–World Bank conference, normally a long and presumably uplifting recitation of accomplishments, the president called attention to a problem to which they had long sought to close their eyes. It was avoided to the point that the very word "corruption" was routinely excised from official reports; the stated rationale was that corruption was a problem for political authorities, not for an institution committed to economic development. Jim went ahead and established the new Department of Institutional Integrity with a professional staff. But I sense resistance was strong from the start and the effort wasn't pushed aggressively.

Things changed rapidly after the Wolfensohn regime and the appointment in 2005 of his successor, Paul Wolfowitz. Paul was known as an intellectual leader among the neocon hardliners in the Bush administration. He had strongly supported the invasion of Iraq and was not warmly received by old-timers at the World Bank. Their concerns deepened when he embraced a more aggressive fight against corruption, appointing an energetic and committed associate, Suzanne Rich Folsom, to undertake the effort.

A combination of policy and personal antagonism soon materialized. Findings that a large but almost totally ineffective World Bank–sponsored health program in India was rife with corruption were mishandled. Failure to notify the Indian government in a timely matter embarrassed both the bank and, by far, its largest client.

The bank's board demanded a review of the Integrity Department and its programs. For reasons I cannot recall, I was once again approached to chair the review. Satisfied by the high quality of five other members proposed by the board, I agreed. The Independent Panel Review of the World Bank Group Department of Institutional Integrity became yet another "Volcker panel."

I soon discovered that the bank's internal management is characterized by a highly forthright and vocal staff. Its apparent dissatisfaction with Mr. Wolfowitz and his appointee was openly and forcefully expressed. Accusations that he was improperly involved in negotiating a promotion and pay increase for his girlfriend, who worked at the bank, soon became a means of forcing his resignation. He was replaced by the conservative and highly respected ex-deputy secretary of state Robert Zoellick, who immediately acted to calm the waters.

Our review proceeded with harmony and mutual respect among the committee members. Ben Heineman, the experienced general counsel of General Electric, provided a needed and tested framework for a successful anti-corruption effort. Sir John Vereker, drawn from the British senior civil service where his roles included serving

as Bermuda's governor, surprised me after my earlier disappointment
with Britain's Serious Fraud Office. He contributed strongly both to
the substance and concise articulation of our report. Gustavo Gaviria
from Colombia and John Githongo from Kenya brought a strong
and needed perspective on corruption from the developing world.
Walter Van Gerven, a distinguished law professor, could speak with
authority from a European Union point of view.

We managed to interview virtually every senior bank official.
Some were clearly resistant to change; others were forthcoming. A
new general counsel was particularly helpful, perhaps because she
found the World Bank's existing internal organization, in her word,
"bizarre." Early on President Zoellick straightforwardly told me that,
given the turbulent and divisive mood of the bank, he would have to
accept the panel's recommendations without question. He did.

My (perhaps biased) sense is that we set out institutional arrangements suitable not only for the World Bank but for other international organizations called upon to administer complicated, costly,
and politically sensitive programs. My associates had the right experience and a common goal.

I signed the report. The unfinished business was to find a respected new leader for the Institutional Integrity Department and
to assure that person would be placed at a suitably high level in the
bank hierarchy. The ability to deal with the other senior executives
as an equal and with access to the bank's president was essential to
show that the attack on corruption was central to the World Bank's
mission.

The right candidate showed up. Leonard McCarthy had led the
anti-corruption effort in South Africa with broadly acknowledged
success—but also against strong opposition. He was ready for a new
challenge outside his country. Through the Zoellick presidency and
into that of Dr. Jim Yong Kim, the bank's anti-corruption responsibilities have been clearly articulated.

In 2006 there was a major breakthrough. The powerful multina-
tional engineering firm Siemens AG was raided by German law enforcement and discovered to have been paying bribes to participate

in international contracts over the course of years. Hundreds of millions of dollars were involved. German authorities, long passive in discovering and preventing international bribes (bribes were a permitted, tax-deductible expense in Germany before 1999), were no longer ignoring the issue.

Large settlements with international organizations and internal management turmoil brought the issue front and center, not just for development institutions but for governments as well. The World Bank itself won a $100 million settlement from Siemens and blacklisted a Siemens subsidiary for four years.

Another clear signal was the World Bank's 2012 decision to bow out of an international effort to finance the Padma Bridge project in Bangladesh, a huge undertaking that the bank staff found prone to corruption. It was a strong signal of an end to passivity with respect to project management.

Reforms at the World Bank, under the leadership of President Zoellick, Leonard McCarthy, and his close associate Steve Zimmerman, helped lead to a more disciplined effort to combat corruption by other development agencies, including the Inter-American Development Bank in Washington.

Will progress be lasting?

Dr. Kim has repeatedly expressed his strong personal support. Promising initiatives have been undertaken to implant anticorruption considerations in the program design at an early stage. Cooperative efforts with other institutions are needed to reinforce the common cause. No doubt, success will be a continuing challenge. I have learned enough to know that occasional speeches and internal analysis are not enough. There is a need to demonstrate success in nailing down specific examples of misdeeds. Joint efforts among the development institutions to set standards and to pursue difficult cases involving constituents large and small must be sustained. The efforts need to be on the agenda of the various boards, with successful efforts publicized.

I greatly regret the World Bank has not continued the oversight board that my group recommended after its initial and successful five-year term. Leonard McCarthy has now left to develop a private advisory service. His successor's authority, with the full backing of the board and president, will be critical.

Dealing with corruption is difficult, often seemingly unrewarded. It also is critically important for an institution in which discipline and authority should go hand in hand with the provisioning of resources by its member states and ethical standards more broadly.

All in all, I was pleased with the work, at the very least a modest success. My fellow panel members presented me with a stuffed parrot to honor my chairmanship. And in 2007, at age eighty, that seemed a reasonable way to end my career as "Mr. Chairman." Or so I thought.

The "name carrier" with my father (*right*) and grandfather (*left*). *Personal collection of Paul Volcker*

"Buddy" with two of my sisters, Virginia *(left)* and Ruth *(right)*, enjoying some time at the beach in Cape May. *Personal collection of Paul Volcker*

On the Princeton varsity basketball team in 1948. I barely made it. *Courtesy of University Archives, Princeton University Library*

With Barbara *(second from right)* and New York Fed colleagues, the campaign "chairman" celebrates the election of Madeline McWhinney *(second from left)* as Federal Reserve retirement system trustee. *Personal collection of Paul Volcker*

Joining US Treasury Secretary Douglas Dillon *(center)* and Under Secretary for Monetary Affairs Robert Roosa *(right)* in January 1962. *Personal collection of Paul Volcker*

To Paul Volcker
With appreciation and best wishes, *Richard Nixon*

Charls Walker *(left)* and I meet with President Richard Nixon and Treasury Secretary David Kennedy at the White House in early 1969. *Official White House photo; personal collection of Paul Volcker*

"An historic day." Standing in front of the Aspen Cottage at Camp David on August 13, 1971, with *(from left in front of the terrace)* Pete Peterson, Arthur Burns, Herb Stein, Paul McCracken, John Connally, and George Shultz. Mike Bradfield is at left in the back. *Official White House photo; personal collection of Paul Volcker*

My swearing-in as Fed chairman, with President Carter *(left)* and Barbara *(second from right). Official White House photo; personal collection of Paul Volcker*

Meeting with President Jimmy Carter in the White House. *Official White House photo; personal collection of Paul Volcker*

Meeting with President Reagan in the Oval Office, with Donald Regan *(second from left)* and James Baker *(right)*. *Official White House photo; personal collection of Paul Volcker*

Starting my second term as Fed chairman in August 1983, on a fishing trip in Blooming Grove, Pennsylvania. Sworn in by Curtis "Hank" Barnette, general counsel of Bethlehem Steel. *Personal collection of Paul Volcker*

The Trilateral Commission in action!
With Asia-Pacific chairman Kiichi
Miyazawa *(left)* and European
chairman Otto Lambsdorff *(right)*.
Personal collection of Paul Volcker

With my two immediate successors
at the Fed, Alan Greenspan *(right)*
and Ben Bernanke *(left)*, in 2005.
*Photo by Britt Leckman. Photo courtesy
of Federal Reserve Board*

At the opening of the Barbara Volcker Center for Women and
Rheumatic Diseases at New York's Hospital for Special Surgery. *From
left:* My daughter-in-law, Martha, seated with Jennifer, and Janice
standing with Jimmy in front of a portrait of Barbara with the center's
director, Dr. Michael Lockshin *(right)*. *Personal collection of Paul Volcker*

With Anke, meeting President Obama. *Official White House photo; personal collection of Paul Volcker*

At the Taj Mahal with Anke in 2007. *Personal collection of Paul Volcker*

"If you keep at it, eventually you'll catch a big one." Ristigouche Salmon Club fishing guide Brian Irving holds my thirty-seven-pound catch, my biggest ever. *Photo by David LeBlanc, Executive Director, Restigouche River Watershed Management Council*

My fishing wall at home in New York. © *Erica Berger*

The "wise old parrot" in my office, a gift from my colleagues on the Independent Review Panel of the World Bank Group's Department of Institutional Integrity. © *Erica Berger*

chapter 14

SETTING STANDARDS

*A*mid the complexities of today's world, it is hard to avoid accounting issues—personal, corporate, and international. Somehow, I've been involved in all three areas. In each I've seen a degree of erosion in the trust that should be at the heart of the auditing profession, its very *raison d'être.*

I respect many of the leaders in the field, both in the private sector and certainly in the US Government Accountability Office (the GAO). I came to value the forensic accountants who played an important role investigating the claims on Swiss banks by Holocaust victims and corruption in the UN's Oil-for-Food program. In both, the internationally respected forensic accountant Frank Hydoski and his colleagues demonstrated what experience and technical skills can produce in terms of hard evidence.

Unfortunately, in other areas of accounting there have been too many grounds for skepticism and concern, too many incentives to cut corners, too many conflicts of interest.

Stubborn Resistance to International Standards

Sometime in the middle of 2000 I got a call from Arthur Levitt, then chairman of the US Securities and Exchange Commission. He had been working with an ad hoc group of national securities regulators toward a common goal: establishing a single set of accounting standards to be applied internationally with discipline and sophistication.

The concept had long made sense to me, so I could hardly reject his invitation to start putting the concept into practice. A newly formed group of distinguished business, accounting, and financial leaders from around the world would lead the way.

It became the nineteen-person board of trustees of the London-based International Accounting Standards Committee Foundation, in turn charged with appointing and overseeing a board of professional accountants: the International Accounting Standards Board. The major accounting firms agreed to provide a third of the needed financial resources. The rest would, at least initially, be volunteered by international businesses, investment groups, financial institutions, and central banks that would presumably benefit from a successful effort.

Choosing the right chairman of the professional board, a person who could lead experienced and strong-minded accountants drawn from around the world, would be crucial to its success. Sir David Tweedie, retiring as head of Britain's Accounting Standards Board (now known as the Financial Reporting Council), was virtually everyone's first choice. Establishing high-quality international standards had been his dream, so he was willing to embrace the challenge.

Uppermost in my mind, and indeed of the committee generally, was the need to bring the United States along. The SEC by law had official oversight of US accounting practices. It had long shared with the accounting profession, most American businesses, and certainly members of the US Financial Accounting Standards Board (FASB) the view that the United States generally accepted accounting principles (GAAP) were the gold standard. The only reasonable path to international consistency would be for the world to adopt the US standard.

That view, which rather overstated the special intellectual merit and political sanctity of GAAP even in the United States, would certainly not be accepted easily elsewhere.

Accounting standards, after all, were not an American invention. The US rule book, running to thousands of pages, was seen as far too detailed and onerous by other countries. It was another example of the penchant of American regulators, and those who are regulated, for exhaustively spelled-out rules. Scotland, the old home of accounting, and the UK more generally, had gotten along with setting out principles, to be interpreted and applied responsibly by accounting professionals.

The SEC, perhaps influenced by the enthusiasm of Arthur Levitt, seemed willing to explore the merits of a common international approach even if they viewed adoption by US companies as unlikely in the near term. It helped that a past SEC chairman and American business leaders joined the committee. Many international businesses were intrigued, and so was the American Institute of Chartered Professional Accountants. US members had a heavy weighting on both my oversight committee (the IASC Foundation Trustees) and the decision-making board (the IASB).

Chairing the trustees was, at least at the start, a pleasure. I knew several of the trustees drawn from around the world, as well as the American participants. We all shared a common vision. I happened to run into an old Princeton student who was open to a new challenge. Tom Seidenstein became director of operations for the London-based board, keeping me informed of the organizational challenges and our progress or lack thereof.

In fact, quite a lot of progress was made quickly. Established European Union law provided procedures for adopting international standards, subject to review and a limited "opt out" for a particular rule provided to a few financial institutions. Jurisdictions including Australia and New Zealand, with a long history of standard setting and robust capital markets, followed. SEC chairman Christopher Cox and his chief accountant were on board, Japanese authorities became interested, and so did a number of developing countries. Within three or four years more than a hundred countries agreed, in principle, to adopt the new standards, at least as an option, for their companies' accounts.

The international board made a point of its independence by requiring that company accounts recognize the cost of stock options, an effort that in the United States had been thwarted by strong political opposition. But that initiative, however intellectually justified, did not change mindsets. The SEC leadership seemed to pull back. A few influential US auditors and activist groups (and ultimately FASB's oversight body) sowed doubt about the willingness and ability of emerging, or even well-developed, countries to follow international rules in a disciplined way. More importantly, the commitment of David Tweedie and most of the IASB toward a principles-based approach couldn't be easily reconciled with GAAP's detailed rules.

There were also questions, raised by those reluctant to participate, about the international board's governance and the lack of official participation. In anticipation of their concerns, leaders of the five most relevant international economic bodies were asked (and agreed) to review the board of trustees' composition.

In 2005, towards the end of my five-year term as chairman, some of the obstacles seemed to be receding. I was hopeful that a measure of success could soon be achieved, at least in permitting the international standards to be an option for internationally active US companies. In fact, an increasing number of nations had indicated they would sign on. The American and international boards agreed to work toward a common standard in some new and complicated areas. In 2007 the SEC stopped requiring foreign companies registered in the United States to reconcile their International Financial Reporting Standards accounts with US GAAP—a long-desired outcome.

Progress has been slow. Some US-based international businesses that initially supported the move toward uniform standards seemed to lose interest as the possibility of full-scale adoption stalled. More support from US officials, businesses, and auditors will be necessary if the standard is to be truly global. After all, US dominance of world capital markets is still strong, if diminishing. It doesn't make sense to let the rest of the world write what will become the international rule book without active US participation. As things stand, that participation has, in fact, been reduced on both the oversight and rule-making boards.

The effort is still alive. I'm told that dedicated members of the United States and international accounting standards boards meet regularly and are making progress on some common projects, including working with the SEC. I remain hopeful that their perseverance will help end the gridlock.

Breakdown: Enron and Arthur Andersen

Little did I suspect that my entry into the world of accounting would soon bring me to the dark side.

I happened to know and admired Ken Lay, the chairman of Enron. He briefly was a Wolfensohn client and regaled me with the remarkable progress being made in transforming Enron from a gas and electricity supplier into a leading-edge, technology-driven company on the brink of revolutionizing the global utilities industry. The company was a poster child for consulting firm McKinsey & Company, from which it recruited chief executive officer Jeffrey Skilling.

Revolution indeed. After a decade of frenetic expansion, cracks in the façade began to develop. Huge losses were disguised in an elaborate array of special purpose entities. The practice had been aided and abetted by the venerable accounting firm Arthur Andersen, which certified Enron's accounts.

Skilling's abrupt resignation in the summer of 2001 fueled growing suspicions about the company's financial stability. Happily for me, Ken didn't press an invitation for me to help out. By the end of the year Enron filed for bankruptcy, at the time the biggest by a US company.

It was a sorry affair. Investigations by Congress, the SEC, and US prosecutors revealed a trail of fraud that led to the imprisonment of top executives, including Skilling. Ken died of a heart attack before he could be sentenced. All in all, Enron was a case study in modern management incentives and practice run wild.

Arthur Andersen was considered the leading US auditing firm, one that had long promoted itself as a paragon of solid midwestern business virtue. Founded in Chicago in 1913, it had developed partnerships around the world. Arthur Andersen himself, and his successor Leonard Spacek, became globally renowned as highly principled leaders of the accounting profession. They stood for upholding standards and minimizing conflicts.

Over time, however, the firm's old-school auditing partners had been challenged by younger, more aggressive associates. They had a vision of a more lucrative business, built by providing companies with a long list of consulting services. A bitter internal fight ensued that Wolfensohn, a decade earlier, and other advisory firms could not reconcile. Eventually the growing, profitable consulting practice was split off into a new firm named Accenture.

The remaining Arthur Andersen firm then made a strategic error. It set about rebuilding an internal consulting practice at substantial cost.

Even before the Enron disaster, Andersen's auditing practice had been tarnished by other failures. In mid-2001 the firm agreed to pay a $7 million fine—at that time the largest ever paid by an accounting firm—to settle an SEC suit over its failed audit of Waste Management Inc.

The Enron debacle raised the threat of another investigation and, at the very least, an official reprimand. In desperation—and it was indeed a desperate situation—the firm called upon me to chair an independent oversight board in early February 2002. I could pick two partners to help with the effort. On paper at least, we were essentially given full control of the firm's policy and personnel. With the expert (and voluntary) draftsmanship of Wachtell Lipton lawyers, it must have been one of the most sweeping grants of executive authority in American business history. Joined by Chuck Bowsher, former head of the US Government Accountability Office and himself a former Andersen partner, and the highly respected Roy Vagelos, recently retired chief executive officer of Merck & Company, I felt we were equipped to make an impact.

It was not to be. The lead Andersen partner, Joseph Berardino, was consistently helpful and cooperative. He knew what was at stake. But when it came to garnering the full support of the organization, we soon discovered that there was no coherent inside group ready to step in. Members of the formal management board were geographically dispersed and seldom met. Their authority over the individual partners was limited. Partnerships outside the United States had their own way of doing things.

I remember being struck by the marketing material, in Andersen's distinctive orange, given to me at an early meeting. The first page listed the firm's services. Auditing was nowhere near the head of the list. After all of the conflict over the preceding decade and the heavy cost of rebuilding a consulting practice, the internal stresses remained. To exaggerate a bit, auditing seemed to have become the caboose to the consulting train.

Then an existential threat appeared: possible indictment by the Department of Justice. I had been assured in earlier discussions that that possibility was remote. How could an indictment that would effectively put one of the Big Five accounting firms out of business be in the public interest? In a flight of personal hubris, I had convinced myself that the firm, or at least part of the firm, could be reformed into a model for the profession under the benevolent oversight of our independent advisory board.

A group of mostly younger partners was willing to maintain the name and to attempt remaking the company as an audit-only firm. It would lose many of its old clients. It would need to be a much smaller firm, with a core of experienced auditors as partners. The possibility of going forward with a new approach, basically resurrecting the original Arthur Andersen, seemed real. But there was simply too little consensus among the partners, too little sense of common interest, and no strong internal candidate to assume leadership.

Alas, any faint hope of resurrection was lost.

The Justice Department did indict Arthur Andersen on the pretext of discovering that one of its lawyers had instructed partners to destroy documents relevant to the investigation. I wasn't looking forward to overseeing a company under indictment. The United States lost one of its Big Five auditors. Ironically, the subsequent conviction was later overturned. The charges against the firm, as opposed to the individual partners, should never have been brought.

The business tragedy was brought home to me when I was invited to speak about the affair at Arthur Andersen's alma mater. My lecture, calling for reforms including international accounting standards and a greater focus on auditing responsibilities, was delivered in honor of Leonard Spacek near Northwestern University's Arthur Andersen Hall. It seemed a bit surreal.

Sarbanes-Oxley and the PCAOB

The Enron-Andersen affair was the climax of a wave of corporate and accounting scandals around the start of the new millennium. Tyco International and WorldCom were the largest and most publicized, but there were many others. In lengthy testimony with David Tweedie before the Senate Banking Committee in early 2002, I pressed my friends in Congress for legislation that would provide clarity about auditors' responsibilities and enhance their independence. There was bipartisan disgust at the state of financial reporting and Congress was roused to action. It acted to stiffen requirements for corporate governance and accounting.

By mid-2002 the so-called Sarbanes-Oxley Act was passed with a near-unanimous vote. President George W. Bush, signing the bill, called it "the most far-reaching reforms of American business practices since the time of Franklin Delano Roosevelt." That may be an exaggeration, but it did call attention to the urgent need for a response to what I had called in my congressional testimony "an exploding crisis in a once-noble profession."

The legislation did prohibit accounting firms from providing most consulting services to an audit client. It was that egregious conflict of interest, evident with Arthur Andersen and others, that undercut auditing discipline. Tax consulting, a particularly lucrative source of revenue, was still permitted and a full range of consulting services could be developed for and marketed to nonaudit clients. The ideal of enforcing auditing-only firms wasn't achieved. No way was found around the conflict implicit in the fact that auditors are chosen by and paid by the management of the companies they're auditing. (In the UK, a recent parliamentary report urged a forced breakup of the biggest accounting firms. The issue won't go away.)

Potentially more important was the new Public Company Accounting Oversight Board (PCAOB), a quasi-public watchdog under the general aegis of the SEC. The PCAOB was given authority to establish standards, to review particular audits, and to impose penalties for failure to meet the defined standards. It seemed to go to the heart of the matter.

In concept, Sarbanes-Oxley was important and broadly supported legislation. Even the *Wall Street Journal*, a persistent foe of new regulations, endorsed it, citing the Arthur Andersen lapses. I received an invitation to chair the new PCAOB initiative, but I had finally learned to say no. A strong advisory board was appointed, on which I agreed to serve for a time.

Unfortunately, concerns remain as to whether the PCAOB is adequately funded and forceful enough in its disciplinary efforts. In particular, questions persist as to whether it is sufficiently rigorous in its inspections and enforcement, micromanaged rather than effectively overseen by the SEC, and too exposed to forceful lobbying by the profession it regulates.

As I write these words, I have been following the series in the *Financial Times* about the crisis in the UK's auditing profession, brought to attention by the sudden collapse of a company. Much of it seems familiar.

More personally, a recent memorial service for Uwe Reinhardt, one of Princeton's leading economics professors and an old friend, drove home the point. Uwe was not lost in abstract theorizing or advanced mathematics. His proudest teaching moments were the insights he was able to provide to undergraduates about how the real world worked, including the ways by which corporate accounts can be used to shade, or even to obscure, the truth.

The program distributed at his heavily attended memorial service highlighted his parting reminder to accounting students: "I teach accounting because democracy rests on accountability. Accountability isn't possible without responsible accounting."

chapter 15

THE NEW FINANCIAL WORLD

Breakdown and Reform

By *the end* of my chairmanship at the Fed, the need for change in the laws governing the structure of banking and financial markets had become apparent. Investment banks began transforming from small, risk-averse partnerships into swashbuckling publicly traded companies. Firms that had focused on advising corporations and underwriting their securities were building trading capabilities of their own. Hedge funds and leveraged buyout funds (now called "private equity") all began to emerge.

Even inside the traditionalist Federal Reserve we had debated removing some of the broader restrictions on banks. We requested looser restraints on interstate banking, a long-overdue change. The Fed's acceptance of a lenient interpretation of some provisions of the 1933 banking act, known as Glass-Steagall, began to erode the separation of commercial banks from investment banks. Specifically, in several instances we allowed trading and underwriting of corporate securities in bank holding company subsidiaries as long as those subsidiaries were not, in the language of the law, "principally engaged" in such activity.

At one point, I thought we were close to agreeing with then Treasury secretary Don Regan on proposing new legislation that would extend limited authority for banks to engage in real estate and insurance brokerage, activities that would not present a risk to capital. But that kind of half step didn't incite action.

The pace of change accelerated in the 1990s and early 2000s, propelled in part by technology. Increasingly, trading became the economic engine of the investment banks. The new derivatives seemed to open opportunities in the name of reducing risk. Incentive pay systems and highly lucrative year-end bonuses invited ultra-aggressive risk taking. Private-equity firms and hedge funds multiplied. Commercial banks felt left out.

The End of Glass-Steagall

The changes in the industry came to a head about a decade after I left the Fed. In April 1998 John Reed's Citibank agreed to merge with Sandy Weill's Travelers Company, which had a broad insurance underwriting business and owned the Smith Barney investment bank. The deal was in direct defiance of the barriers still imposed by Glass-Steagall. With Federal Reserve support it quickly became apparent that the law would be overturned.

I had two principal concerns at the time. One was to maintain the separation of banking from commerce (that is, business that's not primarily financial in nature), which had come under vigorous attack. Retailer Sears Roebuck led the charge. It had acquired the Dean Witter Reynolds stock brokerage company in the early 1980s, a combination sometimes mocked as "socks and stocks," and operated a small savings and loan operation in California. It wanted to build a banking franchise. I well recall its practice of inviting members of Congress to Chicago on weekend lobbying visits.

I testified before Congress, mustering all the arguments I knew for maintaining the bank-commerce distinction. The main concerns were unavoidable conflicts of interest, undue concentration of local economic resources, and excessive economic power. How, for instance, could independent merchants compete with a bank-owned competitor in small cities and towns? Even in big cities, large banks owning businesses would be placed in conflict with their own customers, taking on hard to identify new risks in the process. (Ultimately, General Electric's aggressive, and once highly profitable, finance subsidiary GE Capital helped illustrate the point when it disclosed a $15 billion shortfall in its insurance reserves in January 2018.)

The dogged efforts of Iowa congressman Jim Leach were the key to ensuring that the so-called Gramm-Leach-Bliley law (named after Leach, Texas senator Phil Gramm, and Virginia Rep. Tom Bliley), which ended the Glass-Steagall restriction on trading and other financial activities in commercial banking organizations, did maintain the distinction between banks and commerce that I viewed as essential. That distinction exists to this day, although a loophole or two involving trading in commodities is still sometimes exploited.

My other concern with Gramm-Leach-Bliley was whether the Federal Reserve would retain strong authority over the newly defined "bank" or "financial" holding companies. The biggest at that point was the newly created Citigroup, which included a bank (Citibank), a broker-dealer (Salomon Brothers), and an insurance company (Travelers). With their subsidiaries still subject to supervision by other regulatory agencies (such as state insurance regulators and the Securities and Exchange Commission), confusion as to the ultimate authority over particular activities within the holding companies seemed sure to arise. In fact, it has. Jim Leach was only partly successful in making sure the legislation maintained the Fed's primary role as the overseer of the entire bank holding company. (A decade later, in the wake of the financial crisis, he ruefully told me that his support for repeal of Glass-Steagall had been a mistake.)

The World of Derivatives

I cannot claim expertise, or even close familiarity, with the rapid development and application of "financial engineering." Along with other members of my generation, I was struck a couple of decades ago by the enthusiastic presentation of a young London investment banker to a high-level business conference at the Villa d'Este in

Lake Como, Italy. He concluded with a strong warning: businesses, particularly financial businesses, that were not fully aware of and capable of using the new instruments of finance would be doomed to failure.

I found myself sitting in the audience next to William Sharpe, a 1990 Nobel laureate in economics whose "Sharpe ratio" has become a widely accepted measure of risk-adjusted returns for fund managers. I nudged him and asked how much this new financial engineering contributed to economic growth, measured by GNP. "Nothing," he whispered back to me. It was not the answer I anticipated. "So what does it do?" was my response.

"It just moves around the [economic] rents* in the financial system. Besides it's a lot of fun." (Later, at dinner, he suggested the possibility of small ways in which economic welfare could be advanced, but I felt I had already gotten the gist of his thinking.)

One aspect of financial engineering soon took off. Credit default swaps, originally designed to provide banks with an efficient way to insure their own loan portfolios, proliferated as trading instruments. The use of tradable derivatives supported the so-called securitization of loans, including the bundling of packages of risky "subprime" mortgages, subdividing the risk for sale to investors. Only a few wise men, or "fuddy-duddies," raised doubts. In his 2002 letter to shareholders, Warren Buffett called derivatives "financial weapons of mass destruction, carrying dangers that, while now latent, are potentially lethal."

I stayed on the sidelines, not sure I understood all the pitfalls. As the new chairman of the Group of Thirty, a long-established group of experienced policymakers and business leaders, I did face a decision. As mentioned earlier, I was presented with the draft text of a long report on derivatives that a G-30 study group had prepared. It reflected the active participation and thinking of important banks and their advisors. The report enthused about the positive potential for the new instruments for risk management. It also cautioned

---

*Economic rents are unearned income, such as when land prices increase as population density rises.

about the potential dangers, the need for strong internal controls and adequate capital.

The sense of the proposed introduction, however, and of the study as a whole, was overwhelmingly positive. We were entering a new financial age. A new cliché was deployed: technology would permit "slicing and dicing" of credits so the element of risk would be efficiently transferred to those most able and willing to bear it.

I insisted that we tone down the enthusiasm. But it became all too easy for some to be lulled into the belief that the risks were somehow being dispersed away by the magic of financial engineering. Instead, we were led down the path of financial crisis by institutions large and small, careless of risks that had, indeed, been removed from their sight but soon reappeared in a different guise. The ultimate cost of moving around the "rents" was enormous.

Storm Clouds Gathering

Meetings, formal and informal, of groups worried about chronic federal deficits and dire fiscal states are part of Washington life. I recall meeting with one such group early in the new century and fielding a question over my shoulder as I was leaving:

"Paul, how long before we really face a really big financial crisis?"

"A 75 percent chance of a crisis within five years," was my casual response as I went out the door. At least one member of the press was there.

I was not at all casual when I prepared a careful speech the next year before a big Stanford University audience. Its title, "An Economy on Thin Ice," captured the mood.

Prices were stable. The economy was growing. But it was seriously out of balance: too much consumption, too little savings, big fiscal deficits, and another large deficit—approaching an unimagined 6 percent of GDP—in the external current account. We were plainly living beyond our means, easily financed by floods of foreign capital. It all presented conditions "as dangerous and intractable as any I can remember, and I can remember a lot." I added the warning that "at some point, the sense of confidence in capital markets that today so benignly supports the growing world economy could fade." Unfortunately, in the end it would likely be a financial crisis, rather than policy changes, that would force "adjustment."

In my first meeting with Ben Bernanke after he assumed the chair of the Federal Reserve Board in February 2006, I half jokingly mentioned my casual five-year forecast. There were just a few years to go! He politely smiled.

It was two years later when Tim Geithner, the president of the Federal Reserve Bank of New York and a former Treasury Department under secretary, visited my apartment. Bear Stearns was collapsing, struggling to fund itself amid growing market doubts about the value of subprime mortgages. A failure of one of Wall Street's Big Five investment banks clearly would have serious implications. My only advice, perhaps obvious, was that he'd better find a merger partner quick.

It took a strenuous weekend's work for Tim, Ben, and Treasury Secretary Hank Paulson to complete a complicated takeover by JP-Morgan Chase. An essential element to the deal was a truly extraordinary commitment by the Federal Reserve to guarantee some $30 billion of assets from Bear Stearns's mortgage desk. A supermajority vote by the board was required to support an emergency loan to a nonbank under Section 13(3) of the Federal Reserve Act, a provision that had long been a virtual dead letter. In particular, I was well aware that use of Section 13(3) lending had been refused to a near-bankrupt New York City in 1975. The point was that the Fed should not be looked to as lender of last resort beyond the banking system.

Just weeks after the Bear Stearns rescue I spoke at the Economic Club of New York. One line in my speech attracted the most attention, not least of all by Tim, who was seated beside me. The Fed, I said, had acted at the "very edge of its lawful and implied powers" in its rescue of Bear Stearns. Then, and now, I didn't want to encourage indiscriminate use of such untraditional authority. I went on to sketch out some needed reforms in the system.

The financial markets settled down again after the Bear Stearns affair, but I was increasingly uneasy. Given our past experience, former Bush Treasury secretary Nick Brady and I would, from time to time, put our heads together. We were both concerned that Bear Stearns would be only the leading edge of the gathering crisis. The two big mortgage agencies, Fannie Mae and Freddie Mac, were under pressure. Money market funds seemed vulnerable and strange excesses seemed to be appearing in the derivatives market. Along with Gene Ludwig, the former comptroller of the currency, we formulated a plan: establish a governmental agency other than the Fed that would be equipped to buy assets and inject capital into vulnerable institutions, following the pattern of the Resolution Trust Corporation that helped clean up the savings and loans in the later 1980s and early 1990s (itself modeled on the Reconstruction Finance Corporation established in 1932 by the conservative Republican Hoover administration).

By the time our proposal was publicized, the bankruptcy of Lehman Brothers had escalated the problems at individual financial institutions into a full-scale systemic breakdown. It justified truly extraordinary use of Fed and Treasury authorities as well as the politically controversial but desperately needed legislative support for the $700 billion Troubled Asset Relief Program (TARP).

What we all learned, sophisticated in the complexities of financial engineering or simply veterans of earlier crises, was that we were in the midst of a financial breakdown that would lead to the Great Recession of 2008. The financial Humpty Dumpty had fallen off the wall and all the government's existing agencies couldn't put the system back together again. It would take years of effort to re-create a safe operating order, not just in the United States, but in Europe as well.

Equally predictably, the reforms introduced to protect that new order would before long be chipped away. Here we are, a decade after the crisis, and the scurrying lobbyist chipmunks are nibbling away in the name of efficiency and simplification (good, in itself), but with the ultimate aim of weakening the new safeguards.

Meeting Mr. Obama

Like so many others, I was caught up in late 2007 and early 2008 by a sense of frustration about the path of the country and its leadership. Hope for the future was epitomized by the sudden appearance on the political scene of the young Barack Obama. His very presence in the chase for the presidency seemed to substantiate the dreams of racial equality once expressed in Rosa Parks's Alabama bus ride and Martin Luther King's "I Have a Dream" speech at the Lincoln Memorial. The potential seemed to extend to practical problems of governance made critical by the financial crisis.

I agreed to join a small dinner arranged by the Obama campaign in Washington with interested but skeptical Wall Streeters. I was impressed enough to tell Senator Obama as I left that, while I could not publicly support him right away, I might get in touch later. I soon had a long conversation in Chicago with Austan Goolsbee, the University of Chicago professor who had for some time been Obama's informal economic advisor.

I often read that I am a Democrat. That was true sixty years ago, when I was captivated by Adlai Stevenson. But once in a high-level role at the Treasury or Fed, I tried (not quite successfully) to avoid political labeling: it was a sense of a pox on both parties. The one and only exception I had made was speaking as eloquently as I could for Bill Bradley during his short-lived presidential primary campaign against Al Gore in 2000. After all, I had been among the many who had urged the reluctant man to run. In addition to his strong political abilities, he was a loyal Princetonian and an infinitely better basketball player than I was (despite being a couple of inches shorter).

In any event, in January 2008 I issued a strong endorsement statement for Senator Obama and subsequently appeared at a few campaign events.

Not long after the election, I received a call at home. The president-elect had two questions. Was there any possibility that I would be interested in becoming Treasury secretary? Well, I thought, at eighty-one I could establish a new high-water mark for age. But I had had enough; did I really want to take on the challenge? My reply was that I certainly was not prepared to serve for a full term. One or even two years didn't make sense. I think he anticipated, and agreed with, that response.

The real question was, what did I make of the other two people under consideration, either for Treasury secretary or White House economic advisor? (Apparently there were no other candidates.) While I knew both, I was not informed of their substantive thinking about handling the crisis. What I did know is that they had quite different personalities and leadership potential that should govern his decision. The appointment of Tim Geithner to be Treasury secretary and Larry Summers as director of the National Economic Council, was a reasonable division of talents.

The Obama Advisory Board

I took part in some of the planning sessions with the new economic team, which included Austan Goolsbee and Christina Romer, the new chair of the Council of Economic Advisers, as well as Summers and Geithner. At the most important meeting, which seemed to set the size of the new fiscal program, the incoming director of the Office of Management and Budget took a seat next to me. "Hi, I'm Peter Orszag, I was in your Princeton seminar twenty years ago."

A generation had passed.

Shortly before taking office, Mr. Obama suggested that I lead the new President's Economic Recovery Advisory Board (PERAB) that he planned to establish to provide an avenue for independent, nonpartisan economic advice.

So there I was, "Mr. Chairman" once again.

I had no illusions about the weight such a board would carry, especially when I was notified that the meetings had to take place in public and the membership had been spread over political interests. The potential for competition and conflict with cabinet-level officials and advisors could also be challenging, but the position did provide a vehicle for keeping in touch with some old congressional contacts. It also allowed me to introduce one former Wolfensohn associate into the world of Washington. Anthony Dowd, a graduate of the US Military Academy at West Point and by now expert in the world of private equity and the management of small business, proved indispensable. In addition to organizing meetings, researching policy questions, and contributing to several useful reports on corporate taxation, mortgage finance, and rebuilding infrastructure, Tony proved to be a tenacious advocate and negotiator. He kept me in close contact with the legislative process, and, along the way, achieved recognition for his judgment and effectiveness.

The PERAB provided a seat at the table when financial regulation reform would be discussed. For me, that extended into the Oval Office as well.

Dodd–Frank, Regulatory Reform, and the Volcker Rule

I am sure Tim Geithner and Larry Summers would have been content if I disappeared. The potential for conflict in policy approaches was real.

But the timing for me was propitious. Just before the new president took office, the Group of Thirty released a rather comprehensive set of proposals titled "Financial Reform: A Framework for Financial Stability." While endorsed by a working group drawn from a number of countries, the report pretty well reflected my own thinking as its principal author. Elements of the report became widely discussed in the reform debate.

Much was made of the need for common and higher capital standards not only for big banks operating internationally but for all "systemically important financial institutions." The call for a solution to the overlapping or sometimes absent authorities overseeing the complex and sprawling markets was particularly relevant to the United States. A strong role for central banks, given their focus on financial stability, was emphasized. This reflected common ground within the administration. But, even if agreed, such broad generalities did not add up to a specific legislative proposal.

The president was impatient. He (innocently, in my view) demanded that his new Treasury secretary make a public presentation of his strategy—oblivious to the fact that specific proposals had not been fully debated and vetted internally. The result was a painfully difficult effort by Secretary Geithner to set out, as best he could, a rather vague outline of plans to stem the financial crisis. Stock markets tumbled on doubts about how the plans would work in practice.

The fact that Tim could, within a few weeks, quietly rebuild his authority and influence internally and externally provided to me, as to others, a clear sign of his character and competence.

Indeed, his strongest personal contribution to the reform effort has been widely accepted and copied. The basic idea was to require regular stress tests to evaluate the resilience of systematically important financial institutions that might pose a risk to the entire financial system in an extreme and unexpected circumstance such as an extended recession or a financial crisis *à la* 2008. Such tests are now embedded in regulation and supervisory practice in the United States as well as in other parts of the world.

The fact remained that Chairman Barney Frank of the House Financial Services Committee, and a little later Chairman Chris Dodd of the Senate Banking Committee, were moving ahead with their own priorities. In a sense, the administration—preoccupied by efforts to restore financial market stability and stimulate the economy, as well as the politically sensitive issues of consumer protection, health-care legislation, and the General Motors and Chrysler bailouts—was forced to play catch-up in financial reform.*

As chair of the PERAB, I participated in much of the internal debate and became familiar with the views of some members of the Senate committee. We pushed for some key points, largely drawn from my G-30 report, about regulatory structure, dealing with the

---

*The sense of prevailing uncertainty and desperation in early 2009 was demonstrated to me by some congressional suggestions that I be named "economic czar" as well as by a request that I temporarily chair American International Group Inc. (AIG), the giant insurance company that had been rescued by the Fed. I was uninterested in both cases; the PERAB role provided an adequate platform.

too-big-to-fail issue, and curtailing speculative trading and other proprietary activities creating undue risk for banking organizations benefiting from the federal safety net.

We kept the PERAB's financial reform recommendations to the president informal—and therefore nonpublic—to avoid open conflict with the Treasury's and White House's own proposals.

In June, President Obama proposed a sweeping overhaul of the US financial regulatory system, including the cherished new consumer financial protection agency. He also emphasized the need for greater Federal Reserve oversight of the major financial institutions and more effective interaction among the various agencies.

To my mind, several key issues were unresolved, including really effective reorganization of the regulatory structure, the appropriate role of money market funds, and, critically, restraints on speculative trading by government-protected commercial banks, which now included major investment banks that had been allowed to convert to banks with Fed supervision and support at the height of the crisis.

I'd lived through enough financial crises, and enough Federal Reserve Boards and chairmen, to know that there had been repeated lapses in attention paid to potential threats to financial stability.

The Federal Reserve is not the only bank regulator and not the only culprit. However, by the nature of its broad responsibilities, it is, or should be, uniquely concerned with exercising effective oversight. And it is also true that the day-to-day, month-to-month, year-to-year work of detecting risks and enforcing needed discipline had not always received the attention required. Nor, at least until recently, have other banking agencies been effective. It is, after all, technically difficult and politically sensitive work.

Moreover, beginning before the turn of the century, too much financial activity had migrated away from banks and beyond the direct surveillance and policy interest of any of the banking regulators. The Financial Stability Oversight Council (FSOC) now established as part of the Dodd-Frank Act is itself a recognition of the problem. However, it is a weak and politically fraught effort to coordinate all of the regulators, each of which has its own turf and political priorities.

In the absence of more sweeping reform, I insisted, as best I could, on the need to maintain and focus the Fed's attention and strengthen its supervisory capacity. The legal vehicle would be to designate a Federal Reserve Board member as vice chairman with the particular responsibility of both heading the Fed's own supervision function and of regularly reporting to the Congress on the adequacy of existing policies and approaches.

Doubts were raised about giving such responsibility to a single board member. What would happen if he or she clashed with the chairman? But disagreements on the board, as I well know, can be healthy as well as destructive.

The new position, while now a part of the 2010 Dodd-Frank financial reform legislation, took years to be formally filled. In the interim, the function was substantially performed by a strong sitting governor, Daniel Tarullo. Randal Quarles, the first of President Donald Trump's appointees to the Reserve Board, was sworn in and specifically tasked with financial supervision in October 2017. Incidentally, Quarles carries forward the historic connection of Utah's Eccles family with the Federal Reserve. His wife, Hope Eccles, is a relative of former Federal Reserve chairman Marriner Eccles, who cared a lot about the regulatory process. I trust those ties will help reinforce his sense of dedication to the high priority of financial oversight. Irrational exuberance threatening the stability of the system is an old story. Time and again, looking back, the question "Where were the supervisors?" hasn't had a good answer.

The massive Dodd-Frank legislation did not deal adequately with the more fundamentally disjointed regulatory structure. It was judged as a matter too complicated and too politically fraught for the congressional committees to tackle in the midst of seemingly more urgent parts of the legislation.

I understand that reluctance. But the overlaps, the inconsistencies, the blind spots in the existing framework are widely understood by the regulators themselves, by the regulated institutions, and indeed by the leaders of the congressional committees. Given my current preoccupation with identifying areas of government ineffectiveness and inefficiency, this stands out as an area demanding attention. All too likely, it will be set aside until the next crisis again fully exposes the weaknesses.*

Another controversial and well-publicized rule amid the complexities of Dodd-Frank bears my name. It aims to ameliorate some of the conflicts of interest and inappropriate incentives inherent in proprietary trading and the ownership and management of private equity and hedge funds by commercial banks. The mind-bending complexities of the new financial technology combined with the modern practice of incentive payments that reward employees for particular deals practically invites malpractice, whatever the pious institutional statements about the priority placed on client relationships and an ethical culture. In fact, rewards for successful proprietary transactions, inherently speculative and often in conflict with client interests, will tend eventually to color the overall atmosphere and the reward systems in banks, even beyond the trading rooms.

My view, widely shared, is that it is inappropriate for an institution that benefits from the federal "safety net" (for example, access to Federal Reserve liquidity, FDIC insurance, and less tangible comforts) to engage in risk taking unrelated to the essential banking functions of deposit taking, lending, and serving customers while sharing in operating a safe, efficient, and necessary payments system.

For months, my proposal that proprietary trading be banned from commercial banks seemed to attract little attention inside or outside of the Obama administration. In the absence of administration backing, Tony Dowd spent the summer and fall meeting with members of Congress and their staffs, winning some support on the Senate Banking Committee.

At a *Wall Street Journal*–sponsored conference in December 2009, my sense of frustration boiled over. I spent the afternoon listening to bankers and traders warning that regulations must not inhibit trading and "innovation." My impulsive reaction to their comments was later printed in full in the *Wall Street Journal:* "I mean: Wake up, gen-

---

*The Volcker Alliance in April 2015 issued an analysis of the problem and set out possible reforms in a report titled "Reshaping the Financial Regulatory System."

tlemen. I can only say that your response is inadequate. I wish that somebody would give me some shred of neutral evidence about the relationship between financial innovation recently and the growth of the economy, just one shred of information." I predicted that my proposal of keeping certain speculative activities outside of the commercial banking system was "probably going to win in the end."

To that point, I received no evidence. But my forecast proved accurate. Shortly before Christmas, I received a call from Vice President Joe Biden.

"How is your proposal on proprietary trading going?"

"It's a good proposal, but I have no horses."

"Forget about that. I'll be your horse."

As simple as that.

I later learned that the vice president won Obama's support for my proposals at a key meeting in which the president admonished his economic team for the slow pace of financial reform. It helped that Biden was able to say that I already had won over several key senators, led by Oregon's Jeff Merkley and Michigan's Carl Levin.

On January 21, 2010, President Obama called a press conference to promote the reform legislation. I was lined up with a few of his officials. He announced his administration's support for a ban on speculative activities within commercial banks, "which we're calling the Volcker Rule, after this tall guy behind me."

Well, that was a total surprise. For better or worse, I became involved in the difficult legislative process. It was a key element in the final package of Dodd-Frank, heavily lobbied and with only tepid support from within the administration itself. But in the end, only limited exceptions were made in the final effort to assure the sixtieth Senate vote.

Nowadays, I no longer have to debate "the Rule." The simple idea that "thou shall not gamble with the public's money" seems to be accepted in principle. Many of the objections raised—that it hampers lending, that trading liquidity would be lost, that "spreads" would widen, even that the Volcker Rule would curb economic growth—have been shown to be lobbyists' fictions.

Markets are operating smoothly. Liquidity is ample. Bank profits have fully recovered from the 2008 crisis. The economy itself is
doing just fine, with the unemployment rate close to a record low.
And once in a while, a banker will himself suggest to me that the
environment in trading rooms has changed constructively—a little
more respect for potential conflicts, less urgency in reaching for a
special deal. But I have no doubt that, one way or another, traders
will test the limits.

The Challenge of Effective Regulation

What is not simply a lobbyist's fiction with respect to the Volcker
Rule is the fact that the supporting regulations, long delayed in pub-
lication by the need to coordinate actions by five different agencies,
are exceedingly detailed. They were unnecessarily applied to small
banks not apt to engage in significant trading activity.

It is also true that concerns about regulatory complexity are
common and not limited to financial regulation. Pictures of the
thousands and thousands of pages of federal regulation are grist for
election campaign mills. I cringe, like others. But then I also cringe
a bit when I receive, each year, the eighty or so pages explaining precisely my rights and the policy limitations in my "simple" household
insurance policy.

I learned the key element of the problem when I took office as
Fed chair. While at the New York Fed, I had heard a steady stream of
complaints from bank executives about the Fed's Truth in Lending
regulation. That conceptually simple regulation sought to address
what in principle should be a reasonable objective: banks should
provide customers a clear and consistent definition of interest rates,
loan maturities, and other elements in their loan and credit card
documents. It was a long regulation, attempting to explain what was
necessary in every possible scenario. Is interest compounding daily,
monthly, annually, or maybe not at all? What about holidays? How
much notice of change is appropriate?

The regulation was a board matter. As soon as I was chairman I called the staff together and suggested (in the end demanded) that they review the regulation and shorten it to a hundred pages or less. They pleaded that it was impossible. I insisted.

Sometime later they returned with a hundred-page document. "Okay," I said. "Put it out for comment."

Every one of the many comments we received from banks was pleading for something to be added: accept our particular method of calculation, redefine exactly what approaches to compounding are acceptable, what automatic rollover could be permitted or refused. No doubt, some of the same banks that had complained about the rule's length in the first place complained again, pleading for more "clarity."

Place that concern into the massively larger and infinitely more complex trading market of the twenty-first century. And add to that the multiple jurisdictions with their own versions of what is important in their regulatory role, and indeed there was reason to demand simplification of the Volcker Rule.

I am convinced that is possible. What's critical, of course, is that any change protect the core principle: "Thou shalt not gamble with the public's money."

There is no force on earth that can stand up effectively, year after year, against thousands of individuals and hundreds of millions of dollars in the Washington swamp aimed at influencing the legislative and electoral process. Indeed, the growth of money in politics is a major challenge to the democratic ideals we express. We have learned time and again that years of financial stability and economic growth tend to involve easing of regulations and supervisory discipline. We see that at work as I write in 2018, with pleas for reduced capital standards for banks and a narrowing of the number of megafinancial institutions subject to more intrusive surveillance.

Can we learn to do better?

chapter 16

THE THREE VERITIES

Tranquil Cape May, New Jersey, September 5, 1927

Tumultuous New York, New York, September 5, 2018

Geographically, Cape May and New York City are not far apart, just 160 miles by turnpike and parkway without a red light.

Chronologically, my personal journey over ninety years has been full of twists and turns, punctuated by long detours on which I encountered some notable challenges that still need attention.

As a child, I was insulated from the Great Depression by a strong and secure family.

As a teenager, I felt inspired by Winston Churchill standing up almost alone against Nazi tyranny and by FDR's Declaration of the Four Freedoms, culminating in a truly "American" victory in World War II.

As a student, I was exposed to the best that great universities had to offer and began to understand varied perspectives on the political and economic world.

As an adult, I spent most of my life in government, in the Treasury and Federal Reserve, proud to be part of a self-confident and powerful country destined to lead the free world.

I loved being in Washington in the 1960s and 1970s with my young family. We had many good friends, most of them in public service. We shared a certain pride in helping to shape economic policy, contributing to the American ideals of liberal democracy, open markets, and the rule of law.

Today, the environment is different—radically so. The historic rise of China and the resurgence of populist extremes and autocratic governments challenge our leadership and ideals. Here at home, the intensity of ideological division, even within our long-established political parties, presents a huge and unfamiliar challenge.

We've come to question all of the hallmarks of our great society: our public educational system and respected universities, the once "reliable" free press, even scientific expertise. The legitimacy of our courts, the Congress, the presidency itself—all of the basic institutions of constitutional democracy have been cast into doubt.

The once honored phrase "good government" is now viewed as an oxymoron rather than an accepted objective of American society. Cynicism is pervasive.

I know one thing for sure. I no longer want to visit Washington, the city in which I gladly spent most of my career and that was once seen as home by my family. What not so long ago was a middle-class, midsized city dominated by an ethic of public service today simply oozes wealth and entitlement. Not a financial center like New York or a technology hub like Silicon Valley, Washington money is directed toward shaping public policy and laws to benefit specific interests. And it shows in the escalating demand for office space, luxury hotels, high-priced apartments and restaurants to serve a multiplying force of lawyers and lobbyists.

Washington's surrounding counties reportedly are now at the top in their residents' average income per capita. I don't know how many senators and congressmen are counted among those residents these days, or what their incomes may be. I do know they spend inordinate amounts of time "dialing for dollars" to finance costly campaigns and less time in Washington socializing with colleagues, seeking areas for compromise and consensus.

We face a huge challenge in this country to restore a sense of public purpose and of trust in government. It will require critically needed reforms in our political processes and leaders who can restore and preserve a consensus upon which our great democracy can depend.

That is a challenge for energetic men and women new to the political world. But this now-aged bureaucrat can still set out some key lessons learned in decades of public service. That, in fact, is the reason I finally decided to write this memoir, concluding with what I term "the Three Verities."

Stable Prices

Early in my second term as Fed chairman, a colleague complained during an Open Market Committee meeting that we'd been accused of being "knee-jerk inflation fighters." My immediate reply was that was "a pretty good reputation," a sign we were making progress.

Trust in our currency is fundamental to good government and economic growth. The influence extends far beyond our shores, given the role of the dollar and the American financial system in the world.

Our monetary system, like that of almost all countries, rests on a fiat currency. There is no gold or other valued hard asset into which a paper dollar (or bank deposit) can be exchanged at a fixed price. Implicitly, we take for granted, or should, the stability of our currency in terms of what it can buy today, tomorrow, and for years ahead—groceries, a home, or maybe even a bond that promises to pay a fixed amount of dollars into the future.

Maintaining that expectation, that confidence, is a fundamental responsibility of monetary policy. Once lost, the consequences can be severe and stability hard to restore. Interest rates rise, savings are squeezed, the currency declines in foreign-exchange markets. Some traders and speculators may win but wage earners and those on fixed incomes, like most retired people, will fall behind.

The United States had a taste of that in the "stagflation" of the 1970s, culminating in the highest rate of price increases in our peacetime history. As is typically the case, the inflation process came to feed on itself as expectations of price increases contributed to more inflation. In the absence of other effective options, it was finally extinguished by forceful monetary policies. A crippling recession could not be avoided. Our experience in the mid-1970s, when weak anti-inflation efforts failed, and again in the early 1980s, when a much more sustained effort was required, were reminders enough of the importance of maintaining price stability once it is restored.

Now the environment is quite different. The generation with direct experience of stagflation is passing on. In contrast, over the past thirty years we've maintained sufficient price stability to engrain expectations of little or no inflation into our thinking. Factors such as cheap imports from countries like China have helped, but our monetary authorities have clearly recognized the importance of maintaining price stability. There can be little question that those firmly grounded expectations have contributed enormously in allowing the United States to absorb huge budget deficits and a massive injection of official liquidity during and after the 2008 financial crisis without reawakening inflationary forces.

A lesson from my career is that such success can carry the seeds of its own destruction. I've watched country after country, faced with damaging inflation, fight to restore stability. Then, with victory in sight, the authorities relax and accept a "little inflation" in the hope of stimulating further growth, only to see the process resume all over again. The sad history of economic policy over much of Latin America offers too many examples.

The United States is not Latin America, with its history of recurrent inflation. But it does face an ongoing challenge for monetary and fiscal policy. The now long expansion and full employment with signs of growing pressures on labor markets have, so far, not upset price stability. But it is a crucial period for monetary policy.

The late Bill Martin, as I recalled earlier, is famous for his remark that the job of the central bank is to take away the punch bowl just when the party gets going. The hard fact of life is that few hosts want to end the party prematurely. They wait too long and when the risks are evident the real damage is done.

Central bankers are the hosts at the economic party. Too often, monetary restraint—never popular—has been delayed too long. The inflationary process begins and then the challenge becomes more difficult.

Now, in recognition of the need for discipline, a remarkable consensus has developed among modern central bankers, including in the Federal Reserve, that there's a new "red line" for policy: a 2 percent rate of increase in some carefully designed consumer price index is acceptable, even desirable, and at the same time provides a limit.

I puzzle about the rationale. A 2 percent target, or limit, was not in my textbooks years ago. I know of no theoretical justification. It's difficult to be both a target and a limit at the same time. And a 2 percent inflation rate, successfully maintained, would mean the price level doubles in little more than a generation.

I do know some practical facts. No price index can capture, down to a tenth or a quarter of a percent, the real change in consumer prices. The variety of goods and services, the shifts in demand, the subtle changes in pricing and quality are too complex to calculate precisely from month to month or year to year. Moreover, as an economy grows or slows, there is a tendency for prices to change, a little more up in periods of economic expansion, maybe a little down as the economy slows or recedes, but not sideways year after year.

Yet, as I write, with economic growth rising and the unemployment rate near historic lows, concerns are being voiced that consumer prices are growing too slowly—just because they're a quarter percent or so below the 2 percent target! Could that be a signal to "ease" monetary policy, or at least to delay restraint, even with the economy at full employment?

Certainly, that would be nonsense. How did central bankers fall into the trap of assigning such weight to tiny changes in a single statistic, with all of its inherent weakness?

I think I know the origin. It's not a matter of theory or of deep empirical studies. Just a very practical decision in a far-away place.

New Zealand is a small country, known among other things for excellent trout fishing. So, as I left the Federal Reserve in 1987, I happily accepted an invitation to visit. It turns out I was there, in one respect, under false pretenses. Getting off the plane in Auckland, I learned the fishing season was closed. I could have left my fly rods at home.

In other respects, the visit was fascinating. New Zealand economic policy was undergoing radical change. Years of high inflation, slow growth, and increasing foreign debt culminated in a sharp swing toward support for free markets and a strong attack on inflation led by the traditionally left-wing Labour Party.

The changes included narrowing the central bank's focus to a single goal: bringing the inflation rate down to a predetermined target. The new government set an annual inflation rate of zero to 2 percent as the central bank's key objective. The simplicity of the target was seen as part of its appeal—no excuses, no hedging about, one policy, one instrument. Within a year or so the inflation rate fell to about 2 percent.

The central bank head, Donald Brash, became a kind of traveling salesman. He had a lot of customers. I was reminded of the practical appeal when I read of a colloquy in a July 1996 FOMC meeting about the Federal Reserve's "price stability" target. Janet Yellen asked then chairman Alan Greenspan: "How do you define price stability?" To me, he gave the only sensible answer: "That state in which expected changes in the general price level do not effectively alter business or household decisions."

Janet persisted: "Could you please put a number on that?"

And so Alan's general principle, to me entirely appropriate, was eventually translated into a number. After all, those regression models calculated by staff trained in econometrics have to be fed numbers, not principles.

I understand reasonable arguments can be made for 2 percent as an upper limit for "stability." There is a body of analysis that suggests official price indexes typically overstate increases by failing to account for improvements in the quality of goods and services over time. The point is also made that expectations and behavior are determined by the price of goods, where productivity gains and strong competition restrain price increases, rather than by the cost of services like education and medical care, where productivity gains are slow.

But it is also true, and herein lies the danger, that such seeming numerical precision suggests it is possible to fine-tune policy with more flexible targeting as conditions change. Perhaps an increase to 3 percent to provide a slight stimulus if the economy seems too sluggish? And, if 3 percent isn't enough, why not 4 percent?

I'm not making this up. I read such ideas voiced occasionally by Federal Reserve officials or IMF economists, and more frequently from economics professors. In Japan, it seems to be the new gospel. I have yet to hear, in the midst of a strong economy, that maybe the inflation target should be reduced!

The fact is, even if it would be desirable, the tools of monetary and fiscal policy simply don't permit that degree of precision. Yielding to the temptation to "test the waters" can only undercut the commitment to stability that sound monetary policy requires.

The old belief that a little inflation is a good thing for employment, preached long ago by some of my own Harvard professors, lingers on even though Nobel Prize–winning research and experience over decades suggests otherwise. In its new, more sophisticated form it seems to be fear of deflation that drives the argument.

Deflation, defined as a significant decline in prices, is indeed a serious matter if extended over time. It has not been a reality in this country for more than eighty years.

It is true that interest rates can't fall significantly below zero in nominal terms. So, the argument runs, let's keep "a little inflation"—even in a recession—as a kind of safeguard, a backdoor way of keeping "real" interest rates negative. Consumers will then have an incentive to buy today what might cost more tomorrow; borrowers will be enticed to borrow at zero or low interest rates, to invest before prices rise further.

All these arguments seem to me to have little empirical support. Yet fear of deflation seems to have become common among officials and commentators alike. (Even back in July 1984, as my Fed colleagues and I were still monitoring the 4 percent inflation rate, the *New York Times* had a front-page story warning about potential deflation.) Actual deflation is rare. Yet that fear can, in fact, easily lead to policies that inadvertently increase the risk.

History tells the story. In the United States, we have had decades of good growth without inflation—in the 1950s and early 1960s, and again in the 1990s through the early 2000s. Those years of stability were also marked by eight recessions, mostly quick, that posed no risk of deflation.

Only once in the past century, in the 1930s, have we had deflation, serious deflation. In 2008–2009 there was cause for concern. The common characteristic of those two incidents was collapse of the financial system.

We can't expect to prevent all financial excesses and recessions in the future. That is the pattern of history with free markets, financial innovation, and our innate "animal spirits."

The lesson, to me, is crystal clear. Deflation is a threat posed by a critical breakdown of the financial system. Slow growth and recurrent recessions without systemic financial disturbances, even the big recessions of 1975 and 1982, have not posed such a risk.

The real danger comes from encouraging or inadvertently tolerating rising inflation and its close cousin of extreme speculation and risk taking, in effect standing by while bubbles and excesses threaten financial markets. Ironically, the "easy money," striving for a "little inflation" as a means of forestalling deflation, could, in the end, be what brings it about.

That is the basic lesson for monetary policy. It demands emphasis on price stability *and* prudent oversight of the financial system. Both of those requirements inexorably lead to the responsibilities of a central bank.

Sound Finance

Central banks have been around for a long time. Originally, they were designed to help finance the government. They could also issue currency and provide some discipline over other banks. Alexander

Hamilton's short-lived National Bank of the United States was one example.

That early incarnation failed, a victim of fear that East Coast monied interests would stifle states' economic independence and growth. It wasn't until 1913, after increasingly damaging banking crises, that the United States created a real central bank to issue currency, rationalize bank reserve requirements, provide authority to lend to banks, and develop some national supervision. And it took another twenty years for the new system to reach its full potential.

The structure of the Federal Reserve System was designed to be, and has remained, complex for good reasons. An act of political compromise, the "system" is designed to balance the need for a unified policy with sensitivity to regional interests; independence with public accountability; government control with some narrowly limited private participation.

The Federal Reserve is at times also a controversial institution, inherently so. That controversy centers more on policy and power than on its unique organizational structure. But policy and organization are really inseparable.

The key is "independence." It was not by accident that this was the first point I scribbled in my notes preparing for my first meeting with President Carter. My second point was "policy"—how that independence should be exercised.

The Federal Reserve is bound to be controversial when restrictive monetary policies are needed and when supervision and regulation rein in financial institutions. That is why the system requires protection against what I would call passing or partisan political pressures.

At the same time, the Federal Reserve is unambiguously part of government. Its authority is derived from the constitutional duty of the Congress to "coin money and regulate the value thereof." It is not a part of the administration, subject to "presidential order," whatever the claims of Jim Baker back in 1984.

As a practical matter, 435 congressmen and 100 senators could not be responsible for the day-to-day operational and policy decisions involved in central banking. Neither has Congress wished to delegate that authority to the president. Similar considerations have motivated the creation of other so-called independent agencies, some older than the Federal Reserve. However, none has the range of structural defenses of independence or the breadth of explicit and assumed responsibilities that Congress has provided to the Federal Reserve over the years:

- The Federal Reserve System is self-financed, with ample income stemming from its operations.

- Fourteen-year terms are provided for the seven members of the Board of Governors, who can be removed only for "cause."

- The chairman, as one of the governors, has a four-year term.

- Twelve Reserve Banks with operational and some policy responsibilities are scattered around the country (in a pattern that seems a bit odd today but was politically sensible in 1913).

- Presidents of those twelve regional Reserve Banks are appointed by each bank's directors with approval of the Federal Reserve Board, which also appoints three of the nine directors of each regional board. The remaining six directors are chosen by the private "member banks," subject to a requirement that they represent a variety of interests and experience.

All very complicated in appearance and hard to explain to a dinner partner innocently asking, "What do you do?" It is tempting to consider organizational tinkering. Do we really need twelve Reserve Banks? Do their current locations (including two in Missouri) make sense? Isn't it politically awkward that the individual Reserve Banks are, technically, still owned by private member banks that are subject to Federal Reserve supervision? Is the often-raised suggestion that the Government Accountability Office should "audit" the Fed appropriate?

Each of us who have played a role have our own ideas of what organizational changes might be logical. But change could quickly become a threat. One "tinker" invites another. Ulterior motives underlie seemingly innocuous proposals for change.

That is particularly true of the recurrent demand by some in the Congress for a GAO audit of the Board of Governors and the Federal Open Market Committee. The true intent is clear. It is not to oversee operational efficiency and to assure accurate accounting for expenditures. (Expenditures are already audited by the GAO for the board and privately for the regional banks.) Rather, it is a play for influence over policy.

Large organizational questions do arise that demand attention, not for the Federal Reserve alone but for all of the agencies involved in banking and financial oversight. The array of financial agencies with overlapping authorities and sometimes inconsistent policies is an accident of history. The Comptroller of the Currency was established during the Civil War, when national banking was authorized. State chartered banks came under the supervision of the Federal Deposit Insurance Corporation in 1933 following the banking collapse during the Great Depression. Going back to its creation, the Federal Reserve shares authority over its member banks, whether nationally or state chartered. Only in the 1970s did it gain authority over all bank holding companies, which today dominate ownership of the larger banks. The Securities and Exchange Commission, with authority over independent investment banks, retains responsibility for broker-dealer functions even within bank holding companies and regulates banklike money market funds. The SEC and the Commodity Futures Trading Commission both oversee derivatives. Insurance companies are state regulated. A range of new financial institutions, including hedge funds, have no designated oversight.

Who looks after the whole?

Before the 2008 crisis, the honest answer was no one.

By the nature of its responsibilities for monetary policy, for bank holding companies and for financial stability generally, the Federal Reserve has sometimes assumed or attempted to assume a lead role. But that depended upon particular personalities and interests.

In a way, the present answer is the Federal Stability Oversight Council, created in the 2010 Dodd-Frank legislation. FSOC, under the aegis of the Treasury secretary, was intended to foster consistency and cooperation between the financial agencies. It hasn't worked well. The attempt to enforce common rule-making is worthy but weak. Importantly, a regulatory system built when traditional banks dominated financial markets is simply out of touch with key elements of modern finance, firms driven by trading, securitization, and derivatives. New credit entities perform banklike functions. Corporate debt levels are rising inexorably out of the reach of existing supervision.

I know quite literally of no agency head, no banker, no other experienced participant who doesn't believe the present system has both serious overlaps and gaps. Its excesses and inconsistencies in oversight and enforcement make the financial system vulnerable to manipulation and breakdown. One cannot read the laments of Treasury secretaries Paulson and Geithner, and chairman Bernanke, without recognizing their frustration in dealing with the financial crisis.

So what to do? What to do in particular about the Federal Reserve, which by law and practice has the broadest responsibility? It alone manages monetary policy, controlling the money supply and influencing interest rates. It participates directly in the massive market for government securities, buying and selling in virtually unlimited amounts in pursuit of its policy objectives. It has direct regulatory and supervisory authority over the big bank holding companies. It maintains contact with foreign monetary policy and regulatory authorities. In emergencies it can marshal huge resources.

The range of its involvement in banking and in financial markets—and the simple fact that it is looked to as the guardian of financial stability by the Congress and public alike—make it natural that the Fed's responsibilities have in practice been extended beyond those explicitly listed in law.

There has been, and should be, growth in the staffing of the Fed, both in Washington and in the regional banks, reaching beyond commercial bank supervision to oversight of the financial system more generally. But informal oversight, however competent, is not the same as clear responsibility and authority. And Federal Reserve leadership, both at the board and at the banks, has sometimes been reluctant—or even opposed—to undertaking supervisory efforts that might detract from the primary responsibility for monetary policy.

Again, an anecdote involving former Fed chair Janet Yellen illustrates the point. During her testimony to the government inquiry into the financial crisis, she was reminded that, as president of the San Francisco Fed, she had raised concerns about the spread of subprime mortgage lending. San Francisco was a hot spot, so it was perhaps natural that Ms. Yellen picked up at a relatively early stage credit excesses that were less noticed elsewhere. Evidence for the importance of regional representation!

The question naturally followed: "What did you do about it?" The answer, condensed, was that the San Francisco Fed had no authority.

What about the Fed in Washington? It missed it too, even when Ms. Yellen and one or two other insiders (quietly) raised the issue.

Wasn't the activity taking place in bank holding companies under Fed supervision? Yes, but typically in nonbank divisions, such as the broker-dealer, where other regulators had primary responsibility.

In her November 2010 interview with the staff of the Financial Crisis Inquiry Commission, Governor Yellen explained it this way: "We were focused on the banking system, and I don't think we were sufficiently looking at the risks within the entire financial system."

Well, it wasn't long before subprime mortgages capsized the ship of finance!

As chairman of President Obama's Economic Recovery Advisory Board, I had a seat at the table when regulatory reform was discussed. My own experience with repeated financial crises left me with two particular priorities in addition to the widely agreed need for higher commercial bank capital standards, for broad oversight of financial markets, and for authority to resolve, or wind down, failing banks in an orderly manner, consistent with their ultimate liquidation.

Best known because of the label attached was the so-called Volcker Rule, aimed at proprietary (that is, noncustomer-driven) trading by banks. The simple idea is that institutions benefiting from the protections inherent in the federal safety net should not be speculating with what is ultimately and widely understood public support.

(During the crisis, the established role of the safety net had been stretched far beyond insuring retail deposits and providing solvent banks with easy access to the Fed's discount window. For instance, the Troubled Asset Relief Program, or TARP, permitted the Treasury to use taxpayer money to stabilize financial institutions and even the auto industry.) The new rule would be fleshed out by informal supervisory oversight, with the presumption that the five relevant agencies* could come to agreement on the needed regulations.

The political reality is that each agency has its own leadership, staff, constituencies, and congressional committee oversight. Each agency brings a different sense of urgency to oversight and enforcement. In the case of the Volcker Rule, five years passed before there was an agreed regulation extending over thousands of pages.

My second contribution was simpler and more straightforward. I felt the Federal Reserve needed to be prodded and equipped to effectively and consistently exercise its broad responsibility for the stability of the financial system. To assure attention, I proposed that the president should designate, and the Congress should confirm, one of the Fed's seven board members as vice chairman for supervision. He or she would be directly accountable to the Congress by means of a semiannual report on the state of the financial system.

A little awkward, perhaps, for the Fed chairman. However, the responsibility for rule making and supervision would continue to lie with the chairman and the board as a whole. The point is that making one board member by law explicitly accountable for minding the store should ensure that the system as a whole cannot escape its oversight responsibilities.

After a long lapse, the position has been filled. Mr. Randal Quarles, I will be interested in seeing how you manage the job!

The much broader and more fundamental organizational question is how to resolve the overlaps and lacunae between the agencies.

---

*These five are the Federal Reserve, Office of the Comptroller of the Currency (OCC), the Federal Deposit Insurance Corporation (FDIC), the Securities and Exchange Commission (SEC), and the Commodity Futures Trading Commission (CFTC).

The Volcker Alliance has issued a report that sets out one possible approach. It would combine the supervisory functions over the financial system into one entity, the board of which would include representatives of each of the relevant agencies. That new entity might be led by, or be closely associated with, the Fed's new vice chair for supervision. In the interest of maintaining checks and balances, rule making (the regulatory function) could be led by the Fed, subject to review and comment by the other agencies in the FSOC or otherwise.

Obviously, a number of other approaches could be considered. Before the crisis, then Treasury secretary Paulson went some distance in developing an approach that was similar in some respects. After the financial crisis, the UK put the Bank of England in charge of the new Prudential Regulation Authority, essentially providing a close relationship of day-to-day supervisory authority to monetary policy. Other approaches are a matter of debate in the European Union.

The key issue is the extent to which the full load of oversight, supervision, and regulation should be placed on the central bank. Effectiveness and efficiency argue for consolidation. The desirability of getting a variety of viewpoints and checks and balances needs to be taken into account. However, the central bank, with its inherent interest in market stability, its range of regulatory and supervisory responsibilities, and its relative independence from political pressures, must not and cannot sensibly be removed from active participation.

The experience of the United Kingdom is an object lesson. In restoring the operational independence of the Bank of England about twenty years ago, its supervisory authority was placed in a new sister agency. The practical result was an unfortunate delay in recognizing the underlying market excesses and the system's vulnerability to the failure of a little-known but aggressive bank.

The UK government quickly reversed course, placing the supervisory role back squarely in the bank's jurisdiction.

A friend pointed out to me recently that the Federal Reserve, so far almost uniquely among major federal agencies, hasn't had its basic organization and functional responsibilities threatened by the Trump administration.

I'd like to think that, over the years, the Federal Reserve has in fact maintained the respect of the Congress and presidents alike. In an environment in which trust in government is dangerously low, the Fed still retains a high degree of credibility. In that respect, it is a national asset.

It is not above accountability.

It is not free from error.

It does need the attention of the Congress to ensure it is equipped to maintain responsible and economical administration of its authorities. And it does need to be shielded from partisan politics.

Taken all together, it remains a precious asset for the country in troubled times.

Good Government

Good government. That's a phrase we don't hear much anymore.

If we do, what likely comes to mind is the dictum of Ronald Reagan: "Government is the problem." With a high degree of certainty as I conclude this memoir, I can state that government—the democratic government in which we take pride—is indeed in trouble at every level.

Poll after poll delivers the message. Only 20 percent or so of the population trusts the federal government to do the right thing most of the time. Congress fares still worse in public opinion. Even the courts and the press, the so-called fourth branch of democratic government, are in poor repute.

It's not just a matter of polling and opinion. Paul Light, the distinguished professor of public administration, in an issue paper prepared for the Volcker Alliance, identified forty-eight highly visible breakdowns in government performance since the beginning of this century—breakdowns important enough to receive substantial interest in the national press. His examples include the failure

to coordinate known pieces of intelligence that could have anticipated the September 11 attacks; the inability to respond effectively
to Hurricane Katrina in New Orleans; the inadequate inspection of
a Gulf of Mexico oil rig; and on to—my home field—our inability
to understand and foresee the financial system's vulnerability before
the 2008 debacle. Since his 2015 paper, there have been many more
examples.

I understand that some management lapses are inevitable in the
complex, interdependent world in which we live. Policies conflict.
Politics—crude electoral politics—intrude. But Professor Light's
careful analysis points toward some distressing conclusions. The
number of breakdowns has increased over time, perhaps because
the government is trying to do more than its resources and competence permit. The trend appears independent of administrations,
Republican or Democrat. The causes vary widely. Sometimes policy
is misconstrued. Financial and human resources are inadequate. The
responsible organization is weak in structure and leadership.

We should not, and cannot, tolerate extending this record of serious lapses in public management—not if we want to restore a sense
of respect and trust in government and respect for its mission.

Ronald Reagan, in pointing out government failures and arguing that it is too big, also implicitly recognized that government
is, in fact, necessary. He certainly supported providing resources for
national security, the huge slice of our federal budget that the military and our intelligence agencies represent. He didn't campaign to
end Social Security or some form of Medicare. Nor did he want to
shut down agencies such as the Centers for Disease Control and the
National Institute of Health, which protect us from epidemics and
fund the research necessary to identify, treat, and prevent disease.

We can and should debate the size of government, the range of
its responsibilities, and which programs deserve financing. We also
need an effective and fair system of taxation to pay for what we conclude we need.

Those are matters for the political process. Once they are determined, it is up to the administration and management to produce the

results. Alexander Hamilton made the point more than two hundred years ago in his Federalist Papers: good administration is the key to good government. What has changed is the complexity, the rapidly changing technology, the multiplicity of programs, the intensity of political and lobbying pressure.

Seventy years ago, the problems of local government that my father encountered were simpler. He took pride in public service and in doing the job well. An engineer, he approached government as a science, one that required training, expertise, and discipline to be practiced successfully. It was an approach that served his town's citizens and taxpayers well.

The US government—at the local, state, and federal levels—spends close to 40 percent of our total economic output. Identifying our needs and how to meet them effectively is an enormous challenge that requires special skills, sophisticated technology, and most of all good judgment.

Against that challenge the federal government today employs about the same number of civilians as when I joined the Kennedy administration in 1962. (The US population meanwhile has nearly doubled. GDP and federal spending have soared to more than thirty times their 1962 levels.) We rely today on outsourcing, or contracting out to private business and some nonprofit organizations, for both more repetitive and routine operations but also for some of the highest technological challenges imaginable—for security, for space, for national health, for the environment.

Are we doing what we can do, what we must do, to be reasonably sure those jobs are being done well? Who is really equipped to judge what to outsource and what to do in house? How do we direct and oversee the thousands and thousands of contractors? For sure, it requires education, experience, and, above all, concern for doing it right.

Take the straightforward challenge of our infrastructure needs, about which we read so much and do so little. What should we build or rebuild? To what extent does good public policy and the need for efficiency require joint efforts—federal, state, local, and private? Do we have the right managers in place? Are they trained and educated appropriately? Can we make solid estimates of cost?

I'm afraid that too often the answer is no.

It is not that successive administrations have failed to pay lip service to the need for reform.

Within my experience, President Nixon emphasized "management by objective," the then fashionable approach of business consultants.

President Carter lauded "zero-based" budgeting.

President Clinton assigned Vice President Gore to undertake a more comprehensive effort of "reinventing government."

President George W. Bush undertook one major structural effort, combining related agencies into a new Department of Homeland Security—and then failed to insist on competent leadership.

We didn't have polls a century ago. Government was smaller, with a much narrower range of responsibilities. The technology was relatively primitive by today's standards. But complaints about government go back as far as the birth of the republic. At times, corruption has undermined confidence in fairness and competence. Eventually there was a response, typically spread over a number of administrations.

The assassination of President James Garfield in 1881 helped to introduce civil service reform. The first independent agencies go back to the nineteenth century. The Republican Theodore Roosevelt and the Democrat Woodrow Wilson both had strong views on effective government, the former with respect to matters as far apart as national parks and anti-trust policy, and the latter to government administration generally and the Federal Reserve in particular. The New Deal in the 1930s and Herbert Hoover at the behest of Presidents Truman and Eisenhower in the late 1940s and 1950s largely built the organization and the personnel structure we have today.

Schools and universities had a major role in "good government." Public administration programs proliferated, particularly in state-supported universities, but in some of the oldest and most established universities as well. Harvard, Princeton, and Yale, the Ivy

League triad, were encouraged by large contributions to develop
new programs of their own.

Sadly, that sense of energy, of initiative, that developed over
decades has dissipated. University donations and endowed profes-
sorships are much more likely to be devoted to questions of policy—discussion and debate about foreign and international affairs
or about the pros and cons of social programs. National educational
policy, international cooperation, and other challenging subjects are
attractive to scholars and students alike. But policy alone, no matter
how brilliantly conceived, doesn't get the job done.

My plea is very simple. At the end of the day, good policy is dependent on good management.

That is the central credo and mission of the nonpartisan Volcker
Alliance that I founded in 2013. By sponsoring research on public
management, by bringing together leading civil servants and academics, we hope to foster new approaches toward more effective and
efficient government at the federal, state, and local levels.

Fortunately, there is evidence that the challenge of public service
remains attractive for at least a small cadre of talented young people,
both those early in careers in government or those just beginning to
consider a professional career.

They share a common concern. Are relevant training programs
available? Are the university curricula relevant to emerging needs?
Indeed, is there any consensus on the approaches and talents that are
needed? How can new technology, including big data, be brought
to bear on management issues? What should be done in house or
contracted out? Does the structure of the civil service need serious
review in the light of today's technology and lifestyles?

Earlier in this memoir, I described my disappointment with the
response to the substantial recommendations of the two national
commissions on the public service that I chaired. In those days we
thought a quiet crisis was building. The crisis we see around us can
no longer be characterized as quiet.

Is it impossible that amid all the sound and fury in our national
politics today—the erosion of trust in government, the clear need for

collaboration among federal, state, and local authorities, the challenge of technology—a revival of interest in effective public management might find a response?

A Longer Perspective

Unavoidably, I end this memoir with a sense of deep concern. The rising tide of progress toward open democratic societies—the world in which I have lived and served—seems to be ebbing away.

Parts of Europe are becoming responsive to authoritarian leadership. Latin America, where some countries struggle to build consistently strong democracies, remains burdened by repeated economic breakdowns. The great potential in Africa and Asia is too often undercut by corruption, a cancer on development. Potentially most significantly, China and Russia seem determined to set out competing economic and political models.

Here at home, deep-seated economic, social, and cultural divides have eroded trust in our democratic processes. Attacks on the press and on science—indeed on any kind of expertise or established fact—have hampered our capacity to lead. Critical questions of environmental and immigration policy go unresolved. Long-established institutions for trade and national security are being threatened.

Perhaps it is time to remember that our nation has been challenged before. Within the ninety years of my life, we've faced depression, a world war, assassinations, unnecessary counterproductive wars in Vietnam and the Middle East, vicious race relations, double-digit inflation, terrorist attacks.

My mother, who lived for almost a century, died in 1990. I recall bemoaning to her, during some earlier occasion of despair: "Where is our proud country headed? Why can't we get things done?"

Her response, to me, remains the only convincing answer:

"The United States is the oldest and strongest democracy in the history of the world. In two hundred years it has survived a lot.

"Get back to work."

CREDIT WHERE CREDIT

IS DUE

I'*ve scattered* names of presidents, cabinet secretaries, chairmen, bosses, associates, and staff—some prominent, some not—throughout this memoir. Several have been close friends, in government and in the private sector.

Here, I want to make a special point to acknowledge a few who have worked side by side with me at critical points in my public life. Most have been long-term civil servants. All of them have been dedicated to the challenge of effective government.

Two were with me for more than half my working life. I lost them both in 2017.

Mike Bradfield

It was almost fifty years ago when Mike Bradfield was assigned to me as assistant general counsel for international affairs in my days as under secretary of the Treasury. A decade later, he joined me at the Fed as general counsel, building a strong division and proving himself as an indispensable advisor in regulatory and congressional affairs. He practically ran "my" investigation into the treatment by Swiss Banks of the deposit accounts of Holocaust victims after World War II. He later organized the Volcker Alliance legally and otherwise. I came to rely on him as a valued counselor on more run-of-the-mill, and some not so routine, family legal issues.

Dewey Daane

I had an even longer history with Dewey Daane, starting when he was my immediate superior in the Treasury Department in 1962. Almost a decade older than I and an earlier graduate of Harvard's Littauer School, the graduate school of public administration, he became a particularly close friend during his long years as a governor of the Federal Reserve Board. We traveled together to many more international meetings than I can count. He loved the title of "governor," which sometimes got him a better airline seat than a mere under secretary. To some degree, the Volcker family continued to participate in Dewey's life after he retired from the Fed and settled down to his last decades of banking and academic life in Nashville, Tennessee, with his beloved wife, Barbara.

Civil Servants at Their Best

Bill Taylor died too early in 1992, age fifty-three. He was at the peak of his career as the chairman of the FDIC, an appointment that recognized the stature he'd attained in the Fed and outside as, in my view, Washington's premier bank supervisor. As I rose to chair the Federal Reserve, I was fortunate he was there when we were called upon to deal with one financial crisis after another. Responding to a request by Treasury Secretary Nick Brady, he later helped to untangle the savings and loan debacle in the late 1980s. With sly wit and exceptional leadership, he taught us all about the world of finance beyond textbooks and economic theorizing.

Two long-term Fed staffers, former Associated Press reporter Joe Coyne and the Jesuit-trained Don Winn, protected me from missteps with the media and politicians. Among other things, each in their own way reminded me to resist the recurrent temptation of all of us in high office to equivocate (or even prevaricate) when meeting with the antagonistic press or Congress. Civil service at its best.

Jerry Corrigan was with me in the front office for those critical years after I returned to the New York Federal Reserve Bank and later when I was chairman of the Federal Reserve Board and the attack on inflation was at its dramatic peak. As financial crises kept intruding, Jerry had a talent, rare among academically trained economists, for springing into action and responding forcefully and convincingly in the face of uncertainty, political attacks, and lobbying pressure. When he was out in Minneapolis for a few years as the Reserve Bank president, we would steal time together so I could introduce him to fly fishing in the Rockies, part of his district!

His brightest few hours perhaps came even later when, as New York Fed president, he encouraged (or demanded) that banks step up and support the money market after stock prices dropped more than 20 percent on a single day, 1987's "Black Monday." Out of the Federal Reserve myself by then, I could only watch in admiration.

Steve Axilrod, Sam Cross, Ted Truman—key Federal Reserve and Treasury officials during my watch—each epitomize the sense of commitment, and I trust of satisfaction, that can be found in civil service professionals of the highest caliber.

And how could I ever forget Catherine Mallardi, who sat right outside the door of my Washington office for eight years? The embodiment of discretion, efficiency, and dedication that characterized the very best of that long-serving cohort of young women who were first drawn to Washington as teenagers during World War II.

On the Outside

I can't possibly record all of the men and women who have worked with me, befriended me, or even provided constructive opposition over the long years in private life.

Jim Wolfensohn provided a fine transitional avenue back into private finance through the investment bank boutique he established. I share his pride in the way Wolfensohn & Company did business. The small group of partners, both senior and junior, the associates, and analysts all reflected, and still reflect, quality. I can't list them all, but they have my appreciation.

What can I say about Dick Ravitch and his close associate Don Rice, who rescued me when I left investment banking by inviting me to join in a small office suite in Rockefeller Center? More than twenty years later, I sit in the same chair. I soon learned that, over the years, Dick has come to know everyone of political significance in New York City and State—and in many other states as well. He ran the enlarged Metropolitan Transportation Authority for a few years and in those days, the trains (almost always) ran on time. He was key to managing New York City's near bankruptcy. There is no man in this country more concerned with the crushing pressures on city and state finances, ranging across the United States and now to Puerto Rico as well.

Ernie Luzzatto has tended to all of my personal legal and sometimes complicated tax responsibilities for at least thirty years. I am eternally grateful.

This book describes the high morale and energy of the entire Oil-for-Food staff under Reid Morden but fails to note the sense of commitment of former assistant US district attorneys Mark Califano, Sue Ringler, and Michael Cornacchia as well as now US district court judge Jeffrey Meyer. They provided the talent, the energy, the experience that made our report both meaningful and accurate. They collectively opened my eyes to the importance of disciplined intelligence, getting the facts right within the legal process.

Two relatively young men have to me come to exemplify the talent, energy, and judgment we need for the future.

Tony Dowd, I still think of as a youngster. It was only thirty years ago when I met him as an associate at Wolfensohn. More than once he saved me by strongly advising against purchasing a floundering fly shop in the Berkshires. Two decades later he read of my pre-election connection with Barack Obama and volunteered to help. After the election he was my key aide on the President's Economic Recovery Advisory Board, far more disciplined than I was in communicating with the administration, congressional staffs, and financial industry executives. He tirelessly applied himself to the negotiations and to drafting important legislation. Later, with Mike Bradfield, he launched the Volcker Alliance. Still indispensable, he is now applying his entrepreneurial talents to private businesses. His inbred sense of public service and discipline honed at West Point will never leave him and I am confident someday a stint in a high-level government position is in order.

It was a young University of Chicago economist, Austan Goolsbee, who first led me to Barack Obama. He held my hand during my time as chairman of the Economic Recovery Advisory Board, and survived Washington with great humor and common sense. He teaches, he writes, he communicates, and we need him and his kind back in public service.

The Volcker Alliance

One cannot sit here in 2018 without a strong sense of concern about the future of this country, and more particularly the state of public service. Distrust and ill-will permeate attitudes toward government. Too many of the best in the assailed bureaucracy, both in Congress and in key administrative posts, have left too soon, doubting that their voices could be heard or that their goals could be achieved.

That needs to change. And it won't be easy.

As a signal of my concern, I decided to establish a foundation with a mission impossible: Can we stimulate others—particularly schools of public policy, of management, of administration—to rethink how government can and should respond to the needs of the twenty-first century?

Today, the small staff is hard at work, led by Tom Ross, who brings to the effort his long-honored experience as a judge and educational leadership in his home state of North Carolina. Paul Light and Don Kettl, two leaders in the fight, have worked with me in the past and now again as advisors to the senior staff. Bill Glasgall and Gaurav Vasisht, steeped in the challenges of state and local management and financial reform, have a full agenda. Emily Bolton, for a while caught between careers in ballet and public service, is committed to making government work. She first coordinated the Oil-for-Food and World Bank investigations and now she helps the "world go around" at the Volcker Alliance.

AFTERWORD

When I finished writing this book, late in the summer of 2018, it was already clear that the United States—and the world order it had helped establish during my lifetime—were facing deep-seated political, economic, and cultural challenges. I concluded with a bit of reassurance: My mother's reminder that the United States had endured a brutal civil war, two world wars, a great depression, and still emerged as the leader of the "free world," a model for democracy, open markets, free trade, and economic growth. That was for me a source of both pride and hope.

Today, threats facing that model have grown more ominous, and our ability to withstand them feels less certain. Increasingly, by design or not, there appears to be a movement to undermine Americans' faith in our government and its policies and institutions. We've moved well beyond Ronald Reagan's credo that "government is the problem," with its aim of reversing decades of federal expansion. Today we see something very different and far more sinister. Nihilistic forces are dismantling policies to protect our air, water, and climate. And they seek to discredit the pillars of our democracy: voting rights and fair elections, the rule of law, the free press, the separation of powers, the belief in science, and the concept of truth itself.

Without these, the American example that my mother so cherished will revert to the kind of tyranny that once seemed to be on its way to extinction—though, sadly, it remains ensconced in some less fortunate parts of the world.

In the original edition of this book I observed that President Trump had not attacked the independent Federal Reserve, for which I was grateful. To say that is no longer true would be an understatement. Not since just after World War II have we seen a president so openly seek to dictate policy to the Fed. That is a matter of great concern, given that the Federal Reserve is one of our key governmental institutions, carefully designed to be free of purely partisan attacks. I trust that the members of the Federal Reserve Board itself, the members of Congress responsible for Fed oversight, and indeed the public at large will maintain the Fed's ability to act in the nation's interest, free of partisan political purposes.

Monetary policy is important, but it cannot by itself sustain global leadership. We need open markets and strong allies to support economic growth and the prospects for peace. Those constructive American policies have been a large part of my life. Instead, confidence in the United States is under siege.

Seventy-five years ago, Americans rose to the challenge of vanquishing tyranny overseas. We joined with our allies, keenly recognizing the need to defend and sustain our hard-won democratic freedoms.

Today's generation faces a different, but equally existential, test. How we respond will determine the future of our own democracy and, ultimately, of the planet itself. There is a need to "keep at it." It cannot be set aside.

ACKNOWLEDGMENTS

Acknowledgment is a long, four-syllable word, but not enough to convey my appreciation of my co-author. Christine Harper has been with me from start to finish, encouraging, prodding, disciplining, clarifying, correcting, and, not so incidentally, ably writing.

For reasons unknown, she willingly took leave from her responsibilities as a senior *Bloomberg News* financial editor to almost literally lead me by the hand. Get the facts right. Don't rely on fading recollections about whether B followed A, or vice versa. Memories are frail. Check those choice anecdotes with another participant.

After a year, I almost began to think of Christine as a member of the family, maybe a fourth younger sister who somehow had been lost and who thought my public servant father was the real hero. I can only hope that the finished work properly conveys her contributions and eases the way back to her professionally satisfying senior position at Bloomberg. I know for sure why she is so respected in that organization and more widely.

And now for the last time, my assistant Melanie Martha has produced a finished manuscript, transferring my virtually illegible writing into readable text and somehow ensuring that Christine's additions and subtractions are faithfully recorded. Melanie, soon to embark on a career in urban planning, has played a valuable role in organizing my office and my time. I wish her well in her new endeavors.

As mentioned, I relied on assistance from many people who diligently read all or some of this manuscript to help improve my recollections. For that I am especially grateful to Chuck Bowsher, Jacques de Larosière, John Dilulio, Tony Dowd, Edwin Gray, Judah Gribetz, Steve Harris, Frank Hydoski, Donald Kohn, Reid Morden, Bill Rhodes, Tom Seidenstein, and Ted Truman.

I am fortunate to have worked with Toyoo Gyohten and editor Larry Malkin on our 1992 book *Changing Fortunes*, which recounts some of the experiences I had earlier in my career. That book, along with fine biographies of me by Joseph Treaster and William Silber, were helpful references, as was Jeffrey Meyer and Mark Califano's book about our Oil-for-Food investigation, *Good Intentions Corrupted*.

At the New York Fed, Kenneth Garbade and Elizabeth Holmquist were unflaggingly helpful in tracking down economic data that's not always easy to find.

At Princeton University's Mudd Library, archivists Daniel Linke and Sara Logue have played an important part in preserving my papers and helped guide us through the process of combing through them for this project. They can anticipate a few more boxes as my papers accumulate.

My niece Victoria Streitfeld took the time to share a trove of old letters, photos, and other documents saved by her mother, my sister Virginia, that prodded memories. Her brother Andy also provided photos and has worked hard to produce a documentary about me and the Volcker Alliance that helps recognize both the challenge and the satisfaction of public service.

Both of my children, Janice and Jimmy, took time out of their busy lives to answer questions about long-ago events that they remembered better than I did. I am grateful to them for that, but more importantly for the innumerable ways in which they have enriched my life. I could not be a prouder father, grandfather (of three productive young men and one promising young woman), and even now a great-grandfather.

I don't know whether to thank or deplore the initiative of Peter Osnos, the founder of PublicAffairs, for stimulating some memories of the "old" days. It's been more than twenty-five years since he and I worked on *Changing Fortunes*. A memoir was far from my mind, but apparently not from Peter's a year or so ago. His winning argument was to produce Christine Harper as a co-author and, along the way, John Mahaney and a talented team at PublicAffairs who guided the editing and production process.

NOTES

Introduction. *The Wise Old Parrot*

2 *"its aptitude and tendency to produce"*: Alexander Hamilton, James Madison and John Jay, *The Federalist Papers* (New York, New American Library of World Literature, 1961), 414.

3 *"Polls show fewer than 20 percent of Americans"*: Pew Research Center, "Public Trust in Government: 1958–2017," http://www.people-press.org/2017/12/14/public-trust-in-government-1958-2017/.

Chapter 1. *Growing Up*

5 *"Government is a science"*: "1st City Manager in Jersey to Quit," *New York Times*, July 26, 1948, 9, https://timesmachine.nytimes.com/timesmachine/1948/07/26/85298535.pdf.

5 *his childhood in Brooklyn, New York:* Program from retirement dinner honoring Paul A. Volcker, still available on the town's website: http://www.teaneck.org/virtualvillage/Manager/volcker.pdf.

6 *"As the first official in such a capacity"*: "Paul A. Volcker for Municipal Manager of Cape May City," *Lebanon Daily News*, March 25, 1925, 1.

6 *No young Cape May maiden:* A quote attributed to my father at the time was "We cannot see the propriety of the most charming young women, many of them mere children, from other coast cities and inland communities, being sent with pomp and circumstance to Atlantic City, or any other city, once a year to be measured, weighed, appraised and gazed upon by a curious multitude." ("Beauty to Stay Home," *Wilmington Morning News*, June 12, 1925, 7.)

7 *"Do not suffer your good nature"*: The original quote was in a letter from Washington to Colonel George Baylor, January 9, 1777, https://founders.archives.gov/documents/Washington/03-08-02-0018.

8 *The Saturday Evening Post carried an article:* Edward T. Radin, "There's No Crime in Teaneck," *Saturday Evening Post*, July 28, 1945, http://www.teaneck.org/virtualvillage/police/no_crime_in_teaneck.htm.

8   *the US Army selected:* Kalman Seigel, "Teaneck on Film as Model Town,"
     New York Times, September 22, 1949, 28, https://timesmachine.nytimes.com
     /timesmachine/1949/09/22/84279327.pdf.

11   *He once took me out of school:* Here's how my teacher, Bill Moore, told it in
     a 1984 oral history interview: "Well, Paul Jr. was in my homeroom in 217 at
     the high school and he was absent one day and the next day he brought in
     the usual parental note, although it was a bit extraordinary coming from
     the township manager and it was a typewritten letter that read: 'Dear Mr.
     Moore, Please excuse Paul's absence from school yesterday. I took him fish-
     ing. I figure that a day of fishing is worth as much as a day in Teaneck high
     school. Paul A. Volcker, Sr.' Well, I didn't know what to do at first. There was
     nothing on the slip that we use, homeroom teachers use, to pass on to the
     other teachers that says, 'excused, went fishing.' But I excused Paul anyway
     and I have been glad ever since that I did. First of all, I have come to believe
     that Mr. Volcker was absolutely right and secondly, Paul still loves to go
     fishing and I think that a day of fishing with his dad was worth as much
     as a day at Teaneck High school," http://www.teaneck.org/virtualvillage/
     OralHistory2/moorewilliam.html.

11   *It was at Beaver Lake that I heard:* John Drebinger, "61,808 Fans Roar Trib-
     ute to Gehrig," *New York Times,* July 5, 1939, 1, https://timesmachine.ny
     times.com/timesmachine/1939/07/05/112698231.html?pageNumber=1.

13   *the very cream of women's colleges:* One of her classmates went on to marry
     Henry Morgenthau Jr., FDR's Treasury secretary.

Chapter 2. Getting an Education

17   *"training and education of men and women":* Form 4653, "Notification Con-
     cerning Foundation Status," signed by Charles Robertson on August 20,
     1970. Cited in Doug White, *Abusing Donor Intent: The Robertson Family's
     Epic Lawsuit Against Princeton University* (Paragon House, 2014), 96.

17   *twenty years later, it changed again:* Karin Dienst, "Princeton's informal
     motto recast to emphasize service to humanity," October 24, 2016, Prince-
     ton University website: https://www.princeton.edu/news/2016/10/24/
     princetons-informal-motto-recast-emphasize-service-humanity.

20   *President Truman remembered feeling cheated:* Federal Reserve transcript
     of the Federal Open Market Committee's January 31, 1951, meeting, p. 24,
     https://www.federalreserve.gov/monetarypolicy/files/FOMChistmin1951
     0131.pdf.

23   *and Willy Fellner:* Fellner, a visiting professor from Wesleyan, impressed
     me in particular one day when, in contrast to so many of my professors,
     he expressed uncertainty about a broadly accepted economic doctrine. He

made it apparent that there were problems in economic theory, including interest-rate analysis, for which he, a leading scholar, didn't know the answers.

24   *"All of us have seen":* Associated Press, "Morgenthau's Talk to Monetary Conference," *New York Times,* July 2, 1944, 14, https://timesmachine.ny times.com/timesmachine/1944/07/02/85184564.pdf.

24   *known for its corrupt local politics:* At the time, Kansas City was notorious for the power of its Pendergast political machine.

Chapter 3. Early Experience

31   *"just when the party was really warming up":* In the second to last paragraph of this 1955 speech he attributes the idea to another, unidentified, writer. See https://fraser.stlouisfed.org/scribd/?item_id=7800&filepath=/files/docs/historical/martin/martin55_1019.pdf.

33   *sixteen inches shorter:* Friedman was five feet, three inches tall, according to Milton Viorst, "friedmanism, n. doctrine of most audacious U.S. economist, esp. theory 'only money matters,'" *New York Times,* January 25, 1970, 196, https://www.nytimes.com/1970/01/25/archives/freidmanism-n-doctrine-of-most-audacious-us-economist-esp-theory.html.

33   *Much later I depended on:* September 12, 1979, letter to Milton Friedman from Paul Volcker papers, MC279, Box 1, September 1979 folder, Seeley G. Mudd Library, Princeton University archives.

33   *a report that, in his nineties:* Simon London, "Lunch with the FT, Milton Friedman: The Long View," *Financial Times* magazine supplement, issue no. 7, June 7, 2003, 12–13.

34   *had served in an Office of Strategic Services:* Charles Kindleberger, an economist best known for his 1978 book *Manias, Panics, and Crashes: A History of Financial Crises,* described the unique Office of Strategic Services unit of economists that he led, and in which Roosa served, in this oral history conducted for the Harry S. Truman Library. See https://www.trumanlibrary.org/oralhist/kindbrgr.htm.

36   *The dealers themselves were:* There's a helpful Federal Reserve research paper on the history of primary dealers at https://www.newyorkfed.org/media library/media/research/staff_reports/sr777.pdf?la=en.

40   *The combined Chase Manhattan:* Bank of America, allowed by California to establish branches throughout the state, was also large but was disparaged as a savings bank in commercial bank clothing.

42   *The comprehensive commission report:* The report was presented to President John F. Kennedy in June 1961. (John F. Kennedy: "Remarks to the Members of the Commission on Money and Credit," June 19, 1961. Online by

Gerhard Peters and John T. Woolley, American Presidency Project, http://www.presidency.ucsb.edu/ws/?pid=8195.)

44 *that wasn't where my heart lay:* A colleague, who ranked well above me and no doubt had his eye on future Chase leadership, asked me one day: "Where do you think you could go in the bank?" My model at the time was Citibank's strong economics department, where there were three people that held a lot of respect in the profession. One of them was vice chairman of the bank. So my answer was that I might like to become vice chairman of the bank and be, not a line officer, but a consultant, a consigliere. In a big institution with a lot of decisions to be made, it would be an honorable role and comfortable financially.

Chapter 4. Off to Washington

45 *running a balance-of-payments deficit:* The United States ran a balance-of-payments deficit for most of the 1950s, but foreign governments were willing to hold dollars and converted relatively little into gold. When foreign currencies became freely convertible in 1958, more capital moved overseas to earn higher interest rates and foreign central banks demanded more of the influx of dollars be converted into gold. See Federal Reserve Bank of St. Louis, "The United States Balance of Payments," March 1961, https://fraser.stlouisfed.org/files/docs/publications/frbslreview/rev_stls_196103.pdf/.

45 *he would not devalue the dollar:* Wayne Phillips, "Kennedy Pledges He Will Maintain Value of Dollar," *New York Times*, October 31, 1960, 1, https://timesmachine.nytimes.com/timesmachine/1960/10/31/105454271.pdf.

46 *my Washington opportunity:* My appointment was announced on December 28, 1961, and I started on January 8, 1962. Associated Press, "Fiscal Job Filled," *Wilmington Morning News*, December 29, 1961, 29.

46 *(such as a 5 percent economic growth target):* Walter Heller, head of Kennedy's Council of Economic Advisers, later remembered that Kennedy's first question to him in October 1960 was whether they could really attain the 5 percent growth target they'd promised during the campaign. (JFK Library, Council of Economic Advisers Oral History interview, JFK#1 08/1/1964, https://archive1.jfklibrary.org/JFKOH/Council%20of%20Economic%20Advisers/JFKOH-CEA-01/JFKOH-CEA-01-TR.pdf.)

46 *The tax program the president outlined:* The text of JFK's June 7, 1962, press conference is available at http://www.presidency.ucsb.edu/ws/index.php?pid=8698&st=&st1=. (John F. Kennedy: "The President's News Conference," June 7, 1962. Online by Gerhard Peters and John T. Woolley, American Presidency Project, http://www.presidency.ucsb.edu/ws/?pid=8698.)

48   *our gold stock was $20 billion:* These figures are derived from "Gold Reserves of Central Banks and Governments" charts contained in monthly Federal Reserve bulletins as well as Chart 15.1, "U.S. Liquid and Nonliquid Liabilities to Foreign Institutions and Liquid Liabilities to All Other Foreigners" from the Federal Reserve's "Banking and Monetary Statistics: 1941–1970." All are online at the St. Louis Fed's online FRASER service.

48   *the Treasury had practical support:* The balance of payments deficit and nuclear war were his two biggest worries, Kennedy used to tell his advisors, according to Arthur M. Schlesinger Jr. in *A Thousand Days: John F. Kennedy Jr. in the White House* (Houghton Mifflin Co., 1965, 652–665).

50   *interest equalization tax:* John F. Kennedy: "Special Message to the Congress on Balance of Payments," July 18, 1963. Online by Gerhard Peters and John T. Woolley, American Presidency Project, http://www.presidency.ucsb.edu/ws/?pid=9349.

50   *dollar deposits ordinarily kept in New York:* Clyde H. Farnsworth, "City of London Regains Status as Market for Raising Capital," *New York Times*, November 2, 1963, 45, https://timesmachine.nytimes.com/timesmachine/1963/11/02/89971248.pdf.

51   *(an under secretary's annual salary at the time):* Adren Cooper, Associated Press, "3½ Years of Robert V. Roosa Won't Be Easily Forgotten," *Cincinnati Inquirer*, December 6, 1964, 14D.

53   *"We're going to have a program":* And, indeed, one year after he was reelected, Johnson signed into law the Higher Education Act of 1965. (Lyndon B. Johnson: "Remarks at Southwest Texas State College Upon Signing the Higher Education Act of 1965," November 8, 1965. Online by Gerhard Peters and John T. Woolley, American Presidency Project, http://www.presidency.ucsb.edu/ws/?pid=27356.)

53   *he gave me a draft of a long speech:* "Remarks by Fowler on the International Monetary System," *New York Times*, July 11, 1965, 57, https://timesmachine.nytimes.com/timesmachine/1965/07/11/101555669.pdf.

55   *released a disappointed statement:* Lyndon B. Johnson, "Statement by the President on the Raising of the Discount Rate by the Federal Reserve Board," December 5, 1965. Online by Gerhard Peters and John T. Woolley, American Presidency Project, http://www.presidency.ucsb.edu/ws/?pid=27395.

56   *the dramatic new Chase skyscraper:* The 813-foot building was the sixth-tallest in the world when it opened in 1961. Charles Grutzner, "Chase Opens 64-Story Tower," *New York Times*, May 18, 1961, 24, https://timesmachine.nytimes.com/timesmachine/1961/05/18/101463880.pdf.

Chapter 5. *"The Best Job in the World"*

59 *(dated January 21):* The memo can be found at https://www.nixonlibrary.gov/virtuallibrary/documents/nssm/nssm_007.pdf. (Memo: Henry Kissinger to Secretaries of State, Treasury, Chairmen of the CEA and Federal Reserve, National Security Study Memorandum No. 7; January 21, 1969; Richard Nixon Presidential Library and Museum, Yorba Linda, California.)

61 *The conversation was not prolonged:* After the meeting Kennedy announced that Charls and I had been nominated, adding a statement that the United States wouldn't seek to change the price of gold. (Edwin L. Dale Jr., "Treasury's Chief Rules Out Change in $35 Gold Price," *New York Times*, January 23, 1969, 1.) Other reports said he made assurances the United States would act to curb inflation. (John R. Cauley, "Vows Drive on Inflation," *Kansas City Times*, January 23, 1969, 1.)

62 *At an emergency meeting:* Edwin L. Dale Jr., "7 Nations Back Dual Gold Price, Bar Selling to Private Buyers," *New York Times*, March 18, 1968, 1, https://timesmachine.nytimes.com/timesmachine/1968/03/18/79937229.pdf.

62 *He blamed the franc's weakness:* Henry Tanner, "De Gaulle Orders Austerity Plan, Wage-Price Freeze, Budget Cuts; Blames Spring Strikes for Crisis," *New York Times*, November 25, 1968, 1, https://timesmachine.nytimes.com/timesmachine/1968/11/25/76972133.pdf.

62 *Five months later:* Henry Tanner, "De Gaulle Quits After Losing Referendum; Senate Leader to Serve Pending Election," *New York Times*, April 28, 1969, 1, https://timesmachine.nytimes.com/timesmachine/1969/04/28/90099539.pdf.

63 *His principal intellectual opponent:* Their 1967 debate was preserved in a book by the Washington-based American Enterprise Institute. (Milton Friedman and Robert V. Roosa, "The Balance of Payments: Free Versus Fixed Exchange Rates," Washington, DC, American Enterprise Institute for Public Policy Research, 1967.)

64 *There had been "a lot of discussion":* Clyde Farnsworth, "U.S. Scores Idea of Money Reform," *New York Times*, February, 13, 1969, 63, https://timesmachine.nytimes.com/timesmachine/1969/02/13/77439795.pdf.

64 *Our remaining gold reserves:* Data compiled from "Banking and Monetary Statistics: 1941–1970, Board of Governors of the Federal Reserve System" and from Federal Reserve Bulletin July 1969, https://fraser.stlouisfed.org/scribd/?toc_id=333555&filepath=/files/docs/publications/FRB/1960s/frb_071969.pdf&start_page=144.

64 *the French did devalue:* Clyde H. Farnsworth, "Franc Is Devalued to 18C," *New York Times*, August 9, 1969, 1, https://timesmachine.nytimes.com/timesmachine/1969/08/09/78389549.pdf.

65   *It made for a rather long:* See summary at https://history.state.gov/historical documents/frus1969-76v03/d130. (Foreign Relations of the United States, 1969–1976, Volume III, Foreign Economic Policy; International Monetary Policy, 1969–1972, Document 130.)

66   *We succeeded, but with a reduced amount:* Edwin L. Dale Jr., "I.M.F. Nations Vote for 'Paper Gold' as a World Money," *New York Times*, October 4, 1969, 1, https://timesmachine.nytimes.com/timesmachine/1969/10/04/81867494 .pdf.

68   *"If they aren't willing to accept Iowa beef":* This line and its anti-Japan protectionist sentiment became a prominent feature in his later, and unsuccessful, 1980 presidential campaign. Paul Burka, "The Truth About John Connally," *Texas Monthly*, November 1979, https://www.texasmonthly.com/politics/ the-truth-about-john-connally/.

68   *Arthur Burns's own diaries:* Robert H. Farrell, ed., *Inside the Nixon Administration: The Secret Diary of Arthur Burns, 1969–1974* (University Press of Kansas, 2010).

69   *In early May:* Clyde H. Farnsworth, "Germans Decide to 'Float' Mark in Money Crisis," *New York Times*, May 9, 1971, 1, https://timesmachine.ny times.com/timesmachine/1971/05/09/91298207.pdf.

69   *"Helpful to the solution of any problem":* Paul Volcker and Toyoo Gyohten, *Changing Fortunes* (Times Books, 1992), 74–75.

70   *The world of finance quickly understood:* Clyde H. Farnsworth, "Connally Tells Bankers U.S. Will Defend Dollar," *New York Times*, 28, May 29, 1971, 28, https://www.nytimes.com/1971/05/29/archives/connally-tells-bankers -us-will-defend-dollar-burns-also-at-munich.html.

70   *After a lot of internal debate:* James M. Naughton, "Nixon Vetoes a Works Plan; Bars Tax Cut," *New York Times*, June 30, 1971, 1, https://www.nytimes .com/1971/06/30/archives/nixon-vetoes-a-works-plan-bars-tax-cut -confidence-cited-connally-to.html.

71   *He reported to me by early August:* An account of Connally's discussions with Nixon in the White House, saved on taped recordings, is available at https://history.state.gov/historicaldocuments/frus1969-76v03/d164. (Foreign Relations of the United States, 1969–1976, Volume III, Foreign Economic Policy; International Monetary Policy, 1969–1972, Document 164.)

71   *The activist and ambitious Henry Reuss:* Edwin L. Dale, "Devalued Dollar Is Asked in Study," *New York Times*, August 8, 1971, 1, https://www.nytimes .com/1971/08/08/archives/devalued-dollar-is-asked-in-study-congress -unit-sees-benefits-in.html.

71   *Two months earlier:* Edwin L. Dale Jr., "Shift in Monetary Set-Up Is Proposed in House," *New York Times*, June 4, 1971, 45, https://www.nytimes .com/1971/06/04/archives/shift-in-monetary-setup-is-proposed-in-the -house-reuss-resolution.html.

71   *He rushed back:* An account of their discussions is available at https://history
      .state.gov/historicaldocuments/frus1969-76v03/d165. (Foreign Relations of
      the United States, 1969–1976, Volume III, Foreign Economic Policy; Inter-
      national Monetary Policy, 1969–1972, Document 165.)

72   *All of the discussion was later reported:* William Safire, *Before the Fall: An In-
      side View of the Pre-Watergate White House* (Doubleday, 1975).

73   *justifying the import surcharge:* Richard Nixon: "Proclamation 4074—Impo-
      sition of Supplemental Duty for Balance of Payments Purposes," August 15,
      1971. Online by Gerhard Peters and John T. Woolley, American Presidency
      Project, http://www.presidency.ucsb.edu/ws/?pid=107023.

73   *The State Department wasn't represented:* On an August 2, 1971, White House
      tape, Nixon can be heard telling Connally that any consultations abroad
      about the potential program should be handled by Kissinger: "Under no
      circumstances was the State Department to be consulted as that agency
      represented foreign governments." Foreign Relations of the United States,
      1969–1976, Volume III, Foreign Economic Policy; International Monetary
      Policy, 1969–1972, 455, https://history.state.gov/historicaldocuments/frus
      1969-76v03/d164.

73   *So far as I know, no one really cared:* Amending the Canadian-American
      Automotive Agreement was, however, included among a broader discussion
      of "trade irritants" between United States and Canadian economic officials
      on December 6, 1971. See https://history.state.gov/historicaldocuments/
      frus1969-76v03/d85. (Foreign Relations of the United States, 1969–1976,
      Volume III, Foreign Economic Policy; International Monetary Policy,
      1969–1972, Document 85.)

Chapter 6. Monetary Reform Frustrated

75   *He was instead taking "bold leadership":* Richard Nixon, "Address to the Na-
      tion Outlining a New Economic Policy: 'The Challenge of Peace,'" August
      15, 1971. Online by Gerhard Peters and John T. Woolley, American Presi-
      dency Project, http://www.presidency.ucsb.edu/ws/?pid=3115.

75   *Stocks soared:* "Ebullient Investors Send Stocks Soaring in Record Day's
      Climb," *Wall Street Journal*, August 17, 1971, 1.

75   *Full reform of the system:* A summary of the discussion, prepared by Sam
      Cross, is available at https://history.state.gov/historicaldocuments/frus
      1969-76v03/d170. (Foreign Relations of the United States, 1969–1976, Vol-
      ume III, Foreign Economic Policy; International Monetary Policy, 1969–
      1972, Document 170.)

76   *An emergency Group of Ten meeting:* John M. Lee, "Currency Parley Enliv-
      ens Trading," *New York Times*, September 20, 1971, 39, https://www.nytimes

.com/1971/09/20/archives/currency-parley-elivens-trading-one-result-of
-group-of-10s-meeting.html.

76   *Connally called for a $13 billion swing:* A description of our reasoning is available at https://history.state.gov/historicaldocuments/frus1969-76v03/d76. (Foreign Relations of the United States, 1969–1976, Volume III, Foreign Economic Policy; International Monetary Policy, 1969–1972, Document 76.)

77   *we were looking toward an 11 percent drop:* Clyde H. Farnsworth, "U.S. Ready to End Surtax If Currencies Go Up 11%," *New York Times*, November 30, 1971, 1, https://www.nytimes.com/1971/11/30/archives/us-ready-to-end-sur tax-if-currencies-go-up-11-group-of-10-seeking.html.

77   *That offer, we explained:* Connally's memo to Nixon from Rome outlining our position can be accessed at https://history.state.gov/historicaldocu ments/frus1969-76v03/d211. (Foreign Relations of the United States, 1969–1976, Volume III, Foreign Economic Policy; International Monetary Policy, 1969–1972, Document 211.)

78   *progress had been made:* Clyde H. Farnsworth, "Progress at the Palazzo Corsini," *New York Times*, December 5, 1971, 315, https://www.nytimes .com/1971/12/05/archives/progress-at-the-palazzo-corsini-devaluation -hint-by-us-unlocks.html.

78   *The terms were pretty well settled:* Tad Szulc, "Nixon Agrees to a Devaluation of Dollar as Part of Revision of Major Currencies," *New York Times*, December 15, 1971, 1, https://www.nytimes.com/1971/12/15/archives/pact-with -france-azores-talks-opening-way-to-wide-accord-in.html.

78   *That would depreciate the dollar:* A copy of the memo signed by Pompidou and Nixon is available at https://history.state.gov/historicaldocuments/frus 1969-76v03/d220. (Foreign Relations of the United States, 1969–1976, Volume III, Foreign Economic Policy; International Monetary Policy, 1969–1972, Document 220.)

79   *realigning so many currencies:* Connally said at the press conference after the Smithsonian meeting that the dollar would depreciate by an average of 12 percent against other OECD countries, without providing specific exchange rates. See https://history.state.gov/historicaldocuments/frus1969 -76v03/d221. (Foreign Relations of the United States, 1969–1976, Volume III, Foreign Economic Policy; International Monetary Policy, 1969–1972, Document 221.)

79   *He did so in grand style:* The text of Nixon's statement can be accessed at http://www.presidency.ucsb.edu/ws/index.php?pid=3268&st=&st1=. (Richard Nixon: "Remarks Announcing a Monetary Agreement Following a Meeting of the Group of Ten," December 18, 1971. Online by Gerhard Peters and John T. Woolley, American Presidency Project, http://www .presidency.ucsb.edu/ws/?pid=3268.)

80   *some official intervention was required:* Michael Stern, "Devaluation Fear Spurs a Renewal of Dollar Sales," *New York Times*, February 9, 1973, 1, https://www.nytimes.com/1973/02/09/archives/devaluation-fear-spurs-a -renewal-of-dollar-sales-bonn-buys-up-16.html.

80   *Secretary Connally had resigned:* In his memoir, Connally explained that he resigned after Nixon failed to keep his promise to consult with Connally on appointments to the Treasury. John Connally with Mickey Herkowitz, *In History's Shadow: An American Odyssey* (Hyperion, 1993).

81   *Secretary Shultz unveiled the changes:* Edwin L. Dale Jr., "U.S. Orders Dollar Devalued 10 Per Cent; Japanese Yen Will Be Allowed to Float; Nixon to Submit Trade Plan to Congress," *New York Times*, February 13, 1973, 1, https://www.nytimes.com/1973/02/13/archives/gold-to-be-4222-controls -on-lending-abroad-also-will-be-phased-out.html.

81   *soon jumped sharply higher:* Clyde H. Farnsworth, "Gold Touches $90 as Dollar Erodes in Trade Abroad," *New York Times*, February 23, , https:// www.nytimes.com/1973/02/23/archives/gold-touches-90-as-dollar-erodes -in-trade-abroad-renewed.html.

82   *By early March, speculative pressures:* Clyde H. Farnsworth, "Monetary Crisis Flares Up Again; Dollar Weakens," *New York Times*, March 2, 1973, 1, https://www.nytimes.com/1973/03/02/archives/monetary-crisis-flares-up -again-dollar-weakens-markets-closed-us-is.html.

82   *"Whatever happens to the discount rate":* Clyde H. Farnsworth, "U.S. and 13 Others Adopt Measures on Dollar Crisis," *New York Times*, March 17, 1973, 1, https://www.nytimes.com/1973/03/17/archives/us-and-130-others-adopt -measures-on-dollar-crisis-plans-are.html.

83   *a forward-looking speech:* "Text of Shultz Talk Before International Monetary Fund and World Bank," *New York Times*, September 27, 1972, 70, https://www.nytimes.com/1972/09/27/archives/text-of-shultz-talk-before -international-monetary-fund-and-world.html.

84   *Schweitzer recognized that:* Edwin L. Dale Jr., "Schweitzer of I.M.F. Won't Quit His Post Despite U.S. Stand," *New York Times*, September 24, 1972, 1, https://www.nytimes.com/1972/09/24/archives/schweitzer-of-imf-wont -quit-his-post-despite-us-stand-schweitzer.html.

84   *Secretary Shultz's constructive speech:* Edwin L. Dale, "New U.S. Monetary Plan Asks Wider Fluctuation in World Exchange Rates," *New York Times*, September 27, 1972, 1. https://timesmachine.nytimes.com/timesmachine /1972/09/27/91349838.pdf

85   *Floating would remain as a last resort:* See "Major Elements of Plan X" at https://history.state.gov/historicaldocuments/frus1969-76v03/d239. (Foreign Relations of the United States, 1969–1976, Volume III, Foreign Economic Policy; International Monetary Policy, 1969–1972, Document 239.)

85   *He patiently tested my ideas:* The rather complicated proposal was fully laid out in the 1973 annual report of the Council of Economic Advisers.

90   *Fannie Mae squeaked through:* Kenneth B. Noble, "Fannie Mae Loses $70 Million," *New York Times*, January 19, 1982, D3, https://www.nytimes .com/1982/01/19/business/fannie-mae-loses-70-million.html.

91   *six- or seven-figure compensation:* See November 23, 1973, letter from head-hunter Russell Reynolds seeking a meeting about just such a position at a leading financial firm. Balance of Payments folder 1, Box 23, MC279, Paul Volcker papers, Mudd Library, Princeton University special collection.

91   *when we moved to Cleveland Avenue:* The Cleveland Avenue home in DC was about half the size of my beloved Montclair house. It was located on a fifty-foot lot that had been carved out of the estate of Cliff Folger, founder of the investment bank Folger, Nolan & Company. He later bought the house and tore it down.

Chapter 7. Back to the Beginning

97   *from a 1974 peak near 5,300:* Chart 8, Federal Reserve Bank of New York, annual report, 1979.

99   *declined to bring any action:* Jeff Gerth, "S.E.C. Overruled Staff on Finding That Citicorp Hid Foreign Profits," *New York Times*, February 18, 1982, 1, https://www.nytimes.com/1982/02/18/business/sec-overruled-staff-on -finding-that-citicorp-hid-foreign-profits.html.

100   *"maintain long run growth":* The text of the act, Public Law 95-188, 95th Congress, H.R. 9710 is available online through the Government Publishing Office at https://www.gpo.gov/fdsys/pkg/STATUTE-91/pdf/STATUTE -91-Pg1387.pdf.

100   *The following year, Congress passed:* President Jimmy Carter's comments upon signing the bill are available at Jimmy Carter: "Full Employment and Comprehensive Employment and Training Act Bills Remarks on Signing H.R. 50 and S. 2570 Into Law," October 27, 1978. Online by Gerhard Peters and John T. Woolley, American Presidency Project, http://www.presidency .ucsb.edu/ws/?pid=30057.

100   *He found himself outvoted:* The June 30, 1978, decision to raise the discount rate to 7.25 percent was passed with a three to two vote, in which Miller was in the minority. Steven Rattner, "Miller Opposes Move to 7 ¼% Discount Level," *New York Times*, July 1, 1978, 23, https://www.nytimes.com/1978/07/01/ archives/miller-opposes-move-to-7-discount-level-fed-acts.html.

Chapter 8. Attacking Inflation

102   *rising 13 percent a year:* Clyde H. Farnsworth, "Prices Rose Sharply Again in May, Spurred by Increasing Costs of Fuel," *New York Times*, June 27, 1979,

1, https://www.nytimes.com/1979/06/27/archives/prices-rose-sharply-again
-in-may-spurred-by-increasing-costs-of.html.

102   *and made a speech:* Jimmy Carter: "Address to the Nation on Energy and
National Goals: 'The Malaise Speech,'" July 15, 1979. Online by Gerhard
Peters and John T. Woolley, American Presidency Project, http://www
.presidency.ucsb.edu/ws/?pid=32596.

103   *was not confidence building:* Indeed, by the end of the week, on Friday, July
20, the Fed had to raise the discount rate half a percentage point to 10 percent and intervened in markets to support the dollar.

103   *I got on the shuttle:* The New York–Washington shuttle at that time was a true
shuttle. The planes were smaller, but they were available every hour and if they
filled up, additional planes came into service. It was possible to make the entire
trip, door to door, in less than two hours in those pre-September 11 days.

104   *the board took action:* Karen W. Arenson, "Reserve Raises Loan Rate to
Banks to Record 10½% from 10% Level," *New York Times*, August 17, 1979, 1,
https://www.nytimes.com/1979/08/17/archives/reserve-raises-loan-rate-to
-banks-to-record-10-from-10-level.html.

105   *The vote was split 4-3:* Robert A. Bennett, "Reserve Board, by 4-3, Raises
Rate on Loans to Banks to Record 11%," *New York Times*, September 19,
1979, 1, https://www.nytimes.com/1979/09/19/archives/reserve-board-by-43
-raises-rate-on-loans-to-banks-to-record-11.html.

105   *But the market saw it differently:* A typical comment came from Lawrence
Kudlow, then an economist at Bear Stearns. The split vote "suggests circum-
stantially that future policy adjustments will be of a timid nature." Associated Press, "Fed Boosts Discount Rate But Vote Is Not Unanimous," *St.
Louis Post-Dispatch*, September 19, 1979, 6.

105   *gold hit a new record:* Robert D. Hershey Jr. "Gold Price Soars at Record
Pace in Wild Trading," *New York Times*, September 19, 1979, 1, https://www
.nytimes.com/1979/09/19/archives/gold-price-soars-at-record-pace-in
-wild-trading-hits-37778-at.html.

105   *I myself, some years ago:* Paul A. Volcker, "The Contributions and Limitations
of 'Monetary' Analysis" address delivered before the Joint Luncheon of the
American Economic Association and the American Finance Association in
Atlantic City, New Jersey, September 16, 1976. *FRBNY Quarterly Review*,
https://www.newyorkfed.org/medialibrary/media/aboutthefed/monanal.pdf.

107   *in which he (infamously) expressed doubt:* Clyde H. Farnsworth, "Burns
Cites Limits on Fed Powers," *New York Times*, October 1, 1979, 45, https://
timesmachine.nytimes.com/timesmachine/1979/10/01/112122164.html?page
Number=45.

107   *including that I had resigned or died:* I jokingly referred to these rumors to begin the October 6 press conference: "I will tell you that the major purpose of
this press conference is to show you that I have not resigned—the way the

early rumor had it yesterday—and I am still alive—contrary to the latest rumor." (Transcript of Federal Reserve press conference, October 6, 1979, Paul A. Volcker papers (MC279), folder October 6, 1979 action, Box 29, Mudd Manuscript Library, Department of Rare Books and Special Collections, Princeton University Library.)

107 *I did read this one:* The transcript is available on the Federal Reserve's website at https://www.federalreserve.gov/monetarypolicy/files/FOMC19791006meeting.pdf.

108 *The rate on three-month Treasury bills:* Data on Treasury bills and commercial prime bank lending rates were collected from Federal Reserve Board H.15 reports from 1979 to 1987; data on mortgage rates from weekly thirty-year mortgage rates are from Freddie Mac at http://www.freddiemac.com/pmms. Compiled with help from Kenneth Garbade at the New York Fed.

109 *For half an hour we exchanged views:* Associated Press, "Demonstrators Protest High Interest Rates," *Tampa Times*, April 14, 1980, 11.

109 *The Fed insisted I agree to:* This decision was referenced in the April 15, 1981, Federal Reserve memo "Personal Security" to Volcker from John M. Denkler. Paul A. Volcker papers (MC279), folder memoranda from Michael Bradfield, Box 29, Mudd Manuscript Library, Department of Rare Books and Special Collections, Princeton University Library.

109 *A year later an armed man:* UPI, "Suspect Is Seized in Capital in Threat at Federal Reserve," *New York Times*, December 8, 1981, 19, https://www.nytimes.com/1981/12/08/us/suspect-is-seized-in-capital-in-threat-at-federal-reserve.html.

110 *The president's initial budget:* Jimmy Carter: "Budget Message: Message to the Congress Transmitting the Fiscal Year 1981 Budget," January 28, 1980. Online by Gerhard Peters and John T. Woolley, American Presidency Project, http://www.presidency.ucsb.edu/ws/?pid=32851.

110 *the message of restraint was diluted:* Carter's revamped budget, submitted on March 31, estimated a $16.5 billion surplus. Spending was down just $4.3 billion from the January version and the surplus was mostly from a $12.6 billion oil import fee. Jimmy Carter: "Budget Revisions Message to the Congress Transmitting Revisions to the Fiscal Year 1981 Budget," March 31, 1980. Online by Gerhard Peters and John T. Woolley, American Presidency Project, http://www.presidency.ucsb.edu/ws/?pid=33205.

111 *The president's anti-inflation program:* Jimmy Carter: "Anti-Inflation Program Remarks Announcing the Administration's Program," March 14, 1980. Online by Gerhard Peters and John T. Woolley, American Presidency Project, http://www.presidency.ucsb.edu/ws/?pid=33142.

111 *a mildly critical comment:* Clyde H. Farnsworth, "Volcker Criticized by Carter on Rates," *New York Times*, October 3, 1980, 1, https://timesmachine.nytimes.com/timesmachine/1980/10/03/111177523.pdf.

114 *the threats of impeachment:* Democratic Texas Rep. Henry B. Gonzalez, in particular, introduced legislation calling for my impeachment and the impeachment of the other members of the FOMC. It went nowhere. See https://www.congress.gov/bill/97th-congress/house-resolution/196.

114 *I was invited to address:* "Housing Recovery Tied to Inflation," *New York Times,* January 26, 1982, D11, http://www.nytimes.com/1982/01/26/business/housing-recovery-tied-to-inflation.html?scp=787&sq=volcker&st=nyt.

115 *The markets took off:* Michael Quint, "Interest Plunges, Elevating Stocks to a Record Gain," *New York Times,* August 18,1982, 1, https://www.nytimes.com/1982/08/18/business/interest-plunges-elevating-stocks-to-a-record-gain.html.

115 *its price had been marked down:* I told a version of this story to journalist Andrew Tobias in 1982. He included it in his piece "A Talk with Paul Volcker," *New York Times,* September 19, 1982, 271, https://timesmachine.nytimes.com/timesmachine/1982/09/19/issue.html.

116 *it was a matter of tactics:* Peter T. Kilborn, "Volcker Suggests Federal Reserve May Shift Tactics," *New York Times,* October 10, 1982, 1, https://www.nytimes.com/1982/10/10/us/volcker-suggests-federal-reserve-may-shift-tactics.html.

117 *The president recorded that:* see entry for Tuesday, June 7, 1983 in Ronald Reagan, "The Reagan Diaries" (HarperCollins, 2007), 158.

117 *It split symmetrically:* CQ Almanac, 1983, https://library.cqpress.com/cq almanac/document.php?id=cqal83-1198874.

118 *I was summoned to a meeting:* The 3:30 p.m. July 24, 1984, meeting in the library is recorded in Reagan's daily schedule, although it says Edwin Meese, Richard Darman, and Michael Deaver were present and to my memory they were certainly not. Reagan didn't write anything about the meeting in his daily diary. See https://www.reaganfoundation.org/ronald-reagan/white-house-diaries/diary-entry-07241984/.

Chapter 9. *Financial Crises, Domestic and International*

120 *He famously complained:* "Bank Failures Lag; Patman Is Worried," *New York Times,* June 17, 1963, 48, https://timesmachine.nytimes.com/timesmachine/1963/06/17/89537226.pdf.

121 *Federal assistance was considered:* Robert B. Semple Jr., "Rejection of Pennsy Loan Is Laid to Political Risks," *New York Times,* 1, June 23, 1970, https://www.nytimes.com/1970/06/23/archives/rejection-of-pennsy-loan-is-laid-to-political-risks-sidetracking-of.html.

121 *The sudden shutdown:* Reuters, "Big Bank Closed by West Germany," *New York Times,* June 27, 1974, 65, https://www.nytimes.com/1974/06/27/archives/big-bank-closed-by-west-germany-privatee-institution-herstat-of.html.

121   *So was the failure:* John H. Allan, "Franklin Found Insolvent by U.S. and Taken Over," New York Times, October 9, 1974, 1, https://www.nytimes .com/1974/10/09/archives/franklin-found-insolvent-by-us-and-taken-over -european-group-in.html.

121   *a victim of fraud:* Arnold H. Lubasch, "Sindona Is Convicted by U.S. Jury of Fraud in Franklin Bank Failure," *New York Times,* March 28, 1980, 1, https:// timesmachine.nytimes.com/timesmachine/1980/03/28/112148354.pdf.

122   *Congress created a three-man committee:* Judmi Miller, "Congress Approves a Compromise Plan on Aid to Chrysler," *New York Times,* December 21, 1979, 1, https://www.nytimes.com/1979/12/21/archives/congress-approves -a-compromise-plan-on-aid-to-chrysler-15-billion.html.

122   *New management was brought aboard:* Bernard D. Nossiter, "Chrysler Chairman Will Retire Early," *New York Times,* September 18, 1979, 1, https://www .nytimes.com/1979/09/18/archives/chrysler-chairman-will-retire-early -riccardo-plans-to-leave.html.

122   *They agreed to take the haircut:* UPI, "Chrysler Announces Accord with Banks," *New York Times,* February 26, 1981, D5, https://www.nytimes.com /1981/02/26/business/chrysler-announces-accord-with-banks.html.

123   *Chrysler ended up paying:* Thomas J. Lueck, "Chrysler Tops Bids to Buy Back Stock Rights," *New York Times,* September 13, 1983, 1, https://www.nytimes .com/1983/09/13/business/chrysler-top-bids-to-buy-back-stock-rights.html.

124   *first imposing position limits:* Robert A. Bennett, "Position Limits Adopted in Comex Silver Futures," *New York Times,* January 8, 1980, D1, https://times machine.nytimes.com/timesmachine/1980/01/08/111760374.pdf.

124   *then limiting trades:* H. J. Maidenberg, "Comex Curbs Trade in Silver Futures," *New York Times,* January 22, 1980, D1, https://timesmachine.nytimes .com/timesmachine/1980/01/22/111137098.pdf.

124   *"purely speculative holdings":* Federal Reserve Press Release, March 14, 1980, 3. Papers of Paul A. Volcker (MC279), Folder: Monetary Improvement Program, Box 29. Mudd Library, Department of Rare Books and Special Collections, Princeton University Library.

125   *attracted congressional and public attention:* Paul A. Volcker, Statement Before the Subcommittee on Agricultural Research and General Legislation, U.S. Senate Committee on Agriculture, Nutrition and Forestry, May 1, 1980, https://fraser.stlouisfed.org/files/docs/historical/volcker/Volcker_1980 0501.pdf.

125   *Led by John Bunting:* Mario A. Milletti, "First Pennsy's Golden Boy," *New York Times,* September 25, 1977, 119, https://www.nytimes.com/1977/09/25/ archives/first-pennsys-golden-boy.html.

125   *provided a $1.5 billion rescue:* "First Penn to Receive Rescue Aid," *New York Times,* April 29, 1980, D1, https://timesmachine.nytimes.com/timesmachine /1980/04/29/111234761.pdf.

125 *enough to provide a controlling majority:* Irvine H. Sprague, *Bailout: An Insider's Account of Bank Failures and Rescues* (Basic Books, 1986) 96.

125 *The failure of two:* Vartanig G. Vartan, "Drysdale Securities Out of Business," *New York Times,* June 16, 1982, D1, https://www.nytimes.com/1982/06/16/ business/drysdale-securities-out-of-business.html.

126 *notably to Continental Illinois:* Robert A. Bennett, "Bigger Banks Are Hurt by Failure in Oklahoma," *New York Times,* July 7, 1982, D1, https://www .nytimes.com/1982/07/07/business/bigger-banks-are-hurt-by-failure-in -oklahoma.html.

127 *who had already agreed to:* Robert A. Bennett, "$4.5 Billion Credit for Chicago Bank Set by 16 Others," *New York Times,* May 15, 1984, 1.

127 *needed to restore full confidence:* Winston Williams, "U.S. Puts Together $7.5 Billion in Aid for Illinois Bank," *New York Times,* May 18, 1984, 1, https:// www.nytimes.com/1984/05/18/business/us-puts-together-7.5-billion-in-aid -for-illinois-bank.html.

127 *The de facto guarantee of the FDIC:* The press release included this key sentence: "In view of all the circumstances surrounding Continental Illinois Bank, the FDIC provides assurance that, in any arrangements that may be necessary to find a permanent solution, all depositors and other general creditors of the bank will be fully protected and service to the bank's customers will not be interrupted." Reprinted on p. 70, William H. Isaac, *Senseless Panic: How Washington Failed America* (John Wiley & Sons, 2010).

128 *the FDIC negotiated a second rescue:* Robert A. Bennett, "U.S. Will Invest $4.5 Billion in Rescue of Chicago Bank, Vowing More Aid If Needed," *New York Times,* July 27, 1984, 1, https://www.nytimes.com/1984/07/27/business/ us-will-invest-4.5-billion-in-rescue-of-chicago-bank-vowing-more-aid-if -needed.html.

129 *Newly appointed by President Reagan:* Ronald Reagan: "Nomination of Edwin J. Gray to Be a Member of the Federal Home Loan Bank Board," February 17, 1983. Online by Gerhard Peters and John T. Woolley, American Presidency Project, http://www.presidency.ucsb.edu/ws/?pid=40941.

130 *got caught up in an attempt to browbeat Gray:* Dan Fesperman, "Former Regulator Blames S&L Crisis on Congress," *Baltimore Sun,* November 27, 1990, http://articles.baltimoresun.com/1990-11-27/news/1990331046_1_loan -crisis-ethics-committee-gray.

130 *The ultimate cost to the federal government:* "U.S. taxpayer losses amounted to $123.8 billion, or 81 percent of the total costs." Timothy Curry and Lynn Shibut, "The Cost of the Savings and Loan Crisis: Truth and Consequences," *FDIC Banking Review,* December 2000, https://www.fdic.gov/ bank/analytical/banking/br2000v13n2.pdf.

130 *in today's money:* Calculated from $123.8 billion in June 1989 using the Bureau of Labor Statistics Inflation Calculator: https://www.bls.gov/data/ inflation_calculator.htm.

130   The Best Way to Rob a Bank Is to Own One: University of Texas Press, 2005.

131   *more than twice the capital of the eight largest:* FDIC Division of Research and Statistics, "An Examination of the Banking Crises of the 1980s and early 1990s," ch. 5. "The LDC Debt Crisis," https://www.fdic.gov/bank/historical/history/191_210.pdf.

131   *a fluent English speaker with a graduate degree:* Alan Riding, "Man in the News; Survivor: Jesus Silva Herzog," *New York Times*, August 21, 1982, 29, http://www.nytimes.com/1982/08/21/business/man-in-the-news-survivor-jesus-silva-herzog.html.

132   *the huge consequences a Mexican default:* Edward Cowan, "Loans and Credits for Aiding Mexico Are Mapped by U.S.," *New York Times*, August 21, 1982, 1, https://www.nytimes.com/1982/08/21/business/loans-and-credits-for-aiding-mexico-are-mapped-by-us.html.

133   *he explained to the press:* Robert A. Bennett, "Bankers Pressured to Assist Mexico," *New York Times*, August 21, 1982, 32, https://www.nytimes.com/1982/08/21/business/bankers-pressured-to-assist-mexico.html.

134   *De Larosière instinctively moved rapidly:* Jacques de Larosière has written his own memoir, published in 2017 by Éditions Odile Jacob. The title of the English translation is *50 Years of Financial Crises.*

135   *announced at the October 1985 IMF meeting:* Ronald E. Yates, "Baker's Plan May Be Too Late," *Chicago Tribune*, October 9, 1985, http://articles.chicago tribune.com/1985-10-09/business/8503080744_1_debt-crisis-world-bank-baker-plan.

Chapter 10. Unfinished Business: Repairing the Financial System

139   *some analysts compared the German effort:* James Sterngold, "Dollar Falls Sharply on Bonn Move," *New York Times*, September 22, 1984, 39, https://www.nytimes.com/1984/09/22/business/dollar-falls-sharply-on-bonn-move.html.

139   *the Treasury responded to a plea:* Peter F. Kilborn, "Reagan's New Dollar Strategy," *New York Times*, March 3, 1985, 141, https://www.nytimes.com/1985/03/03/business/reagan-s-new-dollar-strategy.html.

139   *were becoming intrigued by:* Paul Lewis, "Plan Emerging on Currency Rates," *New York Times*, March 18, 1985, D1, https://www.nytimes.com/1985/03/18/business/plan-emerging-on-currency-rates.html.

140   *I was shoved to the front:* Peter T. Kilborn, "U.S. and 4 Allies Plan Move to Cut Value of Dollar," *New York Times*, September 23, 1985, 1, https://www.nytimes.com/1985/09/23/business/us-and-4-allies-plan-move-to-cut-value-of-dollar.html.

141   *A front-page story the next day:* Peter T. Kilborn, "Group of 5 Hints at Effort to Cut Interest Charges," *New York Times*, January 20, 1986, 1, https://www

.nytimes.com/1986/01/20/business/group-of-5-hints-at-effort-to-cut
-interest-charges.html.

141 *a public reprimand was in order:* From a conference I was attending in Tokyo, I released a statement calling Martin's suggestions for a policy shift in
Latin America "incomprehensible" and praised the efforts then under way
by Latin American governments to manage their debt. (Robert A. Bennett, "Volcker Rebukes Martin on 3d-World Debt Ideas," *New York Times*,
June 21, 1985, D2, https://www.nytimes.com/1985/06/21/business/volcker
-rebukes-martin-on-3d-world-debt-ideas.html).

142 *That is what happened in early March:* Susan Chira, "Japan Says It Will Join
in Rate Cut; French, Dutch Follow Lead of West Germans," *New York
Times*, March 7, 1986, D1, https://www.nytimes.com/1986/03/07/business/
japan-says-it-will-join-in-rate-cut.html.

142 *Preston Martin resigned:* Robert D. Hershey, "Martin Resigning from Fed;
Denies Move Is Tied to Dispute with Volcker," *New York Times*, March 22,
1986, 35, http://www.nytimes.com/1986/03/22/business/martin-resigning
-from-fed.html.

143 *hands full with Irangate:* Irangate, also known as the "Iran-Contra affair,"
was a political scandal that involved covert sales of arms to Iran, in violation
of an arms embargo, to help fund anti-communist Contras in Nicaragua
after Congress had prohibited further funding.

144 *it called for a G-5 meeting:* Peter T. Kilborn, "Accord on Dollar Appears
Remote," *New York Times*, 13, February 22, 1987, https://www.nytimes.com
/1987/02/22/world/accord-on-dollar-appears-remote.html.

145 *the dollar was slipping below its band:* Robert D. Hershey Jr., "Volcker Sees
Danger to Economy of U.S. If Dollar Falls More," *New York Times*, April 8,
1987, 1. https://www.nytimes.com/1987/04/08/business/volcker-sees-danger
-to-economy-of-us-if-dollar-falls-more.html.

145 *called for greater attention to exchange rates:* The text of the speech is at https://
piie.com/commentary/speeches-papers/quest-exchange-rate-stability
-realistic-or-quixotic.

147 *At the end of a European tour:* Charles Goodhart, *The Basel Committee on
Banking Supervision: A History of the Early Years, 1974–1997* (Cambridge
University Press, 2011).

147 *announced in early 1987:* Nathaniel C. Nash, "Similar Standards for Banks
Are Set by U.S. and Britain," *New York Times*, January 9, 1987, 1, https://
www.nytimes.com/1987/01/09/business/similar-standards-for-banks-are
-set-by-us-and-britain.html.

148 *the final rules later that year:* Nathaniel C. Nash, "12 Countries Want Banks
to Increase Capital," *New York Times*, December 11, 1987, 1, https://www
.nytimes.com/1987/12/11/business/12-countries-want-banks-to-increase
-capital.html.

148 *completed the third iteration:* Jack Ewing, "Global Regulators Make Move to Prevent Next Financial Crisis," *New York Times*, December 8, 2017, B1, https://www.nytimes.com/2017/12/07/business/global-regulators-agree -on-rules-to-prevent-financial-crises.html.

148 *began to be diluted:* Ryan Tracy and Lalita Clozel, "Plan Aims to Ease Bank Rule on Capital," *Wall Street Journal*, April 12, 2018, https://www.wsj.com/ articles/u-s-proposes-retooling-big-bank-capital-rule-1523478608.

150 *according to one report he thought:* This is based on an eyewitness account of a Republican meeting about my reappointment that's cited in Thomas Ferguson, Paul Jorgenson, and Jie Chen, "Fifty Shares of Green: High Finance, Political Money and the U.S. Congress," Roosevelt Institute, May 2017, http://rooseveltinstitute.org/wp-content/uploads/2017/05/FiftyShadesof Green_0517.pdf.

Chapter 11. After the Fed

155 *"we want to be perceived":* Michael Quint, "Saudi Prince to Become Citicorp's Top Stockholder," *New York Times*, February 22, 1991, 1, https://www .nytimes.com/1991/02/22/business/saudi-prince-to-become-citicorp-s-top -stockholder.html.

156 *We wrote a book:* Paul Volcker and Toyoo Gyohten, *Changing Fortunes: The World's Money and the Threat to American Leadership* (Times Books, 1992).

158 *(almost $300 million in today's dollars):* Calculated with the Bureau of Labor Statistics' Inflation Calculator. See https://www.bls.gov/data/inflation_ calculator.htm.

158 *to support a new graduate program:* A detailed description of the donation and the subsequent dispute over it is available in Doug White, *Abusing Donor Intent: The Robertson Family's Epic Lawsuit Against Princeton University* (Paragon House, 2014).

158 *"comparable to the country's best schools":* Fred M. Hechinger, "Gift of 35 Million Goes to Princeton," *New York Times*, August 6, 1961, 1, https://times machine.nytimes.com/timesmachine/1961/08/06/118046661.pdf.

159 *for "managers or bureaucratic cogs":* This is from the Princeton University website that's dedicated to explaining the mission of the Woodrow Wilson School in the aftermath of the Robertson donation. See https://www.prince ton.edu/robertson/documents/implementing_mission/.

159 *as early as 1970:* Doug White, *Abusing Donor Intent: The Robertson Family's Epic Lawsuit Against Princeton University* (Paragon House, 2014), 97–99.

161 *My understanding is that:* The text of the settlement agreement is available at https://www.princeton.edu/robertson/documents/docs/Robertson_Set tlement_Agreement-Executed.pdf.

Chapter 12. Mr. Chairman in Several Guises

166 *acquiring one of our boutique rivals:* Peter Truell, "NatWest to Buy Gleacher in $135 Million Stock Deal," *New York Times*, October 18, 1995, D2, https:// www.nytimes.com/1995/10/18/business/natwest-to-buy-gleacher-in-135 -million-stock-deal.html.

166 *In May 1996 the firm was sold:* Saul Hansell, "Bankers Trust to Acquire Wolfensohn," *New York Times*, May 23, 1996, http://www.nytimes.com /1996/05/23/business/bankers-trust-to-acquire-wolfensohn.html.

167 *For too many years:* From May 1988 until May 2168 to be precise. See https:// www.nestle.com/media/pressreleases/allpressreleases/recordperformance -25feb00.

168 *possibility of criminal indictments:* In March 1999, almost six months af- ter agreeing to be acquired by Deutsche Bank, Bankers Trust did end up pleading guilty to federal criminal charges that it had used unclaimed cus- tomer money to enhance the bank's own financial performance. Benjamin Weiser, "Bankers Trust Admits Diverting Unclaimed Money," *New York Times*, March 12, 1999, https://www.nytimes.com/1999/03/12/nyregion/ bankers-trust-admits-diverting-unclaimed-money.html.

169 *Hundreds of thousands of foreign students:* Total foreign enrollment reached a record of 1.08 million students in 2016 before dipping in 2017. Nick Ander- son, "Report finds fewer new international students on U.S. college cam- puses," *Washington Post*, November 13, 2017, https://www.washingtonpost .com/local/education/report-finds-fewer-new-international-students-on -us-college-campuses/2017/11/12/5933fe02-c61d-11e7-aaeo-cb18a8c29c65_ story.html?utm_term=.4997869e8653.

169 *thirty or so board members:* A full list is available at https://www.ihouse-nyc .org/about-student-housing-in-ny/board-of-trustees/.

169 *a definitive report on derivatives:* The report is available at http://group30.org/ images/uploads/publications/G30_Derivatives-PracticesandPrinciples.pdf.

170 *the report, published in January 2009:* The report is available online at http:// group30.org/images/uploads/publications/G30_FinancialReformFrame workFinStability.pdf.

170 *the 2015 report:* "Banking Conduct and Culture: A Call for Sustained and Comprehensive Reform," published in July 2015, http://group30.org/ images/uploads/publications/G30_BankingConductandCulture.pdf.

174 *we produced a forceful report:* The National Commission on the Public Ser- vice, "Leadership for America: Rebuilding the Public Service," *Washington Post*, 1989, http://www.washingtonpost.com/wp-srv/opinions/documents/ Leadership_for_America_Rebuilding_the_Public_Service.pdf.

174 *he was sympathetic to our cause:* Robert D. Hershey, "The Government Is Hiring, Which Isn't Easy," *New York Times*, July 23, 1989, 115, https://www

.nytimes.com/1989/07/23/weekinreview/nation-government-hiring-which -isn-t-easy-civil-service-doubts-within-without.html.

174   *and freezing salaries:* "Tonight I call for an across-the-board freeze in Federal Government salaries for one year. And thereafter, during this 4-year period, I recommend that salaries rise at one point lower than the cost of living allowance normally involved in Federal pay increases. Next, I recommend that we make 150 specific budget cuts, as you know, and that all those who say we should cut more be as specific as I have been." (William J. Clinton: "Address Before a Joint Session of Congress on Administration Goals," February 17, 1993. Online by Gerhard Peters and John T. Woolley, American Presidency Project, http://www.presidency.ucsb.edu/ws/?pid=47232).

174   *the long-defunct Bicentennial Commission:* "Government is great at starting things and bad at stopping things. So we're still, believe it or not, you're still paying for a bicentennial commission. That was over in 1976. And there are lots of things. It's a little bit of money, but you can't justify it. It's just terrible." (William J. Clinton: "Remarks and a Question-and-Answer Session on the Economic Program in Chillicothe, Ohio," February 19, 1993. Online by Gerhard Peters and John T. Woolley, American Presidency Project, http://www.presidency.ucsb.edu/ws/?pid=45998).

175   *a follow-on commission:* National Commission on the State and Local Public Service, also known as the "Winter Commission."

175   *its recommendations were even broader:* The report was called "Urgent Business for America: Revitalizing the Federal Government for the 21st Century." A link is available at https://ourpublicservice.org/publications/view contentdetails.php?id=314 .

Chapter 13. The Search for Integrity

177   *his decision pending settlement negotiations:* See chronology in "Swiss Banks Settlement: In re Holocaust Victim Assets Litigation," official website: http://www.swissbankclaims.com/Chronology.aspx.

177   *What soon became known as:* Detail on the composition of the committee is available in our final report: Independent Committee of Eminent Persons, "Report on Dormant Accounts of Victims of Nazi Persecution in Swiss Banks," 1999, http://www.crt-ii.org/ICEP/ICEP_Report_english.pdf.

179   *could and finally did uncover:* "In May 1954, the legal representatives of the big banks coordinated their response to heirs so that the banks would have at their disposal a concerted mechanism for deflecting any kind of enquiry." (Bergier Commission Final Report).

181   *his lasting legacy:* A complete guide to the awards is available at http://www .crt-ii.org/_awards/index.phtm.

182   *"Henceforth, the most comprehensive":* Cited in *The United Nations Security Council from the Cold War to the 21st Century,* David Malone, ed. (Lynne Reinner, 2004), 182.

184   *Weir Group in effect voluntarily disclosed:* "Weir Group Admits Iraq Oil for Food Contracts Were Inflated," *Herald of Scotland,* July 22, 2004, http:// www.heraldscotland.com/news/12497592.Weir_Group_admits_Iraq_Oil_ for_Food_contracts_were_inflated/.

184   *forced the SFO to shut down:* David Leigh and Rob Evans, "'National Interest' Halts Arms Corruption Inquiry," *Guardian,* December 15, 2006, https:// www.theguardian.com/uk/2006/dec/15/saudiarabia.armstrade.

184   *Lord Goldsmith said in Parliament:* A transcript of Lord Goldsmith's statement in the House of Lords on December 14, 2006, is available online at https://www.theyworkforyou.com/lords/?id=2006-12-14d.1711.2.

185   *The committee could itself investigate:* A full report by two senior staff members entitled "Good Intentions Corrupted," with an introduction by me, tells the full story in all of its complexity. It's worth reading for insights into the mismanagement of an international organization. Jeffrey A. Meyer and Mark G. Califano, *Good Intentions Corrupted: The Oil-for-Food Scandal and the Threat to the U.N.* (PublicAffairs, 2006).

185   *the "Volcker Effect":* Press Trust of India, "Volcker Effect: Natwar Singh Removed as Foreign Minister," *Times of India,* November 7, 2005, https:// timesofindia.indiatimes.com/india/Volcker-effect-Natwar-Singh-removed -as-Foreign-Minister/articleshow/1287392.cms.

185   *the "Volcker Report":* Saurabh Shukla, "Volcker Report: Aniel Matherani's revelations leads to Natwar Singh's resignation," *India Today,* December 19, 2005, https://www.indiatoday.in/magazine/nation/story/20051219-volcker -report-aniel-matherani-s-revelations-leads-to-natwar-singh-resignation -786387-2005-12-19.

188   *the "cancer of corruption":* See http://www.worldbank.org/en/about/archives/ history/past-presidents/james-david-wolfensohn and speech at http:// documents.worldbank.org/curated/en/135801467993234363/pdf/99712-WP -Box393210B-PUBLIC-1996-10-01-People-and-Development.pdf.

189   *became yet another "Volcker panel":* See http://www.worldbank.org/en/news/ press-release/2007/09/13/world-bank-president-robert-zoellick-welcomes -volcker-panel-review-world-bank-institutional-integrity-department.

191   *were no longer ignoring the issue:* The Siemens corruption case started with the Munich prosecutor's office before including authorities in several other countries and at international institutions.

191   *The World Bank itself won:* See http://www.worldbank.org/en/news/press -release/2009/07/02/siemens-pay-million-fight-fraud-corruption-part -world-bank-group-settlement.

191   *found prone to corruption:* World Bank statement: http://www.worldbank.org/ en/news/press-release/2012/06/29/world-bank-statement-padma-bridge.

Chapter 14. Setting Standards

194   *It became the nineteen-person board of trustees:* See https://www.iasplus.com/en/binary/resource/0110ascfar.pdf.

198   *In mid-2001 the firm agreed:* Floyd Norris, "Accounting Firm to Pay a Big Fine," *New York Times,* June 20, 2001, http://www.nytimes.com/2001/06/20/business/accounting-firm-to-pay-a-big-fine.html.

200   *My lecture, calling for reforms:* A text of my remarks is available at http://www.kellogg.northwestern.edu/news_articles/2002/volcker_text.aspx.

200   *There was bipartisan disgust:* During my testimony, Alabama Republican Senator Richard Shelby made the following statement: "I just want to repeat what was part of my opening statement, what Dr. Volcker said. He said: 'We have had too many restatements of earnings, too many doubts about pro forma earnings, too many sudden charges of billions of dollars to goodwill, too many perceived auditing failures accompanying bankruptcies to make us all comfortable. To the contrary, it has become clear that some fundamental changes and reforms will be required to provide assurance that our financial reporting will be accurate, transparent, and meaningful.' I could not say it as well as you have, Dr. Volcker." (Transcript of S. Hrg. 107–948, Volume 2—Accounting Reform and Investor Protection Volume 1 S. Hrg. 107–948 Accounting Reform and Investor Protection).

200   *"the most far-reaching reforms":* George W. Bush: "Remarks on Signing the Sarbanes-Oxley Act of 2002," July 30, 2002. Online by Gerhard Peters and John T. Woolley, American Presidency Project, http://www.presidency.ucsb.edu/ws/?pid=73333.

200   *"an exploding crisis in a once-noble profession":* Paul Volcker testimony before the Senate Banking Committee, February 14, 2002. (Transcript of S. Hrg. 107–948, Volume 2 —Accounting Reform and Investor Protection Volume 1 S. Hrg. 107–948 Accounting Reform and Investor Protection).

201   *urged a forced breakup:* Madison Marriage, "Big Four accountancy firms plan for forced break-up," *Financial Times,* May 16, 2018, https://www.ft.com/content/6c07f5d8-591b-11e8-bdb7-f6677d2e1ce8.

201   *the series in the Financial Times:* Jonathan Ford and Madison Marriage, "The big flaw: auditing in crisis," *Financial Times,* August 1, 2018, https://www.ft.com/content/29ccd60a-85c8-11e8-a29d-73e3d454535d.

Chapter 15. The New Financial World: Breakdown and Reform

205   *it disclosed a $15 billion shortfall:* Sonali Basak, Katherine Chiglinsky, and Rick Clough, "GE's Surprise $15 Billion Shortfall Was 14 Years in the Making," *Bloomberg News,* January 25, 2018, https://www.bloomberg.com/news/

articles/2018-01-25/ge-s-surprise-15-billion-shortfall-was-14-years-in-the
-making.

206 *In his 2002 letter to shareholders:* Available online at http://www.berkshire
hathaway.com/letters/2002pdf.pdf.

206 *As mentioned earlier:* See chapter 11.

207 *At least one member of the press was there:* The comment was reported in
Georgie Ann Geyer's Universal Press Syndicate column in August 2004.
Georgie Ann Geyer, "Economic Experts Outline Precarious Financial Sit-
uation," *Daily Spectrum* (Saint George, Utah), August 23, 2004, A6.

207 *I prepared a careful speech:* The *Washington Post* published an adapted ver-
sion of the speech: Paul A. Volcker, "An Economy on Thin Ice," *Washington
Post*, April 10, 2005, B7, http://www.washingtonpost.com/wp-dyn/articles/
A38725-2005Apr8.html.

213 *Stock markets tumbled:* Eric Dash and Jack Healy, "New Plan, Old Doubts:
Investors Register Disappointment, Sending Markets Into a Swoon," *New
York Times*, February 11, 2009, B1, https://archive.nytimes.com/www.ny
times.com/2009/02/11/business/11markets.html.

214 *proposed a sweeping overhaul:* Barack Obama: "Remarks on Financial Regulatory Reform," June 17, 2009. Online by Gerhard Peters and John T.
Woolley, American Presidency Project, http://www.presidency.ucsb.edu/
ws/?pid=86287.

216 *later printed in full:* "Paul Volcker: Think More Boldly," *Wall Street Journal*,
December 14, 2009, R7, https://www.wsj.com/articles/SB1000142405274870
4825504574586330960597134.

217 *"which we're calling the Volcker Rule":* Barack Obama: "Remarks on Financial Regulatory Reform and Consumer Protection Legislation," January 21,
2010. Online by Gerhard Peters and John T. Woolley, American Presidency
Project, http://www.presidency.ucsb.edu/ws/?pid=87436.

Chapter 16. The Three Verities

222 *"knee-jerk inflation fighters":* Federal Open Market Committee meeting
transcript, July 17, 1984, 67, https://www.federalreserve.gov/monetarypolicy
/files/FOMC19840717meeting.pdf.

225 *The new government set an annual inflation rate:* Reserve Bank of New Zealand, Policy Targets Agreement 1990, https://www.rbnz.govt.nz/monetary
-policy/policy-targets-agreements.

225 *a colloquy in a July 1996 FOMC meeting:* Federal Open Market Committee
meeting transcript, July 2–3, 1996, 50–51, https://www.federalreserve.gov/
monetarypolicy/files/FOMC19960703meeting.pdf.

227 *a front-page story warning about:* Peter T. Kilborn, "After Years of Absence,
Deflation Causes Worries," *New York Times*, July 23, 1984, 1, https://www

.nytimes.com/1984/07/23/business/after-years-of-absence-deflation-causes-worries.html.

232   *"We were focused on the banking system":* Janet Yellen interview with Financial Crisis Inquiry Commission, November 15, 2010, https://fcic.law.stanford.edu/interviews/view/201.

233   *permitted the Treasury to use taxpayer money:* Details on the October 2008 TARP legislation are available at https://www.treasury.gov/initiatives/financial-stability/TARP-Programs/Pages/default.aspx#).

235   *Only 20 percent or so:* Examples of these polls include the Pew Research Center's Public Trust in Government survey, http://www.people-press.org/2017/12/14/public-trust-in-government-1958-2017/.

235   *in an issue paper:* Paul C. Light, "Vision + Action = Faithful Execution: Why Government Daydreams and How to Stop the Cascade of Break-downs That Now Haunts It," Volcker Alliance, December 2015, https://www.volckeralliance.org/sites/default/files/attachments/Vision%20%2B%20Action%20-%20The%20Volcker%20Alliance.pdf.

237   *Has nearly doubled:* US Census data projects the total population in 2018 is about 328 million (see https://www.census.gov/popclock/), compared with an estimated 186 million in 1962 (see World Bank data available via the St. Louis Federal Reserve Bank here: https://fred.stlouisfed.org/series/POPTOTUSA647NWDB).

237   *GDP and federal spending have soared:* US annual GDP was about $19.4 trillion in 2017 compared with $605.1 billion in 1962. (Federal Reserve: https://fred.stlouisfed.org/series/GDP#0). Total federal outlays in 2017 were $3.98 trillion compared with $106.8 billion in 1962. (Office of Management and Budget, table 14.2, "Total Government Expenditures 1948–2017").

Epilogue. Credit Where Credit Is Due

242   *an earlier graduate:* Dewey was, in fact, the first PhD in public administration from the Littauer school. See Federal Reserve, https://www.federalreservehistory.org/people/j_dewey_daane.

INDEX

Accenture, 198
accounting
    democracy/accountability and, 202
    forensic accountants, 193
    GAO and, 193, 229, 230
    generally accepted accounting principles
      (GAAP), 194, 196
    trust and, 193
accounting standards, international
    Securities and Exchange Commission
      (SEC) and, 193–194, 196, 197
Aichi, Kiichi, 80
Al-Waleed, Sheikh, 155
American Council on Germany, 42
American International Group Inc. (AIG),
    213n
Andersen, Arthur, 198, 199
Anderson, Roger, 126
Angell, Wayne, 142
Annan, Kofi, 181, 183, 186, 187
Argentina, 135, 136–137
Arthur Andersen accounting firm
    Accenture/split and, 198
    consulting vs. auditing, 198–199
    Enron and, 197, 198–200
    history, 198
    Justice Department indictment/results,
      199–200
    reputation (past), 198
    SEC suit/Waste Management Inc., 198
    Volcker and, xv, 198–199
Ash Council, 67
Asian monetary crisis (1990s), 28
Atlantic City, beauty pageant and, 6–7
auditing firms, 200–201. *See also specific firms*
Australian Wheat Board, 185
Auten, John, 67
Axilrod, Stephen, 106, 243

Bache Halsey Stuart Shields problems/rescue,
    123–124
Bagehot, Walter, 19

Bahnson, Barbara, ix, 30. *See also* Volcker,
    Barbara
Bahnson, Bishop, 43
Baker, Howard, xiv, 149
Baker, Jim
    balanced budget and, 144
    exchange rates and, 143–144
    Latin American debt crisis and, 135
    Reagan's request to Fed/Volcker and, xiii,
      118–119
    as Treasury secretary, xiii, 139–141,
      143–144
    Volcker/Federal Reserve and, xiii, xiv,
      118–119, 135, 149–150, 228
"Baker Plan," xiv, 135
Ball, George, 51
Bank for International Settlements (BIS), 72,
    134, 146, 146n
Bank Holding Company Act (1956), 43
Bank of America, 93
Bank of England, 19, 27, 29, 134, 145, 147, 234
Bankers Trust, xv, 93, 166, 168
Bankhaus Herstatt, Germany shutdown
    (1974), 121
Banking Act/1933 (Glass-Steagall Act/1933),
    41, 120, 149, 150, 203, 205
banks
    commerce separation and, 204–205
    "correspondent" banks, 57, 57n
    "deposit-taking banks" vs. investment
      banks, 41
    overlapping agencies and, 230–231, 233
    regulations (early 1930s to 1950s), 41
    too-big-to-fail debate, 128
    See also specific banks; specific regulators/
      regulation
Barre, Raymond, 78
Barros, Robert, 91
"Basel Agreement," 148
Basel Committee, 146–148
Bear Stearns/rescue, 208, 209
Beaver Lake, New Jersey, 11, 12

*Before the Fall: An Inside View of the Pre-
    Watergate White House* (Safire), 72–73
Belgium and fixed exchange rate, 63
Bennett, Jack, 80
"Bergier Commission," 177, 179, 180
Bernanke, Ben, 156–157, 208, 231
*Best Way to Rob a Bank Is to Own One, The:
    How Corporate Executives and Politicians
    Looted the S&L Industry* (Black), 130
Biden, Joe, 217
Black, William, 130
Bliley, Tom, 205
Blumenthal, Michael, xi, 101, 102, 160
boards, 167–168, 169–172
Bocuse, Paul, 27
Bolton, Emily, 246
bonds (government), 20, 37
bonuses, 43, 171
Bowen, Bill, 152, 160
Bowsher, Chuck, 198
Bradfield, Michael, 70, 73, 132, 180–181,
    240–242, 245
Bradley, Bill, 210
Brady, Nicholas ("Nick"), 135, 209, 242
Brady Plan, 135–136
Brash, Donald, 225
Brazil, 137
Bretton Woods system, ix, 24, 67. *See also*
    International Monetary Fund; World
    Bank
Brill, Dan, 54
Britain, 27, 76, 79–80, 184
Britain's Accounting Standards Board
    (Financial Reporting Council), 194
Brookings Institution's Center for Effective
    Public Management, 160
Brzezinski, "Zbig," 171
Buffett, Warren, 206
Bundy, McGeorge, 51
Bunting, John, 125
Bureau of the Budget, 54–55. *See also* Office of
    Management and Budget; Quadriad
Burns, Arthur, 21
    conflicts with New York Fed directors,
        93–94
    Federal Reserve and, x, xi, 66, 69–70,
        93–94, 97, 100, 102–103, 151
    fixed rate exchange/end and, 72, 82
    FOMC and, 93–94, 95–96
    IMF meeting/presentation, 107
    Munich Conference (1971), 69–70
    Nixon and, 66, 72

Volcker and, 93, 94, 95–96, 97, 112
    warning to Volcker, 112
Bush, George H. W., xiv, 135, 141, 174, 209
Bush, George W., 175, 189, 200, 238

Califano, Mark, 244
Camdessus, Michel, 145
Canada, 73
    Camp David meetings (1971) and, 73
Cape May, New Jersey, 6. *See also specific
    individuals*
capital of banks, 98, 98n, 145–148, 155
Carlock, John, 61
Carter bonds, 101
Carter, Jimmy
    advice/Camp David and, 102
    budgeting, 238
    credit controls/Fed and, 110–112
    Fed/Treasury appointments and, xi
    inflation and, xii, 101, 102, 105–106, 108,
        110–112
    Iranian hostage crisis and, 173
    "malaise" speech, xi
    Volcker and, 103–104, 107, 111n, 228
CEA (Council of Economic Advisers), 46, 51,
    54–55, 55n, 62–63, 71, 114
central banking, 227–235. *See also specific banks*
Champion, George, 41, 42, 43, 44, 55, 57, 58
*Changing Fortunes: The World's Money and the
    Threat to American Leadership* (Volcker
    and Gyohten), 156
"chaos theory" in financial markets, 157
Chase Manhattan Bank, 40, 43, 57–58
Chase Manhattan Bank/Volcker, ix, x, 39–40,
    41 , 42–44, 56–57
China
    exports to US, 223
    monetary reform and, 86
    Nixon trip and, 76
    situation (end of twentieth century), 3,
        172, 221
Chrysler Corporation, 122–123, 123n, 153, 213
Chrysler Loan Guarantee Board, 123
Churchill, Winston, 27, 220
Cincotta, Gale, 109
Citibank
    Al-Waleed and, 155
    approach description, 43, 98, 99
    bad loans (1990s), 155
    capital and, 98, 155
    Chase Manhattan Bank competition/
        comparison, 40, 43, 57–58

Citibank (*continued*)
    conduct/investigations, 99
    dodging taxes, 99
    Latin American debt crisis and, 133, 135
    offering gifts/fine and, 99
    Traveler's Company and, 204, 205
Citicorp holding company, 58
Clausen, Tom, 93, 114n
Clinton, William, 174–175, 238
Cohen, Eddie, 61
Columbia, 135
Commission on Money and Credit, 42
Committee for Economic Development, 42
Committee of Twenty, xi, 85
Commodity Futures Trading Commission
    (CFTC), 124, 230
Conable, Barber, 114n
Connally, John
    "economic weapons" and, 70–71
    "four nos" economic policy, 70
    G-10 meeting (1971), x, 76, 77–78
    International Banking Conference
        (Munich/1971), x, 69, 70
    Nixon and, 67, 70, 71
    Pierre-Paul Schweitzer and, 84
    rate exchange and, 68–69, 70, 71, 72, 76,
        77–78, 79, 144
    Treasury appointment, x, 67–68
    Treasury resignation, xi, 80
    Volcker and, 68–69, 70, 71, 150
Consultative Group on International
    Economic and Monetary Affairs. *See*
    G-30 ("Group of Thirty")
consumer financial protection agency, 214
Continental Illinois
    background problems/attempts to solve,
        125–128, 146
    capital needs/Volcker, xiii, 98, 126
    collapse aftermath, 119
    David Kennedy and, 60
    FDIC and, xiii, 126, 127, 128
    Fed/Volcker and, 126–127
    interest rates and, 119
    management change and, 126, 128
    too-big-to-fail debate and, 128
Cooke, Peter, 147
Cornacchia, Michael, 244
"correspondent" banks, 57, 57n
Corrigan, Gerald ("Jerry"), 96–97, 104,
    147–148, 155, 243
Council of Economic Advisers (CEA), 46, 51,
    54–55, 55n, 62–63, 71, 114

Council on Foreign Relations, New York, 57
Coyne, Joe, 108, 109, 242–243
Cross, Sam, 29, 75, 243
Cuneo, Don, 169
"currency in circulation," 21–22

Daane, J. Dewey/Barbara (wife), x, 66, 75, 242
Dale, Bill, 70
"Danny Deever" (Kipling), 35
Darman, Dick, 139
De Gaulle, Charles, 48, 62, 64
de la Madrid, Miguel, 132, 134
de Larosière, Jacques, 78, 131, 132, 134
Dean Witter Reynolds stock brokerage
    company, 204
Debs, Dick/Barbara, 96
debt management, 37, 39
deflation, 226–227
Dening, Anke, xvi, 165
Department of Homeland Security, 175
derivatives, 169–170, 206–207, 209, 230
d'Estaing, Giscard, 48, 72, 76, 78–79, 81, 86
Dickerson, Nancy, 149
DiIulio, John, 159–160
Dillon, Douglas, x, 45, 46, 51–53, 52n, 61, 150
Dixieland jazz, 15
Dodd, Chris, 213
Dodd-Frank legislation, xvi, 128, 213, 214–216,
    217, 230
Dodds, Harold, 14, 159
Dodgers, ix, 11, 30, 40
Dole, Bob, 150
Dow Jones, 152
Dowd, Anthony, 211–212, 216, 244–245
Dowling, Mercedes "Meechy," 162
Duesenberry, Jim, 23

Eccles, Hope, 215
Eccles, Marriner. Federal Reserve and, 37–38,
    42, 215
econometrics, 23, 25–26, 36, 225
economic law, 18
economic rents, 206, 206n, 207
economy (US), 32, 69–70, 72, 75. *See also specific
    aspects/events; specific individuals*
Ecuador, 134, 136
Eisenhower, Dwight, 30, 238
Emminger, Otmar, 107
Engelhard Minerals & Chemical Corp, 124,
    125
Enron, 197, 198
"equilibrium" and financial markets, 157

INDEX 279

"Eurodollar market" beginnings/effects, 50
Europe
 debt crisis (2011), 145, 148
 exchange-rate management and, 138
 fixed exchange rate and, 67, 81
 See also specific countries
European Commission, fixed exchange rate
 end and, 77–78. *See also specific countries*
exchange-rate management, 138–141, 143, 145

Fannie Mae, 89n, 89–90
Federal Deposit Insurance Corporation
 (FDIC), 120, 125, 126, 127, 128, 155, 230
Federal Financing Bank/securities, 88–89
Federal Open Market Committee (FOMC),
 xii, xiv, 34, 35, 36–37n, 38, 93–94, 95–96,
 103, 104, 119, 222
Federal Reserve, 21n, 233
 "Accord, the" and, ix, 31, 38
 authority/new financial world (starting
  late 1980s), 205
 authority/responsibilities, 205, 229, 230, 231
 borrowing at discount window and, 126n
 bureaucracy of, 96
 creation, 17
 debt management and, 37
 GAO audit and, 229, 230
 gold standard and, 62
 independence and, ix, 31, 35, 37, 38, 42,
  118–119, 122, 228, 229
 interest rates and, 31, 35, 36–37n, 38
 interest rates (from Great Depression to
  early Korean War), 31, 38
 money stability and, 31, 32, 35n
 policies (late 1930s to late 1940s), 20
 political pressure/slowing economy and,
  20
 "punch bowl/party" quote, 31, 34, 66,
  223–224
 raising discount rate and (mid-1960s),
  54–55
 "red line" inflation rate policy/problems,
  224, 225–226
 regulation (following Great Recession
  2008), 214
 reserve accounts and, 35, 35n
 securities markets (2008 financial crisis)
  and, 39
 sound finance (overview), 228–235
 structure, 228–229
 trading desk significance, 35–36
 Trump administration and, 234–235

 vice chairman for supervision, 215, 233, 234
 See also Quadriad; *specific individuals*;
  specific policies
Federal Reserve Act (1935), 38
Federal Reserve Act (1977), 100
Federal Reserve Bank of New York, 21n,
 24, 33, 37, 38–39, 96, 97. *See also specific
 individuals*
Federal Reserve Bank of New York/Volcker,
 ix, 21–22, 34, 35, 36, 37n, 38, 39
Federal Reserve Bank of New York/Volcker
 as president, xi, 39
 bank efficiency and, 97
 banks' capital and, 98
 bureaucracy/plants story and, 96
 Burns and, 95, 96, 97
 Citibank misconduct and, 98, 99
 discount rate (1978) and, 101
 easy money policy problem and, 100
 emergency alarm and, 95
 Latin American countries borrowing and,
  97–98
Federal Reserve bank presidents, selection of,
 39n. *See also specific individuals*
"Federal Reserve float," 21–22
Federal Reserve/Volcker, 2, 18–20, 21
Federal Reserve/Volcker as chairman, 104, 162
 bank capital and, 98
 Carter meeting/appointment, xi, 103–104
 Chrysler Corporation bailout and, 122–123
 Citibank conduct/investigations, 99
 coup attempt/resignation letter and, xiv,
  141–143
 credit controls/unanticipated consequences
  (Carter administration), 110–112
 criticism/protests against inflation fighting
  policy, 109
 discount rate and, xi, xiv, 104, 105, 108
 easy money policy problem and, 100
 Fed losing credibility and, 105
 Hunt brothers and, 124–125
 inflation fighting significance, 150–151
 inflation fighting strategy, xii, xiii, 33, 55, 87,
  105–106, 108, 110–116, 117–118
 last days/resignation letter, 148–151
 Latin American debt crisis and, 130–136
 monetary restraint and, 33
 National Association of Home Builders
  meeting, Las Vegas, 114
 Reagan's request and, 118–119
 reappointment/family deal and, xiii, xiv,
  116–117

Federal Reserve/Volcker as chairman
    (*continued*)
    successor and, xiv, 149
    warnings about Fed (early 1980s), 112
    See also specific events
Federal Stability Oversight Council (FSOC),
    230–231
Feldstein, Martin, 114
Fellner, Willy, 23–24
Ferguson, Roger, 170
Fernand Point's La Pyramide restaurant,
    France, 27
financial crisis (2008). *See* Great Recession
    (2008)
financial engineering, 205–207, 209
financial markets, 157, 203–204, 205–206,
    216–217, 227, 232–233. *See also specific*
    events
Financial Reporting Council (Britain's
    Accounting Standards Board), 194
Financial Services Modernization Act/1999
    (Gramm-Leach-Bliley law/1999), xv,
    205
Financial Stability Oversight Council
    (FSOC), 214
Financial Times, 201
First Chicago, 98, 124
First Pennsylvania rescue/as model, xii, 125,
    127, 146
Fiscal Policy Seminar, 24
fixed exchange rates
    Bretton Woods system and, ix, 24, 67
    Federal Reserve and, 49, 49n
    foreign currency swaps, 49
    freely floating exchange rates/problems
        and, 63–64
    gold committee and, 51–52
    gold reserves levels and, 51, 61–62, 64, 70
    Kennedy and, 45
    "market" vs. "official" price, 61–62
    Operation Twist, 49
    problems/possible solutions, 61–69, 70–71
    Roosa/"Roosa bonds" and, 48–49
    "Triffin dilemma," 48, 54, 64, 65, 87
    US/other countries and, 62, 64, 65, 66, 67,
        68, 70–71, 72, 73–74
fixed exchange rates/end
    Camp David meeting (1971), 71–74
    currency crises continuing and, 101
    Nixon meetings/actions following, x–xi,
        76, 78, 79
    Nixon's August 15 speech and, x, 75

    problems/solutions and, xi, 76–86
    reactions US/abroad, 75–79
    Smithsonian agreement and, xi, 79–80,
        82, 87
    Volcker travels/meetings and, 75–82
Folsom, Suzanne Rich, 189
Ford, Gerald, xi, 173
"four nos" economic policy (Connally), 70
Fowler, Joe
    Federal Reserve discount rate and, 54
    Goldman Sachs and, 93, 93n
    special drawing rights (SDRs) and, 57,
        65–66
    Treasury and, x, 53–54, 57, 61
    Volcker and, 93, 149, 150
France, x–xi, 48, 62, 64, 76, 84. *See also specific*
    individuals
Frank, Barney, 213
Franklin National Bank, New York failure
    (1974), 121
Fraser, Doug, 122
Freddie Mac, 89, 89n, 90
Freeman, Brian, 123
Friedman, Milton, 32, 33, 42, 63, 106, 109, 112,
    117–118
Full Employment and Balanced Growth
    Act/1978 ("Humphrey-Hawkins
    Act"/1978), 100

G-5 ("Group of Five"), xiii, xiv, 83n, 140–141,
    144
G-10 ("Group of Ten"), x, xi, 49, 62, 62n,
    76–79, 83, 146
G-30 ("Group of Thirty"), xvi, 169–171,
    206–207
Garfield, James assassination, 238
Garn, "Jake," 130
Gaviria, Gustavo, 190
GDP, 207, 237
Gehrig, Lou, 11
Geithner, Tim
    Obama administration/Treasury and, 211,
        212, 213, 231
    Volcker and, 208, 212
General Electric, 205
General Electric Capital, 205
General Motors, 213
generally accepted accounting principles
    (GAAP), 194, 196
George, Eddie, 145
Germany, 42, 62, 64, 65, 69, 77, 79, 80–81, 138,
    139

Githongo, John, 190
Glasgall, Bill, 246
Glass-Steagall Act/1933 (Banking Act/1933),
    41, 120, 149, 150, 203, 205
Gleacher & Company, 166
GNP (gross national product), 32, 32n,
    206
Goheen, Robert, 158–159
gold standard. *See* fixed exchange rates
Golden, Ray, 154
Goldman Sachs, 121n, 149
Goldsmith, Lord, 184
Goldstein, Jeffrey, 154
Goldstone, Richard, 182
Goolsbee, Austan, 210, 245
Gore, Al, 175, 210, 238
Gotlieb, Allan, 183
governance of other countries, 157–158, 240
governance of United States
    challenges overview, 2–3, 221, 237–240
    Hamilton on, 236–237
    polarization and, 2
    presidential views/examples, 238
    Reagan on, 172, 235, 236
    strengthening, 172–174, 237–240
    trust problems, 2–3, 145, 221, 235–236
    Volcker Alliance and, 235–236, 239
    Volcker's mother on, 240
    wealth concentration and, 2
    *See also specific components; specific
        individuals*
Government Accountability Office (GAO)
    Federal Reserve audit and, 229, 230
    importance, 193
Graham, Frank, 18–19
Gramm-Leach-Bliley law/1999 (Financial
    Services Modernization Act/1999),
    xv, 205
Gramm, Phil, 205
Gray, Edwin, 129–130
Great Depression, 5, 20, 23, 24, 31, 37, 38, 120,
    129, 220, 230
Great Recession (2008)
    bank capital and, 148
    derivatives and, 170, 206, 209
    Dodd-Frank legislation following, 128, 213,
        214–216, 217, 230
    Federal Reserve/Treasury efforts and, 39,
        49–50
    Great Depression comparisons, 20
    missed signs, 203–209, 232
    too-big-to-fail issue and, 128, 213–214

Volcker's warnings, 207–208
    See also Dodd-Frank legislation; Obama,
        Barack
Great Recession (2008) aftermath
    financial regulation/reform, 2, 148, 170,
        209, 213
    stress tests and, 213
    Volcker and, 207, 209, 210–212, 213–214,
        215–218
Greenspan, Alan, 149
    consulting career beginnings, 31
    Federal Reserve, xiv, 150, 157, 225
    on price stability, 225
    wife, 150
Gyohten, Toyoo, 156

Haberkern, Roy, 42–43
Haberler, Gottfried, 23–24
Hamilton, Alexander, 2, 40, 59, 227–228,
    236–237
Hansen, Alvin, 22–24, 31
Harvard/Volcker
    economics and, 22–24, 25–26
    Harvard Graduate School of Public
        Affairs, ix, 22, 40
Hayek, Friedrich, 17
Hayes, Alfred, 39, 93–94
Heath, Edward, 76
Heimann, John, 98
Heineman, Ben, 189
Hiroshima atom bomb, 9
holding companies, 43, 58
Holmes, Alan, 96
Hoover, Herbert, 238
hubris and US, 3
Hume, David, 117
"Humphrey-Hawkins Act"/1978 (Full
    Employment and Balanced Growth
    Act/1978), 100
Hunt brothers/loans and silver market, xii,
    124–125
Hunt, Nelson "Bunker," 124
Hurricane Katrina response, 175, 236
Hydoski, Frank, 193

I-Houses, 169
Iacocca, Lee, 123
ICI (British chemical manufacturer), 152
Independent Advisory Council, 174
Independent Panel Review of the World
    Bank Group Department of
    Institutional Integrity, 189–192

Indonesia, 137n
inflation
    Carter administration/Fed, 105–106, 108, 110, 111–112
    fighting significance, 150–151
    fighting strategy (Fed/Volcker as chairman), xii, xiii, 33, 55, 87, 105–106, 108, 110–116, 117–118
    importance of fighting, 222
    "money illusion" and, 13
    Nixon administration and, 61, 87
    problem in late 1960s/1970s, 69, 87
    "stagflation," 99, 223
    World War II/Korean War and, 23
    See also price stability
Inter-American Bank financing, 136
Inter-American Development Bank, Washington, 191
interest equalization tax, 50
Internal Revenue Service (IRS), 50
International Accounting Standards Board, xv, 194, 195
International Accounting Standards Committee Foundation, London, 194, 195
International Banking Conference (Munich/1971), x, 69–70
International Financial Reporting Standards, 196
International House, New York, 168–169
International Monetary Fund
    Belgrade meeting, 106, 107
    Camp David meetings (1971) and, 73
    creation, ix
    exchange-rate system and, 25, 73
    international monetary reform and, 83–86
    Latin American debt crisis and, xiii, 131, 133, 134, 135, 136
    Volcker/Per Jacobsson Lecture (1990), xv, 8n, 151
international monetary reform
    conflicting triad with, 86–87
    International Monetary Fund and, 83–86
    Volcker and, 83–86
international organizations, importance of, 181. See also specific organizations
Iranian hostage crisis, 173
Iranian revolution, 102
Iraq. See United Nations Iraqi Oil-for-Food program investigation

Jacobs, Harry, 123–124
Japan
    economic status and, 83, 83n
    exchange-rate management and, 138, 142
    fixed exchange rate/end and, 64, 65, 67, 68, 70, 73–74, 79, 80, 81
    Trilateral Commission and, 171, 172
    undercapitalized banks, 146, 147, 148
Jewish community. See Swiss banks-Nazi victims investigation
John Paul II, Pope/visit to America, 107–108
Johnson, Lyndon, x
    Quadriad meeting/interest rates and, 55
    reelection win, 50
    Treasury and, 53, 54
    Volcker and, 53
    William Martin and, x, 55
Johnson, Manuel, 142, 142n
JPMorgan Chase, 208

Kashiwagi, Yusuke/family, 73–74
Kaufman, Henry, xiii, 21
Kavesh, Bob, 103
Keating, Charles, 130
Keating Five, 130
Kennedy, David, 60, 61, 65, 68, 84
Kennedy, John F.
    assassination, x, 47, 67
    exchange rate and, 45, 62, 64
    Nixon and, x, 60
    Treasury and, 44
    Volcker and, 60
Kettl, Donald, 160, 245–246
Keynes, John Maynard, 17, 22–23
Khomeini, Ayatollah, 102
Kim, Jim Yong, 190, 191
King, Martin Luther, 210
Kipling, Rudyard, 35
Kissinger, Henry
    European travels, 73
    international monetary policies and, 59, 64
    Nixon and, 76
    Volcker and, 59, 64
Knight, Bob, 61
Kohn, Donald, 123
Korean War and monetary policy, 23, 31
Korman, Edward, 177, 180

Laingen, Bruce, 173–174
Lambsdorff, Otto, Count, 171
Lamfalussy, Alexandre, 145
LaRouche, Lyndon/supporters, 109

Latin America inflation history, 223
Latin American debt crisis (1980s), 28, 130–131
   current situation and, 136–137
• loans and, 97–98, 115, 121, 131, 146–147
   See also specific countries; specific individuals/
    institutions
Lay, Ken, 197
Leach, Jim, 205
"Leadership for America: Rebuilding the
   Public Service," 174
Lebanon Daily News, 6
Lee Kuan Yew, 137n
Lehman Brothers, 209
Leigh-Pemberton, Robin, 147
Lenny (Federal Reserve barber), 141
Leutwiler, Fritz
   Nestlé and, 167–168
   Swiss bank investigation and, 176–177, 180
   Volcker and, 167–168
Levin, Carl, 218
Levine, Charles, 174n
Levitt, Arthur, 108, 193–194, 195
Lewy, Glen, 154–155
Liberty bonds, 20
Light, Paul, 174n, 235–236, 245–246
Lincoln Savings and Loan (empire), 130
"Little Boy" atom bomb, 9
lobbyists, 92, 170, 209, 217, 218, 221
London School of Economics (LSE), 26,
   27–29
London/Volcker (early 1950s), ix, 26, 27–29
Longstreth, Bevis, 154
Ludwig, Gene, 209
Lutz, Friedrich, 17
Luzzatto, Ernie, 244

McCarthy, Leonard, 190, 191, 192
McCloy, John J., 42
McCracken, Paul, 68, 70
McKinsey & Company, 197
McNamar, R.T. ("Tim"), 132, 135
McWhinney, Madeline, 33–34, 34n
Mallardi, Catherine, 35, 119, 142, 243
Maloney, Don, 14, 15
Mancera, Miguel, 131, 132, 134
Marshall Fellowship, 19
Martin, Canon, 91
Martin, Preston, Federal Reserve/attempted
   coup and, xiv, 141–142
Martin, William McChesney
   "Accord, the" and, 31
   "bills-only doctrine," 38–39

Federal Reserve/New York and, ix, x, 29, 31,
   35, 49, 51–52, 54, 55, 62, 64, 150
   FOMC, 35
   gold standard and, 62
   Johnson and, x, 55
   Nixon and, 66
   "punch bowl/party" quote, 31, 34, 66,
    223–224
   Volcker and, 35, 49, 51–52
Massachusetts Institute of Technology
   (MIT), 23, 42
Maxwell, David, 89
Merkley, Jeff, 217
Merrill Lynch, 123–124
Mexico and NAFTA, 137
Mexico debt crisis, xii, xiii, 115, 131, 132–135,
   136. *See also* Latin American debt crisis
   (1980s)
Meyer, Jeffrey, 244
Milkowitz, Vic, 34
Miller, G. William ("Bill")
   Carter and, 100, 102–103
   Chrysler Corporation bailout and, 122
   Federal Reserve and, xi, 100–101, 102–103
   Treasury and, xi, 102–103, 106
   Volcker and, 103
Mises, Ludwig von, 17
Mitchell, Andrea, 150
Miyazawa, Kiichi, 171–172
monetary reform, Volcker and, 145
money definitions, 32
"money illusion" and inflation, 13
Moore, George, 43
Moravian community, North Carolina, 42
Morden, Reid, 183–184, 244
Morgan Bank, New York, 58
Morgenstern, Oskar, 17
Morgenthau, Henry, Jr., 24
Morita, Akio, 171–172
Moynihan, Daniel Patrick, 60
"Mr. Chairman," 2
Mundell, Bob, 143
Mundheim, Robert, 123

Nathan, Richard, 159
National Civic League (National Municipal
   League), 14
National Commission on the Public Service,
   xiv, xv, 173–175
National People's Action Group, 109
Nestlé, 152, 167–168
New Deal, 238

New York Fed. *See* Federal Reserve Bank of
    New York
New York Mets, 40
New York State's Erie Canal system, 6
New York Times, 52, 149, 165, 226–227
New Zealand economic policy, 225
Nixon, Richard
    becoming president/inaugural parade
        (1969), x, 59
    credit controls and, 110
    government/reorganization and, 67–68, 238
    inflation and, 61, 87
    John Kennedy and, x, 60
    rate exchange and, x, 65, 71–75, 76
    Watergate scandal/resignation, xi, 86, 87,
        90
    See also specific events; specific individuals
"Nixon shock," 74
North American Free Trade Agreement
    (NAFTA), 137
North Atlantic Treaty Organization
    (NATO), 71, 77

Oak Ridge, Tennessee, 9
Obama, Barack
    Dodd-Frank legislation and, 128
    economic advisory board (PERAB), xvi,
        211–212, 213–214, 213n, 232, 244–245
    hope for the future and, 210
    Volcker and, xvi, 170, 210–211, 217, 244, 245
Office of Management and Budget, 54–55
oil, 121, 125, 126, 131
oil crises (1970s), 85–86, 102
Oil-for-Food program. *See* United Nations
    Iraqi Oil-for-Food program
Open Market Committee. *See* Federal Open
    Market Committee (FOMC)
Organization for Economic Cooperation and
    Development (OECD), 63, 63n, 182
Orszag, Peter, 211
Oxman, Stephen, 154

Padma Bridge project, Bangladesh, 191
Padoa-Schioppa, Tomasso, 145
Parks, Rosa, 210
parrot story, 1–2
Partee, Charles, xi
Patman, Wright, 120, 121
Paulson, Hank, 208, 231
Pearl Harbor attacks/impacts, 14
Peña, Mr. (Volcker's Federal Reserve driver),
    115–116

Penn Central Transportation Company
    bankruptcy (1970), 120–121
Penn Square bank, xiii, 125–126, 128
Peterson, Pete, 68
Petty, John, 61
Philipp Brothers, 125
Pieth, Mark, 182
Placid Oil Company, 125
Pöhl, Karl Otto, 141, 142
political parties and Volcker, 30, 210
Pompidou, Georges, x–xi, 76, 78, 79
Poniatowski, Ann, 165
Portillo, José López, 131, 132, 133–134
President's Economic Recovery Advisory
    Board (PERAB), xvi, 211–212, 213–214,
    213n, 232, 244–245
price stability, 222–227. *See also* inflation
Princeton, 14, 15, 17, 157, 158–162, 175. *See also*
    Woodrow Wilson School of Public and
    International Affairs; *specific individuals*
Princeton/Volcker, ix, 13, 14, 15, 16–19, 20, 21,
    56. *See also* Woodrow Wilson School of
    Public and International Affairs
"private equity," 203
Proxmire, William, 114, 119, 122
Prudential Insurance, 168
Public Company Accounting Oversight
    Board (PCAOB), 201
public service
    future and, 239
    National Commission on the Public
        Service, xiv, xv, 173–174, 175
    Princeton public service education/
        controversy and, 158–162, 175
    "quiet crisis" in, xiv, 173
    Volcker's father and, 173, 237
    See also specific individuals
Puerto Rican governance, 157–158
"punch bowl/party" quote, 31, 34, 66, 223–224

Quadriad, 55, 55n
Quarles, Randal, 215, 233

Ravitch, Dick, 244
Reagan, Nancy, 116, 150
Reagan, Ronald
    air traffic controllers and, 113
    Chrysler bailout and, 123
    "government" and, 172, 235, 236
    Gray and, 129
    Howard Baker and, 149
    Irangate, 143

Preston Martin and, 141
recession/inflation and, 112–116, 117–118
request to Fed/Volcker and, 118–119
Shultz and, 33
Thatcher and, 139
Volcker and, xii, xiii, xiv, 112–113, 114,
    116–117, 118–119, 150
recession. *See* Great Recession (2008)
recession (late 1970s to 1980s), 111
    Fed policy and, 112, 113–116
    Federal Reserve "Saturday package" (1979)
        and, 117, 118
recession (1970s)
    Reserve "dual mandate" and, 99–100
    "stagflation," 99, 223
Reed, John, 135, 155
Regan, Donald
    golfing/Volcker and, 113–114, 114n
    Latin American debt crisis, 134–135
    Treasury and, xii, xiii, 112, 113, 139,
        203–204
    Volcker and, xii, 113–114, 114n, 139, 149
regulation challenges, 218–219
Reinhardt, Uwe, 201–202
Rensselaer Polytechnic Institute, 5–6, 13
Resolution Trust Corporation, 209
Restigouche Salmon Club, 164
Reuss, Henry, 71
Rhodes, Bill, 133, 135n, 160
Rhodes scholarship, 34
Rice, Don, 244
Rice, Emmett, xi–xii
Richardson, Gordon, 134
Ringler, Sue, 244
Ritter, Larry, 42, 103
Robertson, Charles/Marie, 158–161
Rockefeller, David, 42, 43, 47, 56–57
Rockefeller, Nelson, 52–53
Roosa, Robert
    Brown Brothers Harriman partnership
        and, x, 50–51, 93
    exchange rates and, 63, 139
    Kennedy administration and, 44
    New York Fed and, 34, 38
    trading desk and, 35, 36
    Volcker and, x, 34–35, 36, 38, 44, 61, 93
    work/reputation of, x, 46, 48, 49–50, 54, 60
Roosevelt, Franklin D., 220
Roosevelt, Theodore, 238
Ross, Tom, 245
Rossides, Gene, 61
Rotary Foundation fellowship, ix, 26, 27

Safire, Bill, 72, 73
Salomon Brothers, 122, 153, 205
Samuelson, Paul, 23, 42
Sanford, Charlie, 93
Sarbanes-Oxley Act (2002), 201–202
Saturday Evening Post, 8
savings and loans (S&Ls), 128–130, 209
Sayers, Richard, 27–28
Schiller, Karl, 77
Schlesinger, Helmut, 156
Schmidt, Helmut, 80, 81, 106–107
School of Public and International Affairs
    (SPIA), 16. *See also* Woodrow Wilson
    School of Public and International
    Affairs
Schultz, Fred, 104, 152
Schweitzer, Albert, 84
Schweitzer, Pierre-Paul, 73, 84
Scranton, Bill, 174
Sears Roebuck, 204
Securities and Exchange Commission (SEC)
    Citibank and, 99
    international accounting standards and,
        193–194, 196, 197
    PCAOB and, 201
    responsibilities, 230
    Waste Management Inc. suit, 198
Seger, Martha, 142
Seidenstein, Tom, 195
Selig, Bud, 158
Senate Banking Committee, 114, 122, 130, 200,
    213, 216–217
Senate Ethics Committee, 130
September 11 attacks, 235–236
Sevan, Benon, 186
Shapiro, Eli, 42
Shapiro, Harold, 160
Sharpe ratio, 206
Sharpe, William, 206
Shultz, George, 85
    fixed rate exchange/end and, 68, 70, 71, 80,
        81, 82
    Friedman and, 33
    Group of Five, 83n
    international monetary reform/IMF
        meeting and, 82–83, 84
    leaving Nixon administration, 90
    Nixon/administration and, 33, 68, 70, 71,
        80, 81, 82
    Pierre-Paul Schweitzer and, 84
    Reagan/administration and, 33
    Treasury and, xi, 80, 81, 82–83

Shultz, George (*continued*)
    Volcker and, 150
    Whitehead and, 149
Shultze, Charlie, 106
Siemens AG bribes, 190–191
Silva Herzog, Jesús ("Chucho"), 131, 132, 133, 134
silver market, xii, 124
Simon, Bill, 90, 112
Singh, Natwar, 185
Skilling, Jeffrey, 197
Slade, Elliot, 154
Slaughter, Anne-Marie, 161
Smithies, Arthur, 23, 31
Smithsonian agreement, xi, 79–80, 82, 87
Solomon, Tony, 101
    Latin American debt crisis and, 132, 133
Solow, Bob, 23
Soros, George, 156–157
Soviet Union collapse/views, 3
Spacek, Leonard, 198, 200
special drawing rights (SDRs), 57, 65–66, 84, 85
Sproul, Allan, 39, 95
Staats, Elmer, 122
"stagflation," 99, 223
State Department
    Bretton Woods fixed exchange rates and, 51, 73
    Camp David meetings (1971) and, 73
Stein, Herb, 71
Sternlight, Peter, 106
Stevenson, Adlai, 30, 210
stock market crash (1929), 37
Stockman, David, 114
Stokes, Donald, 159
Strong, Benjamin, 37
"subprime mortgages," 206, 232
Sumita, Satoshi, 142
Summers, Larry, 211, 212
supply-side economics creator, 143n
Swiss banks–Nazi victims investigation
    accounting firms, 178, 178n
    "Bergier Commission" and, 177, 179, 180
    class-action lawsuits, 177, 177n
    as Independent Committee of Eminent Persons (ICEP) investigation, 177–181
    Jewish community/priorities and, 176, 177–178
    research/results, 178–181
    Swiss banks/priorities and, 176, 177, 178, 178n

Volcker and, 176–177
"Volcker Commission" and, xv, 177–181
World Jewish Congress and, 176, 177

"target zones" (exchange rates), 139, 143
Tariff Act (1930), 73
Tarullo, Daniel, 215
tax consulting, 201
Taylor, Bill, 155, 242
Teaneck, New Jersey, 7, 8, 10, 10n. *See also specific individuals*
Teeters, Nancy, xi–xii
"term loans" beginnings, 120
Thailand, 137
Thatcher, Margaret, 139
thrift industry. *See* savings and loans (S&Ls)
Tilghman, Shirley, 160–161
Tobin, James, 23
too-big-to-fail issue
    Continental Illinois and, 128
    Great Recession (2008) and, 128, 213–214
Trade Expansion Act (1962), 73
Traveler's Company, 204, 205
Treasury
    "Accord, the" and, ix, 31, 38
    Federal Reserve accounts and, 35, 35n
    Federal Reserve independence and, ix, 31, 37, 38
    Latin American debt crisis and, 131, 132–133, 134, 135
    See also Quadriad; *specific individuals*; *specific monetary policies*
Treasury (Nixon administration)
    fixed rate exchange/end and, 61–79
    team/Democrats on team, 60, 61
Treasury/Volcker
    Federal Financing Bank/securities, 88–89
    interest equalization tax/IRS and, 50
    interventions leading to more interventions and, 50
    move/home and, 46
    offer, x, 26
    position/work, x, xi, 46, 50, 51, 52–53, 54–55
Treasury/Volcker (return)
    auctions/debt securities, 88
    beginnings, 60
    Camp David meetings (1971), 71–74
    fixed exchange rates and, 61–62, 63–67, 68, 69–74
    international monetary policies, 59–60, 61–62, 63–67, 68, 69–79
    leaving, 90

Nixon and, 61
reforms/debt securities, 88–89
responsibilities, 60
work, 58, 59
"Triffin dilemma," 48, 54, 64, 65, 87
Triffin, Robert, 48–49
Trilateral Commission
creation/beginnings, 171
David Rockefeller and, 57, 58n
founding, 57
Japan and, 171, 172
Volcker and, 57, 58n, 171–172
Troubled Asset Relief Program (TARP), 209, 233
Truman, Harry, 20, 25, 238
Truman, Ted, 132, 243
Trump, Donald, 215, 234–235
trust in government, xvi, 2–3, 4, 221, 235–236, 245
Tweedie, David, Sir, 194, 196, 200
Tyco International, 200

United Nations Iraqi Oil-for-Food program, United Nations Security Council and, 182
United Nations Iraqi Oil-for-Food program investigation
Australian Wheat Board and, 185
Britain's Serious Fraud Office (SFO) and, 184
countries cooperating/not cooperating, 184–185
findings/recommendations, 186–187
forensic accountants and, 193
Independent Inquiry (Volcker) Committee, 183–188
India/Singh and, 185
Kofi Annan and, 181, 183, 186, 187
Kojo Annan and, 186
secrecy laws and, 184
team members, 182–188
team reunion (2018), 187–188
United Nations Security Council and, 183
US Congress and, 185–186
Volcker and, xv, 182–188
US Financial Accounting Standards Board (FASB), 194, 196
US Government Accountability Office (GAO), 193

Vagelos, Roy, 198
Van Gerven, Walter, 190

Vasisht, Gaurav, 246
Vassar College, 6
Venezuela, 136
Vereker, John, Sir, 189–190
Vietnam War, 54, 55, 240
Volcker, Adolf, 9
Volcker Alliance, 245–246
creation, xvi, 2, 239, 242, 245
Fed supervision and, 234
governance of United States and, 235–236, 239
government trust and, 233–234, 245
mission, xvi, 2, 4, 245
public service education and, 159
Volcker, Alma, 6, 11, 12–13, 18, 240
Volcker, Barbara, ix, xv, 30, 43 , 91, 116, 123, 143
health issues, 91, 103, 116, 152, 156, 162, 163, 164
son's education and, 91, 163
Volcker, Barbara/Paul
car and, 52n
financial squeeze and, 116, 152
friends in Washington, DC, 91
grandchildren, 162, 163
living arrangements/Fed chairman, 103, 104
moves/homes, ix, x, 30, 40, 46, 56n, 93, 95, 156
reappointment to Federal Reserve/deal and, 116–117
Volcker family/childhood
finances and, 12
fishing/New Jersey lake, 11
heights, 5–6, 10, 10n
parental educational responsibilities, 13
See also specific individuals
"Volcker Group," 64, 67, 83, 87
Volcker, Janice, ix, 40, 76, 91, 104, 162, 163, 164
Volcker, Jimmy, ix, 40, 91, 103, 114–115
Volcker, Louise, 6, 9–10, 26–27
Volcker, Paul, Jr., 40, 68
fishing and, 11, 94, 111n, 117, 126, 132, 164–165, 225, 243
golf and, 164
government pension and, 26, 95
offers after leaving Treasury (1974), 93–94
offers following Fed, 152–153
political parties and, 30, 210
procrastination and, 15, 18, 22, 40, 153
smoking and, 163–164, 165
Volcker, Paul, Jr./childhood
birth/significance, ix, 9
description/traits, 9, 12, 60

Volcker, Paul, Jr./childhood (*continued*)
  education and, 12–13, 60
  father and, 8, 11
  nickname, 9
  senior research paper, 12
  sisters and, 9–10
  summary, 5, 220
  teenage years, 12, 220
  transportation/phone calls at time, 11
  See also Teaneck, New Jersey
Volcker, Paul, Sr., ix, 5, 6–8, 10, 11, 173
Volcker Rule
  creation, 2, 216–217
  description, 2, 216–218, 232–233
  Obama and, xvi
  simplification, 219
Volcker, Ruth, 6, 7, 9, 27
Volcker, Virginia, 6, 10, 13

Wachtell Lipton lawyers, 198
wages for CEOs, 171
Walker, Charls, x, 60, 61
Wall Street Journal, 152, 201, 216–217
Washington, DC
  changes (1960s to present), 91–92, 224
  lobbyists and, 92, 170, 209, 217, 218, 221
  Volcker family views on, 91–92
Washington, George, quote, 7
Washington Post Company, 152
Waste Management Inc., 198
Watergate scandal, xi, 86, 87, 90
Weidenbaum, Murray, xii, 61, 114
Weill, Sandy, 204
Wells Fargo, 170–171
White House's Council of Economic
    Advisers (CEA), 46, 51, 54–55, 55n,
    62–63, 71, 114
White, "Sandy," 154
Whitehead, John, 149
Williams, John, 24, 25
Willis, George, 67, 87
Wilson, John, 39, 40
Wilson, Woodrow, 17, 162, 238
Winn, Don, 242–243
Winter, William, 175
Wojnilower, Albert, xiii, 21
Wolfensohn & Company
  Arthur Andersen auditing firm and, 198
  Bankers Trust and, xv, 166
  Enron and, 197
  Jim Wolfensohn and, 153, 154, 155

staff/clients overview, 154
  strategy, 153, 154–155, 166, 244
Wolfensohn & Company/Volcker, xiv, xv, 153,
    154–155, 166
Wolfensohn, Jim
  Volcker and, 153, 244
  Wolfensohn & Company, 153, 154, 155
  World Bank and, xv, 154, 188–189
Wolfowitz, Paul, xvi, 189
Woodrow Wilson School of Public and
    International Affairs
  academic assignments, 156–158
  public service education/controversy and,
    158–162, 175
  reputation, 16–17
  Volcker teaching/fellow, xi, xiv, 16–17, 91,
    94–95, 152, 156–158
  Volckers' home at, 156
Working Party III, 63, 63n
World Bank, ix, 60, 135, 136, 181
World Bank investigation
  corruption and, 181, 188–192
  Department of Institutional Integrity,
    188–189, 190
  findings/recommendations, 190–192
  Independent Panel Review/"Volcker
    Panel," xvi, 189–192
  Siemens AG bribes and, 190–191
World Jewish Congress, 176, 177
World War II
  atom bomb and, 9
  effects on banks, 42
  effects on England/Germany, 27, 28
  inflation and, 23
  interest rates and, 31
  Princeton students and, 14, 15
  savings and loans, 129
  Volcker and, 5, 220
  women in government and, 243
WorldCom, 200
Wriston, Walter
  bank capital and, 146
  Citibank/approach, 43, 98, 133
  Federal Reserve and, 112
  Volcker and, 98, 146

Yellen, Janet, 225, 232

Zijlstra, Jelle, 72
Zimmerman, Steve, 191
Zoellick, Robert, xvi, 189, 191

ABOUT THE AUTHORS

 PAUL A. VOLCKER (1927–2019) worked in the United States federal government for almost thirty years, culminating in two terms as chairman of the Board of Governors of the Federal Reserve System from 1979 to 1987. Earlier he served as Treasury under secretary for monetary affairs and president of the Federal Reserve Bank of New York.

After leaving the Federal Reserve, Mr. Volcker continued his public service as chairman of the Volcker Alliance; as head of President Obama's Economic Recovery Advisory Board; chair of the investigation of the UN's Oil-for-Food program; and head of the committee formed by Swiss and Jewish organizations to investigate deposit accounts and other assets in Swiss banks of victims of Nazi persecution and to arrange for their disposition.

Educated at Princeton, Harvard, and the London School of Economics, Mr. Volcker is a recipient of honorary doctorates from each of his alma maters, as well as a number of other American and foreign universities.

CHRISTINE HARPER has been a financial reporter and editor for more than two decades. She is the editor in chief of *Bloomberg Markets* and previously was executive editor responsible for overseeing *Bloomberg New*'s global coverage of financial companies.

PublicAffairs is a publishing house founded in 1997. It is a tribute to the standards, values, and flair of three persons who have served as mentors to countless reporters, writers, editors, and book people of all kinds, including me.

I. F. STONE, proprietor of *I. F. Stone's Weekly*, combined a commitment to the First Amendment with entrepreneurial zeal and reporting skill and became one of the great independent journalists in American history. At the age of eighty, Izzy published *The Trial of Socrates*, which was a national bestseller. He wrote the book after he taught himself ancient Greek.

BENJAMIN C. BRADLEE was for nearly thirty years the charismatic editorial leader of *The Washington Post*. It was Ben who gave the *Post* the range and courage to pursue such historic issues as Watergate. He supported his reporters with a tenacity that made them fearless and it is no accident that so many became authors of influential, best-selling books.

ROBERT L. BERNSTEIN, the chief executive of Random House for more than a quarter century, guided one of the nation's premier publishing houses. Bob was personally responsible for many books of political dissent and argument that challenged tyranny around the globe. He is also the founder and longtime chair of Human Rights Watch, one of the most respected human rights organizations in the world.

•   •   •

For fifty years, the banner of Public Affairs Press was carried by its owner Morris B. Schnapper, who published Gandhi, Nasser, Toynbee, Truman, and about 1,500 other authors. In 1983, Schnapper was described by *The Washington Post* as "a redoubtable gadfly." His legacy will endure in the books to come.

Peter Osnos, *Founder*